GW01090472

PRINCELY PAGEANT

Christopher Armstead

PRINCELY PAGEANT

CHRISTOPHER ARMSTEAD

One time Mint Master
Superintendent of Stamps
Chief Electrical Engineer
Director of State Workshops
Warden of Weights and Measures
and Currency Officer
to
His Exalted Highness
the Nizam of Hyderabad
and Berar

Thomas Harmsworth Publishing
London

© 1987 H C H Armstead

First published 1987

by the same author
Geothermal Energy

All rights reserved. No part of this publication may be
reproduced, stored in a retrieval system, or
transmitted, in any form or by any means, electronic,
mechanical, photocopying, recording or otherwise,
without the prior permission of
Thomas Harmsworth Publishing.

British Library Cataloguing in Publication Data

Armstead, H. Christopher H.
  Princely pageant
  1. India—Politics and government—
  1919-1947
  I. Title
  325'.341'0954   DS480.45

  ISBN 0-948807-05-9

ISBN 0-948807-05-9

Printed in Great Britain by
The Bath Press, Avon

To Guendolen
in gratitude for the loving
support she gave me
throughout the years of this
narrative and has continued
to give me thereafter

THE NIZAM'S DOMINIONS

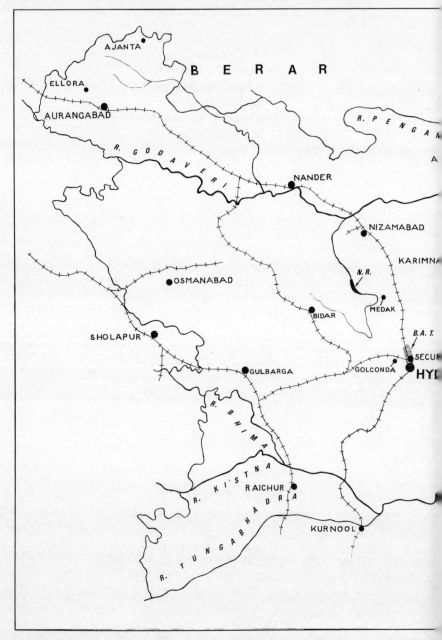

AJANTA

ELLORA

AURANGABAD

B E R A R

R. PENGAN

A

R. G O D A V E R I

NANDER

NIZAMABAD

KARIMNA

N. R.

OSMANABAD

MEDAK

BIDAR

B. A. T.

SHOLAPUR

SECU

GULBARGA

GOLCONDA

HYD

R. B H I M A

R. K I S T N A

RAICHUR

R A I C H U R

R. T U N G A B H A D R A

KURNOOL

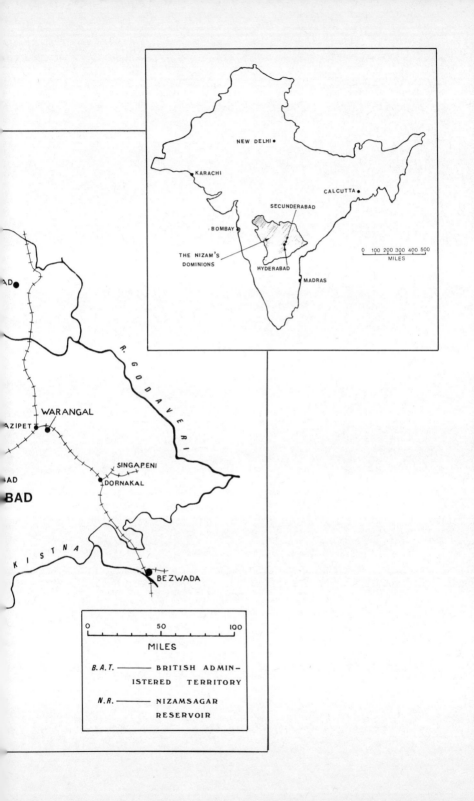

I

Pen portrait of a Prince

In 1967 an old gentleman died in the city of Hyderabad, capital of the Indian State of Andhra Pradesh. His name was Mir Osman Ali Khan. From the simplicity of his dress and the frugality of his ways during his lifetime there had been little to suggest that he had once been the most powerful of all the Indian princes and, allegedly, the richest man in the world. Only a score of years previously he had been known as His Exalted Highness Lieutenant-General Nawab Sir Mir Osman Ali Khan, Rustom-i-Dowran, Arastu-i-Zaman, Wal Mamalik, Sipan Salar, Muzaffar-ul-Mulk, Nizam-ud-Dowlah, Nizam-ul-Mulk, Asaf Jah Bahadur, Fateh Jung, Knight Grand Commander of The Most Exalted Order of The Star of India, and Knight Grand Cross of The Most Excellent Order of The British Empire, Nizam of Hyderabad and Berar, Faithful Ally of the British Government; entitled (with only four other Indian princes) to a salute of twenty-one guns.

In the days of the British Raj, before the birth of Pakistan, the vast Indian sub-continent contained two worlds – British India and Princely India – linked together by treaties. The principalities covered nearly half of the land and supported one-quarter of the population of the whole country. They were many in number, diverse in character and ranged in size from tiny squirearchies to the giants such as Hyderabad, Kashmir and Mysore. Most of the royal houses were Hindu, but the largest and most powerful of all the princely states was ruled by a

1

Muslim, the Nizam of Hyderabad and Berar. It was he alone of all the Indian princes who, after the 1914-18 War, in recognition of the help afforded by him to the British cause, was singled out from a host of 'Highnesses' and honoured by the British Crown with the style and titles of 'His Exalted Highness' and 'Faithful Ally of the British Government'. He was usually referred to, for brevity, as 'HEH', or in Urdu as 'Ali Hazrat'.

Hyderabad State covered an area greater than that of England and Wales combined, or five times that of Switzerland. Its population, including the associated territory of Berar, was more or less equal to that of the four Scandinavian countries together. After the departure of the British, Prime Minister Nehru decided that the State was an anachronism: he invaded it with his armies, dismembered it into three parts and divested the Ruler of his powers. The Nizam's Dominions suffered the same fate as did Poland in the eighteenth century: they were liquidated, the capital city became the provincial centre of a newly created Indian state and all traces of Muslim supremacy were obliterated. The excuse for this drastic action was that more than eighty percent of the old state's population was Hindu, whereas the Ruler and most of his governing hierarchy were Muslim. The fact that in Kashmir the situation was the exact reverse – a Hindu prince ruling over a predominantly Muslim population – did not deter Pandit Nehru from trying to swallow in toto that state also; but he found that less digestible.

The royal house of Hyderabad was founded by Nawab Asaf Jah Bahadur, a military commander appointed by the Moghul Emperor in 1713 AD as Viceroy of the Deccan, with the hereditary title of Nizam-ul-Mulk. The Deccan (which in Urdu simply means 'the South') is the name given to the central plateau of the Indian triangular peninsula. It had formerly been ruled by a succession of Muslim conquering dynasties, the last of which was that of the Qutb Shahi kings whose capital was at Golconda, which stands to this day as a picturesque ruin. Shortly before his death, the Great Moghul Emperor, Aurangzeb, had defeated in battle the last of the Golconda kings, Tana Shah, and had annexed the Deccan. It was Aurangzeb's successor, the Emperor Muhammed Akbar Shah Bahadur, who appointed Asaf Jah Bahadur to the vice-royalty. But by that time the Moghul Empire was already in decline, and it was not long before the Deccan became virtually an independent kingdom, though lip-service continued to be paid to the nominal overlordship of the Delhi emperors.

HEH was the seventh ruler of the house of Asaf Jah. He acceded to the ghadi, or throne, in 1911 AD and ruled as a supreme potentate in all internal affairs of state until he was deposed by Nehru in 1948. In theory he exercised the right of life and death over his subjects, though in point of fact he never sent anyone to the scaffold: his gaols were crowded with criminals 'awaiting his pleasure'. Only in foreign affairs was he subservient to the 'Paramount Power' – the British Crown. Among his other sovereign rights was the privilege of minting his own money and printing his own stamps and security papers. These rights were to have a curious impact upon my life.

In personal habits HEH was, to put it mildly, eccentric. In spite of his millions he lived a life of monastic austerity, eschewing the glittering pomp and circumstance so greatly beloved by many of his Hindu fellow princes. Owner of several royal palaces, he was content to sleep on a pallet bed on the verandah of one of them, and to conduct his state business from the same verandah, the parapet of which served as a desk. His personal budget was reputed to be limited to about one pound sterling a week. Normally he wore simple homespun except on formal state occasions, at which custom decreed that he should appear in a morning coat. It would seem that a single morning coat served for the entire thirty-seven years of his reign. By the time that I appeared in his Dominions, the coat would better have qualified for the jumble sale than for competition with the Savile Row elegance that graced the less exalted backs of some of those in attendance. His favourite mode of locomotion was a shabby old T-model Ford 'Flivver'.

The Nizam had a wide reputation for parsimony. According

3

to his apologists this was undeserved. Nevertheless it cannot be denied that he had a genius for restricting his personal expenditure almost to vanishing point, while at the same time devising original methods of amassing further wealth. If he felt like indulging in a shopping spree, he would select some luckless nawab for the dubious honour of acting as his companion and, incidentally, paymaster. If he condescended to attend the wedding of a high-born subject, his exalted presence would cost the bride's parents a substantial fee in the form of 'unsolicited' nazar – a ceremonial presentation of gold coins. From time to time he would distribute 'gifts' of mangoes grown in the royal orchards. The honoured recipients were expected to register their gratitude by making a suitable cash payment. When a viceroy or other illustrious guest had to be entertained in state, a palace would be refurbished with new chandeliers, curtains and other furnishings at the expense of his government; but after the guest's departure these adornments would be sold and the proceeds credited to the royal personal exchequer. It is not surprising that the vast fortune which the Nizam inherited became even vaster during his long reign.

The Ruler's wealth consisted of Sarf-i-Khas (Crown) lands, palaces and other real estate, and also of immense quantities of bullion and jewels, hoarded in the vaults of his principal palace – King Kothi. These riches included the fabulous Jacob diamond – a $182\frac{1}{2}$ carat stone for which the Nizam was said to have refused an offer of a million pounds and to have used as a paper weight. In 1951 the Indian Government considered the notion of selling the royal jewels, but it was believed that unless the sale were made piecemeal it would have caused the collapse of the world's jewellery market. At one stage a large quantity of currency notes was hoarded in the royal treasury; but white ants, finding paper more palatable than gold or gems, devoured most of the stock. Large sums were placed on deposit with the Imperial Bank of India, but these gave rise to an interesting tussle between avarice and orthodoxy. According to the Muslim creed the charging of interest (usury) is sinful. At regular intervals the bank wrote to HEH to ask whether the accrued interest should be re-invested on deposit or paid otherwise. No replies were ever received to these enquiries so that the interest was neither sinfully claimed nor rashly waived: it just accumulated silently.

There is a legend, possibly apocryphal, to account for the curious naming of the principal palace, King Kothi. This palace was said to have been acquired by the Nizam in his younger days in much the same way as Hampton Court palace had been acquired by Henry VIII. The Hyderabad 'Wolsey' had been a nobleman of ostentatious tastes, named Khader Khan, and had embellished his home liberally with elaborate plaster work embodying his monogram – 'KK'. To have replaced this ubiquitous cypher with the royal initials would have been costly: to let it remain without logical explanation, embarrassing. The problem was neatly solved by the happy marriage of the Urdu word 'kothi', meaning mansion, with the english word 'king'.

HEH was a hard worker who took a keen interest in the minutiae of state affairs, being by no means content to leave everything without question to his ministers. His chief recreations were the writing of Urdu and Persian poetry and the fathering of progeny so numerous that the limited choice of personal names had to be supplemented by letters of the alphabet. These offspring, reputed to number well over a hundred, bore the title of sahibzada (prince) or sahibzadi (princess), but only two of them were officially acknowledged as full members of the royal family. These were the princes Azam Jah Bahadur and Moazzam Jah Bahadur, sons of the Nizam's official First Wife, Dhulam Pasha. The formidable calendar of official state holidays was augmented from time to time by the granting of a special holiday to mark the arrival of yet another baby sahibzada or sahibzadi. Etiquette required that HEH and the Heir Apparent should never speak directly to one another in the presence of the court: even when face to face they had to communicate laboriously through a third party, so that every platitude had to be uttered in duplicate.

In all his eighty years the Nizam never left the shores of India: indeed, he seldom ventured beyond the frontiers of his vast dominions. He owned palaces in New Delhi and in Bombay, but rarely visited them. Once he paid a state visit to the Maharajah of Mysore. He was met at Bangalore station by the Maharajah's Diwan, who told HEH that His Highness had placed his Bangalore palace at his disposal so that he might rest before proceeding to the state capital, Mysore City. HEH declined, on the grounds that his large entourage included many womenfolk who were not properly 'house-trained': he was concerned about His Highness's carpets. At a dinner party which the Nizam gave in a hotel after the ceremonies of the state visit were over, he scandalised the local Establishment by seating next to himself an Anglo-Indian hairdresser to whom he had taken a fancy.

Hyderabad was more than a state: it was an empire in miniature. Acknowledging the Nizam as their liege-lord were a number of princelings, known as jagirdars, some of whom maintained their own private armies and police forces, administered their own local government and even used their own stamps. The prestige of the Nizam's court was supported by a nobility, some of ancient lineage and some parvenu; for the Ruler had the right to create titles. An imposing array of nawabs, rajahs and even one maharajah added lustre to the throne, and the ranks of 'society' in the capital city were swelled by a host of absentee landlords, some of whom openly boasted of not knowing the geographical whereabouts of their jagirs. One observant visitor was constrained to remark that he had never seen such an assembly of Bourbons. Four noble families stood out above all others in rank. These were known as the paigah nobles, roughly equivalent to royal dukes. Into these families alone could princes and princesses of the blood officially marry, as an alternative to a union with some 'foreign' royal house.

The Moghul origin of Hyderabad was reflected in the titles of the nobility – Nawab Wali-ud-Dowlah Bahadur, Nawab Fakhr-ul-Mulk Bahadur, Nawab Vikhar-ul-Umrah Bahadur, Nawab Salar Jung Bahadur – emphasising wealth, war and bravery. Many of the nobility dwelt in vast mansions or palaces, known as devdis.

When in 1924 Kamal Atatürk abolished the Caliphate and deposed the Turkish Sultan, the Nizam found himself in the position of having more subjects than any other Muslim ruler in the world. The prestige of his house was strengthened by the marriage of his Heir Apparent to Princess Dureshevar, daughter of the last of the Turkish Caliphs, His Imperial Majesty Sultan Abdul Majid, and by the wedding of his second official son to the Sultan's niece, Princess Niloufer. The presence of these two very regal young ladies, both of whom had been educated in France, did much to reduce the prevalence of the ancient Muslim custom of keeping upper class women in purdah.

HEH of course had an army. In addition to his regular forces numbering about ten thousand men, there were also the irregular forces which could be mobilised in times of emergency. These irregular forces were truly feudal troops, raised by some of the jagirdars and commanded by a handful of jemadars. Although in British India the term jemadar meant only a sergeant, in the Nizam's Dominions it was a high ranking title. One of these jemadars was no less a man than His Highness the Sultan of Mukalla, an Arabian prince who ruled a sandy kingdom in the Hadramauth and was entitled to a salute of fifteen guns. When in Hyderabad, where he spent about half of each year to enjoy a better climate, he had to shed his regal status and be known by the lesser title of Nawab Saif Nawaz Jung Bahadur.

Every year on HEH's birthday – his lunar birthday, incidentally – the regular army was paraded on the Fateh Maidan, or Plain of Victory, before an assembly of State and British Indian dignitaries. The display of exotic uniforms made a fine spectacle. The Heir Apparent, as Commander-in-Chief, appeared in an attire that would have done credit to the most exclusive of lion-tamers. One regiment, known as the Maisaram Guards, wore a picturesque Arabian uniform and marched to a band of outlandish musical instruments. The name, Maisaram, was a corruption of 'Monsieur Raymond' who, as an eighteenth century French condottiere in the service of an earlier Nizam, had founded the regiment. This birthday parade was one of the few concessions that HEH made to pageantry: it was probably the impression of military might that he enjoyed. The spectators in the grandstand displayed a colourful array of fine-spun saris, 'Ascot' dresses, uniforms, and morning suits and white topis. Probably the most shabbily dressed figure present was that of HEH himself. Unlike so many of his fellow princes he did not indulge in elephant processions or in glittering durbars. The tone of the few ceremonial occasions demanded by custom was somewhat muted by comparison with the equivalent functions in other states. Of pageantry there was plenty in Hyderabad, but this was provided by the nobility rather than by the court.

The government of the Nizam's vast Dominions could be described as one of benevolent autocracy. The traditional method of his predecessors of governing through a diwan, or Chief Minister, was at first abandoned by him in favour of direct personal rule in the manner of the Czars; but in 1919 he established an Executive Council consisting of a President and eight other ministers, all nominated. There was no electorate, and although the Executive Council was given certain powers so as to enable the machinery of state to function, all its actions and orders-in-council were subject to the sovereign prerogative and absolute power of veto by the Nizam. Legislation was enacted by a series of ukases issued in the Persian language (a relic of Moghul tradition) in the form a firman-i-mubarak, or 'auspicious edict'.

Despite the rigidity of this system it worked remarkably well, and in many respects the State could be regarded as 'progressive', particularly in the matter of public works such as roads, railways, water supply and irrigation projects. The imposition of a predominantly Muslim ruling élite over a mainly Hindu population could have been potentially explosive, but it is a fact that Hindu-Muslim conflict was almost entirely absent in Hyderabad even when it reached bloody proportions in British India. Possibly the royal tact in appointing a Hindu to the Council Presidency had something to do with this. For many years this chief administrative appointment in the State was held by a charming old gentleman, His Excellency the Maharajah Sir Kishen Pershad Bahadur, who served his royal master as a loyal rubber stamp and effectively took the wind out of the sails of those critics who, from outside the State, accused the Nizam of imposing Muslim supremacy upon a resentful Hindu majority.

Although the State was autonomous in all internal affairs it was subject by treaty to the Paramount Power and not free to follow its own foreign policy. The link between the Nizam and British India was provided by the Indian Political Service who appointed a British 'Resident', whose functions were dual. He served as a sort of ambassador of the Viceroy accredited to the court of the Nizam; he also administered certain leased territories within the State, notably the enclave of Secunderabad, where British India fulfilled its side of the treaty by providing a military garrison on the doorstep of the capital. The Resident was allotted a splendid Georgian palace in Hyderabad City, a pleasant and less pretentious residence in Bolarum, some ten miles to the north, and a summer retreat in the hill station of Ootacamund in South India.

The State administration was leavened with a sprinkling of European civil and military officers. The Executive Council always included one member, the Honourable Police and Revenue Member, appointed by the Viceroy with the concurrence of the Nizam. Certain key appointments, such as the Director-General of Police, the Chief of Staff of the State Forces, etc. were held by officers 'lent' by British India, and a number of technical and educational posts were also held by Europeans. These included the Mintmastership and many of the Railway officers.

In addition to the Hindu masses and the far less numerous, but powerful, Muslims there were small communities of Parsees and of Anglo-Indians in Hyderabad. The latter enjoyed a unique prestige in the State; a prestige not altogether shared by their brethren in British India where the Anglo-Indian community was chiefly known as an endless source of recruitment for engine-drivers, ticket-collectors and foremen. In Hyderabad, many of the so-called Anglo-Indians were in fact Franco-Indians whose families had been founded by the French adventurers who had accompanied Monsieur Raymond in seeking their fortunes in the service of the Nizams of the eighteenth century. Evidence of their origin was provided by such names as Chamarette, Fallon and even Franswah (sic). The term 'Anglo-Indian' has a totally different connotation from that which applied during my schooldays. Then it conjured up visions of purple-complexioned British colonels whose conversation was enriched by frequent utterances of ' 'pon my soul' and references to PoonAH. Latterly it came to mean a person of mixed British and Indian blood – the older term 'Eurasian' being resented by those to whom it applied. An embarrassing situation once arose when our son was aged about five. My wife was expecting a visit from a certain Anglo-Indian woman and mentioned the fact in the hearing of the small boy, who demanded to know what was an Anglo-Indian. Not unnaturally his mother explained that it was someone who was half English and half Indian. The lady duly arrived at our house to be regaled with coffee and conversation on the verandah and to be subjected to a long scrutiny by our son, whose curiosity could eventually be restrained no longer. 'Mummy!' he said fortissimo, 'her top half is Indian. Is her bottom half English?'

Court life was formal and rigid, but devoid of ostentation.

When not occupied with the perusal of state files in his bed-sitter-office-verandah, in fortifying the royal person with food, drink or sleep, or in dealing with the domestic affairs of his not inconsiderable family, he would meet a few of his close advisers, ministers and courtiers. Apart from the privileged few, scarcely anyone else had direct communication with him – certainly not more than one or two of his few European officers. In all my twelve years in the State I never exchanged a word with him apart from mumbled platitudes when shaking his hand at receptions. The small group of professional courtiers who met him more or less daily were well trained in the arts of sycophancy and flattery. If the Exalted One declared the weather to be cooler, the reflex action of the lesser mortal addressed would be to observe that the Princely perception of the vagaries of the climate was indeed deservedly famous; or if, Nero-like, he were to read his latest poem, it would instantly be compared with the works of Rabindranath Tagore, Iqbal or Omar Khayam to the marked disadvantage of these minor bards. If he asked for a candid opinion he would expect, and receive, a candied opinion. A host of peons, guards, eunuchs and menials, all living near the bread line, populated those parts of the palace that were not occupied by the vast royal family.

HEH had a curious way of talking in triplicate. My first encounter with this mannerism was on an occasion when I had been commanded to attend a formal durbar. I arrived rather early and joined a group of officials, courtiers and nobles who were standing in silence on the terrace outside the Durbar Hall. The reason for the silence was soon apparent: HEH had arrived even earlier and was pacing back and forth like Felix the Cat beneath the deferential gaze of the assembly. Suddenly he caught sight of me and stopped in his tracks. My heart respectfully followed suit. 'Kazim, Kazim, Kazim!' he called. His principal courtier of that name came scuttling up to him. Pointing straight at me and screwing up his face, HEH said 'Who's that? Who's that? Who's that?' Kazim mumbled a reply in respectful tones and I caught the words 'Nazim, Dar-ul Zarb aur Barqi' which were my official designations. 'Oh! I remember. I remember. I remember,' replied HEH, who then resumed his pacing.

The façade of Hyderabad was both picturesque and impressive. A trip to the capital and to such famous places within the Nizam's Dominions as the caves of Ellora and Ajanta, Aurangabad, Daulatabad, Golconda, Gulbarga and Bidar was nearly always included in the itineries of the famous, such as Edward, Prince of Wales, ex-King Alfonso XIII of Spain, the Archduke Franz Ferdinand of Austria-Hungary, Somerset Maugham and Freya Stark (also of the less famous and perhaps of the infamous) when visiting India. The opéra bouffe enacted behind that façade, though often exasperating, was seldom dull. But the substance of the State was brittle: it collasped at the crack of Nehru's whip in spite of a gallant but futile resistance offered by a fiercely pro-Muslim 'army' of volunteer 'Razakars' who were mown down by the advancing Indian troops in 1948. To mollify the ignominy of defeat in that year, the Nizam was appointed Rajpramukh, or titular head of the new state of Andhra Pradesh, by the Indian government; but six years later this position was abolished and the ex-ruler retired, to occupy the remaining eleven years of his life in trying to devise ways and means of holding on the rump of his fortune. He died, a sad and embittered old man, at the age of eighty.

II

India's Coral Strand

Although I was destined to spend many years in the Nizam's service, I was not altogether unacquainted with India when I first went to Hyderabad, having lived previously for three or four years in the very different world of Bombay.

It was pure chance that first took me to India. Ours was not a family steeped in the traditions of the Indian Army, Civil Service or Police – traditions that could lure its sons, generation after generation, to that fascinating yet maddening sub-continent as though by some atavistic urge. No, I came from a family firmly rooted in London and in the Arts, with a capital 'A'. Burlington House was its Mecca. Both my grandfathers were Royal Academicians and several other relatives had attained eminence in the Arts. My father, though quite a gifted sculptor and draughtsman, deviated from the family pattern by becoming a rather fashionable London doctor: but he too lived in the milieu of his forebears in that many of his patients and friends were painters, sculptors and architects. Our only tenuous link with India was through my mother's sister, Aunt Phil, who had married an Indian Army officer whose father, for a short time, had served as Acting Viceroy. But as Aunt Phil was not greatly loved, this vicarious honour passed more or less unnoticed by the rest of the family and was soon forgotten.

As for myself, I was given a conventional Edwardian education with a classical slant at a 'preparatory school for young gentlemen', followed by the tough régime of the Royal

13

Naval Colleges, Osborne and Dartmouth. By the time I was sixteen I was somewhat over-disciplined, thanks to very strict parents, a scholarly but sadistic headmaster at my school and the iron enforcement of blind obedience at the naval colleges. By then I had reached the age of doubts — particularly doubts about myself. But of one thing I was certain: I was not cut out for a naval career, into which I had rashly rushed – with a strong maternal push from behind – at the tender age of thirteen when the First World War held more glamour than horror in the imagination of a small boy.

The timely wielding of the Geddes Axe enabled me, along with some forty percent of my fellow cadets who also felt the lack of an adequate sense of vocation, to doff my uniform with honour, or at least without ignominy. Three years at London University followed by a two-year apprenticeship in a large and famous Lancashire factory qualified me as a fledgling engineer; and within a month of my 22nd birthday I found myself seeking a job. The world was my oyster. A desire to escape from the tentacles of my parents, together with an ardent urge to travel, led me to think in terms of employment abroad; but where? Of the many countries that crossed my mind India held low priority: it was a country about which I knew little, and vaguely associated with Kipling, bugles, be-jewelled princes and snakes.

Yes; it certainly was through no pre-conditioning but by sheer chance that the Fates took me to India – chance in the guise of an advertisement in a technical journal, proclaiming that the Bombay Electric Supply & Tramways Company sought the services of an assistant engineer. The salary offered seemed munificent by comparison with the near-penury to which I had hitherto been condemned by a parsimonious parent. I applied for the job. It was my first application for employment and it was a long shot. The company's London representative and consulting engineer summoned me to Lincoln's Inn, where I was interviewed by him and by one of the firm's directors, Sir Stanley Reed – a former Editor of the *Times of India* and later

MP for Stourbridge. To my utmost astonishment I was accepted.

On 27th November, 1925, with snow on her decks, the RMS *Rawalpindi*, the latest pride of the P&O fleet, sailed from Tilbury, taking me to an entirely new life. Queen Alexandra was buried the same day.

At the time, of course, I could not foresee that I was destined to know two totally different Indias – the Land of the Boxwallahs and the Land of the Nabobs – as different from one another as either was from Bayswater. This oriental meal was to be served up to me in two courses, with a four or five year interval between them.

The voyage to India formed a sort of no-man's land in time, separating two utterly different worlds, itself belonging to neither. It was my first sea voyage and I enjoyed every minute of it. The strange vernacular of the lascars, the exotic and all-pervading smell of their curries, the melancholy mewing of the gulls and the visual contrast of their white wings against the deep blue sky; all these impressions built up the unique atmosphere peculiar to a passage to India in the days before the prosaic plane supplanted the romantic steamship.

First came Gibraltar with its Moorish carpet-sellers, its Spanish shawl vendors, its monkeys and the first glimpse of Africa across the Straits. After that, a short return to winter at Marseilles where we docked for two days. Then off to sea again. The mountains of Corsica; Stromboli in eruption; Messina; a glimpse of Crete; Port Said with its yellowish sea, vivid blue sky and its multitude of small fishing craft. De Lesseps serenely looked down upon us from his pedestal as we steamed into the canal. Thirty-two years later he was to be overthrown by some of Nasser's iconoclastic friends in an orgy of xenophobia. Simon Artzt, 'feelthy peectures', Turkish coffee, Turkish delight, the 'gulli-gulli man' conjuring chicks from the pockets of passengers. The canal with its sand dunes and silhouettes of camels against a setting sun; a small boy passenger spotting an Arab on

the bank, and saying 'Look, Mummy. There's Jesus Christ!'
Sinai; the Red Sea; Aden with its 'mermaids' and King
Solomon's ancient water tanks; and finally the last lap across the
Arabian Sea.

And so we reached Bombay where I said 'Goodbye' to the
good ship *Rawalpindi*. It was only her second voyage. Eighteen
years later she was sent to the bottom of the sea in cold northern
waters by the guns of the German battle-cruiser *Bismarck*.

At last I was independent, self-supporting and completely
free to lead my own life. I was twenty-two, inexperienced and
about to earn the princely salary of eight hundred rupees a
month. I felt on top of the world.

My first impressions of Bombay were most favourable. The
harbour in the early morning looked incredibly beautiful with
the sun rising behind the rugged skyline of the Western Ghats,
and I found a most friendly welcome awaiting me.

At Ballard pier I was met by the deputy general manager of
the tramway company and was driven to the flat of the general
manager, my future burra sahib, who had hospitably invited me
to stay with him for three or four days until I had found my legs.
On arrival I was allotted a servant, a Hindu, and was instructed
as to how I should treat him. I was to work him hard, tolerate no
impertinence, swear at him as much as I wished, but never hit
him. This last injunction struck me as superfluous. I was to
address him as 'Boy', provide him with two sets of white clothes
and two turbans, and take him with me whenever I went to a
dinner party so that he could help serve at table. I surrendered
my baggage to my 'boy' and devoted my attention to other
matters.

My burra sahib first gave me a lecture on the perils of the sun.
I must never venture outdoors before 4.30pm without a topi on
my head. After that hour it was not considered comme il faut to
be seen in a topi: a felt hat was to be worn until the sun was below
the horizon, even if one were playing tennis or bathing in the
sea. To steer a safe course between the Scylla of sunstroke and

the Charybdis of social gaffe required some accurate clock-watching round about half-past four. If one set forth before that hour it was necessary to take with one a topi-bag to contain the felt hat until 4.30 and the offending topi thereafter.

After this sermon my boss took me on a grand tour of the offices to introduce me to my future colleagues, both European and Indian. To drive home his recent lecture he solemnly deviated from his course round every sunbeam that slanted through the windows. I dutifully followed in his tracks as though he were King Wenceslas. Everyone was very kind. My duties were explained to me and I was primed on social obligations which seemed to be of greater importance. The stratification of Bombay society was precisely laid down, and admission to the various clubs depended upon one's *stratum* rather than upon one's character. Apparently my education and origins were such that I would be eligible for membership of any club I chose, but as club subscriptions were expensive it would be unwise for me to join any at first except the Bombay Gymkhana, which was primarily a young man's club and a sine qua non. I was told that after three years the Royal Bombay Yacht Club should be my next goal and that after ten or fifteen years I would doubtless be expected to join the most exclusive of all clubs in India – the Byculla. Between the third and tenth or fifteenth year there would be the Bombay Club, the Willingdon Club and one or two other, more exotic clubs such as the Orient. I could not understand why *anyone* should want to belong to so many, but for the time being this problem did not concern me. I joined the Bombay Gymkhana, which became more or less the focus of my social life for the next three and a half years. There was another club for Europeans called the Commercial Gymkhana. I was advised never to cross its threshold: it was for people in the *retail* trade which, of course, was quite beyond the pale. Later I learned that the general manager of a large Bombay store happened to be an Old Etonian: he was debarred from all the Bombay clubs except the Commercial Gymkhana. It was from those committee members of the more socially acceptable clubs whose speech was most conspicuously innocent of aspirates that the loudest insistence on this 'blackbalderdash' came!

I had come to India armed with many introductions, and became immediately immersed in an endless round of dinner parties; but first I had to be initiated into the mysteries of 'calling'. In the case of the Governor, the Chief Justice and certain other exalted officials whose peons wore scarlet and gold liveries, this meant 'signing in the book' and leaving cards. For lesser fry, the dropping of cards sufficed. A single man was expected to leave two cards when calling on a married couple – one for the husband and one for the wife. When a married couple called on another couple it was necessary to leave one joint card (from Mr and Mrs Smith) and one single card (from Mr Smith); the theory being that both Mr and Mrs Smith called on Mrs Jones but only Mr Smith called on Mr Jones. Mrs Smith would have been considered 'forward' if she too had called on Mr Jones.

A few days after my arrival in Bombay I joined a 'chummery' with three other men. One was a grass widower whose wife was in England. As senior member, who did the house-keeping and kept the chummery accounts, he was known as the 'chummery bitch'. The other two members were, like myself, bachelors, one of whom was a dipsomaniac. Unfortunately I had to share a bedroom with the dipsomaniac. He was a likeable fellow in his way, when sober, but could be very trying at times when he was much the worse for drink. During my years in Bombay I lived in four different chummeries. It was always the same story: three would be all right and the fourth difficult. I would hesitate to deduce from this a statistical law that 75% of the human race are basically pleasant and only 25% unpleasant; but in Bombay there seemed to be some evidence for such a law. Mercifully, one is not too squeamish in one's early twenties.

Bombay was, and perhaps still is for all I know, a pleasant city but for its climate, which is quite horrible except for about six weeks round about New Year. When I first landed the weather was at its best and I saw the city through rose-tinted spectacles. The curious mixture of architecture – bogus Venetian gothic, East India Company Georgian and Brighton Pavilion Saracenic – contrived to make a not unattractive ensemble. Local atmosphere was provided by the indefinable smells, the cawing of innumerable crows, the snake charmers on the Apollo Bunder, the horsedrawn gharries, the hooting cars, the clanging trams, the respectable Hindu carrying his inevitable umbrella and wearing his dhoti so that his sock suspenders were clearly visible, the maimed beggars and the general colourful bustle. In those days the Back Bay reclamation scheme had not been undertaken, and the sea shore with its palm trees came up to the very edge of the Oval and the Cooperage. Now, these are separated from the sea by a forest of characterless blocks of flats.

I had not been in Bombay for more than a week or two before I was summoned to lunch at Government House. I reckoned it would take me fifteen minutes to get there by taxi, and as the invitation was for one o'clock I sent my boy out for a taxi at 12.35. The minutes went by and he failed to return. I became molto agitato. In those days there were two classes of taxi in Bombay and I had forgotten to specify the kind I wanted. Eventually a broken down old bone shaker, with a huge '2nd' on the door chugged up, driven by an unshaven Pathan of villainous appearance. It was by then too late to do anything about it, so off I went. At the imposing gates of Government House, scarlet and gold clad lancers of the Bodyguard sprang to attention as we rattled up to the red-carpeted entrance. The lunch was very formal. The Jam Sahib of Nawanagar (Ranjit Sinhji, the famous cricketer) was a fellow guest. Their Excellencies entered ceremoniously after all the guests had assembled, and we trooped into lunch. Afterwards, Sir Leslie

19

Wilson took up a position on one sofa and Lady Wilson on another, and the guests were brought forward one by one and presented by an ADC. I felt rather nervous but found Sir Leslie most human. As I had come to Bombay armed with an introduction to him we were able to talk of mutual friends. Then, at a prescribed signal, the band played the national anthem. We all rose and the Wilsons departed. By implication we had been politely but firmly dismissed. The guests assembled at the top of the flight of steps leading down to the portico. A splendid Rolls Royce drove up to remove His Highness the Jam Sahib. Next, heralded by a backfire and much rattling, my disreputable taxi arrived. 'And whose carriage is this?' asked an astonished ADC. I slunk down the stairs feeling like a Bateman cartoon.

My normal routine was to be woken by my boy with chota hazri – a cup of tea and a banana, of all improbable mixtures. He would then raise the mosquito net, prepare my bath and lay out my clothes. He seemed to expect to dress me, but that I could not endure. After a bath and shave I would go to the office for an hour, returning to the chummery for breakfast at about 9 o'clock. My work might take me to any part of the city, which I soon learned to know well; and before long I became the proud owner of a small car, so I could easily return home for tiffin at one o'clock. Owing to the importance attached to health and social life, leaving the office at four o'clock in the afternoon for a game of tennis was condoned so long as it did not happen more often than twice a week. Otherwise we went home at half past five. The evenings were usually spent at the club until dinner at 8.30, either in the chummery or at a party elsewhere. I learned to speak the hackneyed jargon of the pukka sahib and to drink chota pegs – whisky drowned in soda; too many, no doubt. A bachelor evening might be rounded off with a visit to the cinema (silent films of course), or sometimes to the more disreputable quarters of the city. One of the city 'sights' was a drive along Saklaji Street, where the prostitutes were displayed in cages, clamouring for custom as one drove past. Wise men did not disembark in Saklaji Street.

A month or two after my arrival in India my chief invited me to the Byculla Ball. This was a tremendous event. No man could attend, unless a club member, who had been a resident of Bombay for more than six months (during which time one was termed a 'griffin'). It was therefore a function to be witnessed only once in a lifetime unless one rose to the affluent stage of membership. There was an oriental splendour about this ball. At supper we were fanned in Cleopatran style by inscrutable long robed and turbanned servants, and the tables were arranged around huge illuminated blocks of ice onto which electric fans played. A wide choice of dancing partners was provided by the 'Fishing Fleet' – an uncharitable term applied to the daughters of officials, officers and business men who visited India during the 'cold weather' to join their parents and to test the matrimonial market.

One day I was sent for by my chief who greeted me with a long doomsday face. 'I have a very serious matter to raise with you, young man,' he began. 'You were seen yesterday driving along Queens Road in an open car at a quarter past four wearing a *felt hat*. Did I not warn you never to discard your topi before 4.30?' By that time I had discovered, by a process of trial and error supported by hunch, that the Great One's views on sunstroke dated from the nineteenth century and were poppycock. 'Oh!' said I. 'Ten minutes later I might have been seen playing tennis *bareheaded*.' He threw up his hands in horror. 'God help you: I wash my hands of you.' I might mention that on my many visits to the tropics since the Second World War, I never wear a hat of any kind, even at noon, and make no claim to be unique in this respect.

The surrounding countryside outside the city of Bombay was then very pleasant, and I went on many long walking

21

expeditions at week-ends. My usual companion was a Norwegian, Torleif Ahlsand, illogically but affectionately known to his friends as 'George'. Later, George became Norwegian Consul-General in India and he remained one of my lifelong friends until he sadly died in Oslo at a good old age in the 1970s. We explored together Salsette Island from end to end and scaled several peaks of the Western Ghats, such as Cathedral Rock and The Duke's Nose (so named for its resemblance to the profile of the Duke of Wellington who, as Sir Arthur Wellesley, had campaigned in the neighbourhood during the Mahratta wars). To get to the Duke's Nose it was necessary to take the Poona road or rail up the Bhore Ghat, which is not unlike a miniature edition of the Grand Canyon of Colorado, and to stay overnight at Lonavla or Khandalla. These two little places are minor hill stations frequented during the hot weather by Bombay wives. Few people venture far away from them, but it is rewarding to do so because there are, or were in my day, some primitive people living in those hills who still used bows and arrows. Cathedral Rock, not far from Kalyan, is so-called for obvious reasons: it is an imposing mountain with a flat table top and a spire. In olden times it had been used as a robber fortress. The ascent through its lower insect-infested and wooden slopes was hot work. Then, about two-thirds of the way up, the vegetation cleared and the precipitous sides of the plateau and spire towered above. At this point there was a small shrine, seated by which we saw an old man in deep meditation, with his legs crossed and soles facing skywards. Two other, younger Indians were nearby. This 'crowd' rather surprised us as we had fully expected to find no one on such a wild mountain. One of the younger Indians told us that the old man was their 'guru' and that he had come all the way from the Himalayas, on foot, to visit this shrine and that he intended to stay there until he died. This was expected to happen in a week or ten days' time. I have no idea whether their expectations were realised. The scramble upwards to the plateau was rather hair-raising, as the only footholds were the worn-away remains of ancient steps carved out of the rock face. Climbing the needle was beyond our capabilities.

There were also several interesting caves to be seen not very far from Bombay, used as Buddhist temples centuries ago before the influence of Gautama had declined in India and found greater favour in Ceylon, Burma and the Far East. There were also a few Hindu cave temples to be found. Every tourist of course knows the Elephanta caves in Bombay harbour, but scattered over the Western Ghats there are other less well known but equally impressive rock temples. George and I also sought out some of the old Mahratta fortresses that are strategically placed along the ridge of the Western Ghats. The old Portuguese fortress of Bassein we visited too: it lies on the coast just to the north of Salsette Island. Peopled then with a few squatters and many snakes it made a picturesque ruin. The arms of illustrious Portuguese commanders and proconsuls still adorned the ancient walls. The west coast of India was, of course, colonised by the Portuguese before the British had gained a firm foothold. Bombay itself was a wedding present to King Charles II, as part of Katherine of Braganza's dowry.

Motoring in the Bombay countryside brought its unusual experiences. A chicken once ran across the road and disappeared beneath my wheels before I could do anything about it. Fierce clucking was to be heard from under the floor boards. As I brought the car to a standstill to see if I could rescue the unfortunate bird there was a piercing squawk, and out she ran, apparently unhurt but completely naked, leaving a trail of feathers in the wake of the car. Another time, during the monsoon, I was driving between showers with the hood down. I was wearing shorts and my knees were higher than my hips. Something that I took to be a large twig fell onto me from a tree, and contrived to drop inside one leg of my shorts. Glancing down I was horrified to see a scaly tail swishing about around my knee. Bringing the car to a rapid halt I more or less somersaulted out of it in a split second. The uninvited guest was

23

a large iguana, which was now perched on the gear lever, its tongue darting in and out. Then there was the occasion when I was driving in a friend's car up the Bhore Ghat during a heavy rainstorm. Bad visibility made it necessary to drive very slowly. Suddenly two figures loomed ahead: they were field coolies wearing hoods of sacking on their heads as a protection from the rain. The driver pulled up as quickly as possible but just bumped gently into one of the men. His hood remained visible above the top of the bonnet of the car. We jumped out, expecting to see the victim crucified on the radiator, but although the hood was held against the car by the force of the wind there was no sign of either cooly. Then we heard a moan; the two coolies were at the side of the road. One was obviously unharmed. The other, though groaning, showed no signs of injury. No cuts or bruises were visible and he seemed uncertain as to where to rub his pains. One of our party produced a rupee. The groaning immediately stopped and was replaced by a grin from ear to ear. We piled back into the car, soaked to the skin, and were just driving off when a shout from behind stopped us. The 'victim's' friend came forward to demand a further four annas (about 2 new pence). 'What for?' we asked. 'Doctor's fees' was the reply.

The most popular place for a week-end visit was the beautiful beach of Juhu – in those days sparsely populated but now, I understand, extensively built over. There were other, even more attractive beaches further afield. Then there was the harbour to be explored. George was a keen yachtsman and I often 'crewed' for him in his crafts, named consecutively *Viking I*, *Viking II* and *Viking III*. During one of his leaves to Europe, George ordered a new mast for, I think, *Viking II*. When he returned to Bombay he met a friend before he had had a chance to inspect his boat. The friend commented on the replacement of George's mast. 'How did you know about it?' said George. 'Oh!' was the reply, 'It is quite a famous landmark in Bombay harbour: it is called the "corkscrew".' After a day on the water it was pleasant to

His Exalted Highness Lieutenant-General Nawab Sir Mir Osman Ali Khan, Rustom-i-Dowran, Arastu-i-Zaman, Wal Mamalik, Sipan Salar, Muzaffar-ul-Mulk, Nizam-ud-Dowlah, Asaf Jah Bahadur, Fateh Jung, GCSI, KGBE, Nizam of Hyderabad and Berar, Faithful Ally of the British Government, the seventh and last of the ruling Nizams.

His Excellency The Maharajah Sir Kishen Pershad Bahadur, for many years President of the Nizam's Executive Council (effectively Prime Minister) mostly during the 1930s – a Hindu in a predominantly Muslim hierarchy. *(Photos: Raja Deen Dayal)*

Her Imperial Highness The Princess Durreshevar, wife of the Prince of Berar and daughter of the last Caliph of Islam and Sultan of Turkey. Her imperial title was not officially recognised in Hyderabad State where she was a simple Highness, like her husband.

His Highness Prince Azam Jah Bahadur, Prince of Berar, elder of the two official sons of His Exalted Highness The Nizam, and Commander-in-Chief of the Hyderabad State Forces.

Prince Moazam Jah Bahadur, second official son of His Exalted Highness The Nizam. The golden crest (turrah) on the turban (dastar) could be worn only by the ruler or princes of the blood.

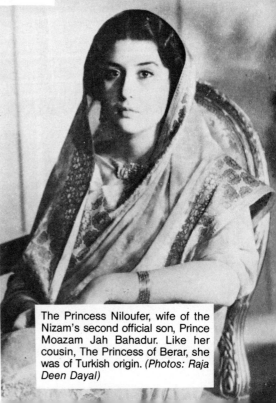

The Princess Niloufer, wife of the Nizam's second official son, Prince Moazam Jah Bahadur. Like her cousin, The Princess of Berar, she was of Turkish origin. *(Photos: Raja Deen Dayal)*

spend an evening on the Yacht Club lawn. I also used to crew sometimes for the Chief Justice of Bombay, Sir Amberson Martin – a charming man ashore, but very hot tempered afloat.

Few cities can have changed so much in little more than half a century as Bombay – unless it be Hong Kong. When I lived there the whole of Cumbala Hill and most of Malabar Hill were given over to bungalows of the 'up-country' type and to the palaces of the wealthy Parsees and Indians. Each had a large garden and stabling. Now, the blocks of flats crowd so closely together that one can almost shake hands with the occupants of the next block opposite. Pali Hill was then a spacious and 'horsy' suburb having a real nineteenth century atmosphere, but the city now spreads far beyond it and the airport has swallowed the once pleasant country district of Santa Cruz.

I bent myself to the task of learning the language and engaged the services of a munshi who taught me the elements of classically correct Urdu; I even mastered the Arab-Persian script. But the fact that few Bombay Indians spoke anything but the local ungrammatical 'bat', except the educated ones who spoke fluent English anyway, discouraged me. For lack of practice I never became very proficient. Many of my fellow countrymen acquired an impressive fluency in what they believed to be 'Hindustani' that was understood by the lower orders. C'était magnifique, mais ce n'était pas Urdu. I could never whip up enough enthusiasm to master a pidjin language.

As the cold weather passed and the city stoked up, I learned to know the agonies of 'prickly heat', an irritating rash that afflicts those whose skins, like mine, are incapable of sweating profusely. The advent of the monsoon, despite a drop in temperature, made matters worse at first; for until the rains set in properly the first early showers were followed by clouds of steam rising from the streets, like stifling blankets. Even the monsoon proper brought only slight relief. Then came the second hot weather from mid-September to December, and

25

finally the blessed respite of a few weeks of really pleasant climate. The Bombay monsoon is a repulsive season, because mould and mildew grew on stored clothes and attacked books, aided and abetted by silver fish. The second hot weather came as a relief because it seemed much healthier: one could swim again at Juhu, even though the stench of 'Bombay duck' drying in the sun was sometimes overpowering.

The Divali Festival in October or November is an impressive sight. It is celebrated in most parts of India, but particularly in the West, and is a festival of light. In every Hindu house and shop all the lamps that can be afforded are lit – oil or electric – and the whole city looks like a vast Christmas tree. It was an anxious time for my company, as the load upon the electricity system was very severe and elaborate precautions had to be taken to prevent 'black-outs'. Another curious festival, Ganpati, took place every year at the end of the monsoon, when thousands of images of the elephant-headed deity, Ganesh, were cast into the sea at Chowpati sands.

I was once a guest at a party given by a wealthy European at his 'shack' on the sea shore some thirty miles or so to the north of Bombay. He had just bought a brand new and expensively smart car. The party drove out in the early morning in various other cars while the new car, because it had to be driven slowly at first, was to follow with the lunch. After a good deal of swimming we were all becoming rather hungry, but there was no sign of the lunch. At about three o'clock a terrified Indian driver staggered in, his clothes awry and his teeth chattering. 'Sahib, Sahib, the new car is wheels uppermost by the roadside and I was nearly killed but thanks be to God I am still alive though much shaken.' With complete sang froid our host quietly removed the pipe from his mouth and said 'Damn the car! Where is the lunch?'

There were many Goanese in the Tramway Company. At one time I was acting for the head of the department for constructing and maintaining the overhead wires for the tramcars, and my foreman was a worthy Goan. When filling in some papers for one of the linesmen, also a Goanese, I said to the foreman 'He's a Christian, isn't he?' 'Indeed no, Sir' was the indignant reply, 'He is a Wesleyan.' Shortly afterwards the foreman died and I had to attend his funeral. It was expected of me to gaze respectfully upon his remains before he was boxed up. Having had but little experience in the viewing of corpses I must confess that the swarms of flies did not make the spectacle any easier to stomach. This craze for viewing corpses seems to be widespread in India. On several occasions later, when I was living in Hyderabad, dead employees would be brought to me so that I might gaze upon them before burial or cremation. I found the custom both macabre and embarrassing.

Once I was invited to a Goanese wedding in Bombay. Being the only European present I was given a seat right up in the front pew. When the bride and her father arrived at the church the air was suddenly shattered by the brassy strains of 'Colonel Bogey' played uncertainly by a Goanese band that had hitherto escaped my notice, concealed as it was behind the pulpit. The bridegroom came over to me and said 'This is European music, Sir, especially in your honour.'

After my third year in India there was a change of Governors in Bombay. Sir Leslie Wilson went home and his successor, Sir Frederick Sykes, reigned in his stead. Now the Sykes's were acquainted with my parents, and it therefore came as no surprise to me when, on arrival at a Government House ball, I was told by an ADC to reserve No 4 dance for 'Her Ex.' After each dance the governor and his wife would seat themselves on a gilded throne with his or her partner on a humbler chair by the side. When the band struck up for No 4 dance I was led up to Lady Sykes's throne and formally presented. I bowed from the cervical vertebrae, asked her for the pleasure of the dance and took the floor with her. My partner was the daughter of Bonar Law, and a most charming person: she quickly put me at my ease. But the ease was soon shattered by the unexpected breaking of my sock-suspender – a horrible piece of leg furniture that mercifully became obsolete with the advent of the nylon sock – which trailed across the floor as we gyrated. Other dancers kept on treading on the damn thing so that it alternately stretched and snapped back at me – 'ping', 'ping'. The wretched device held. If only it had broken and torn itself adrift I could have shamelessly denied all knowledge of it before the cock crowed thrice, but No! Eventually there was nothing for it; I had to relinquish the Excellent waist and make a dive to free myself of the offending gadget and stuff it in my pocket. Lady Sykes was superb: she carried on a chatty conversation without batting an eyelid as though nothing were more normal than for her dancing partners to divest themselves of sock suspenders in the middle of the ballroom floor.

All that I have so far said about Bombay may have given the impression that life was one continuous round of gaiety. This was not so. It is true that we all played hard, but some of us at least also worked hard. In the Tramway Company I was moved from department to department, often 'acting' for a senior man during his absence on home leave. Gradually I acquired a certain amount of experience of a wide, rather than deep, nature; but I felt myself to be out of the main stream, professionally speaking, of the engineering world. I thought it would be unwise to make my professional bed in Bombay. There were many examples before me of sleek, prosperous Englishmen who had settled in the city for thirty or forty years and who had acquired a good deal of money, position and prestige – even knighthoods. It was not for nothing that British India was known as the Paradise of the Middle Classes. Somehow the prospect of becoming an eminent Bombay citizen, even if I were to succeed as such, did not appeal to me; and I decided within two years that I would not renew my contract when it ran out after three years. I had gained something from my stay in India, though it was difficult to say

what. The somewhat unusual experience of driving a tramcar
when testing out a new braking system would scarcely count as
an asset when the time should come for me to apply for more
ambitious appointments. Nor was it likely that the fact that I
had become a licensed plumber would ever stand me in good
stead professionally! This peculiar qualification in no way
implied that I possessed even the rudiments of plumbing
knowledge or skill: it was a highly artificial ruse whereby my
firm could get its building plans approved by the Municipal
Engineer if the drawings bore my signature. For a short time I
had been in charge of the company's buildings, and on
discovering that a plumber's license could be obtained without
embarrassing tests or exams I had hit upon this perverse plan for
short-circuiting bureaucracy.

At any rate I knew a little more about the world, though
scarcely any more about engineering. That was one of the things
that bothered me. I began to feel that after three years I would
have sucked Bombay dry of all the experience it could usefully
offer me, and that surrender to an obvious future could only lead
to a comfortable, but empty life. Meanwhile I decided to enjoy
life and drink the Bombay cup to the dregs. I was more
prosperous than I had ever been before (and seldom since) and I
was making many good friends.

It was obvious that Bombay was not typical of India, and so I
put my local leaves to the best advantage by seeing as much of
the country as possible. I could not then know that I was
destined to spend many more years in India: I thought I would
soon be saying 'Goodbye' to the country for ever. So I visited
Poona and Mahableshwar, Bangalore, Ootacamund, Madras,
Benares, Sanchi, Delhi, Fatehpur Sikri, Cawnpore, Lucknow,
Bhopal, Agra and, of course the Taj Mahal. Nor did I neglect to
visit Portuguese Goa, where I spent four delightful days with
George and four other friends. We took all six cabins in one of
the small steamers that ply along the West coast, and departed
one Thursday before Easter. After a 24-hour journey, putting in

at small ports on the way, we reached Panjim one morning and put up at a picturesque, but airless little hotel at Marmagoa. The colony of Goa was renowned for two principal exports – mangoes and cooks – both excellent; also for brass bands, not so excellent. The public notices were written in Portuguese, which no one could read. The architecture was vaguely Manoelene. The place was a fantastic blend of Europe and Asia. There were cathedrals and monasteries in profusion; for had not Goa been the Christian capital of the East three or four hundred years before? The mutilated remains of St Francis Xavier are enshrined there in the cathedral of Bom Jesus and are periodically displayed to the Faithful when the pope feels the urge to give the saint an airing. His tomb has three keys. One is in the Vatican; one in Lisbon; the third *was* with the Portuguese Viceroy in Goa, but I know not where it is now. All three keys were needed to open the tomb.

One thing marred the fascination of Goa — *snakes*. They were everywhere. I saw more snakes in Goa in four days than in fifteen years elsewhere in India. Some years later I met an Englishwoman who had lived in Goa for six months when her husband had been assigned there by his employers, one of the leading banks. She was recovering from a nervous breakdown brought about by snakes. Snakes in the bed, snakes in her shoes, snakes coiled round the backs of chairs, snakes everywhere!

Snakes apart, one could feel the presence of Vasco da Gama and the Iberian renaissance in Goa, even though in a decayed and ruined form.

There was little mixing between Indians and Europeans in Bombay in those days, other than in business relationships. Each race had its own clubs; only a few, principally the Willingdon, were open to all races and creeds. Some Indians complained about the exclusiveness of the European clubs; but this was not entirely consistent, for no European would have been admitted to a Hindu club. I got to know a rather pleasant Anglo-Indian couple named Smith. He was very dark: she was a peroxide blonde. They were known as the blacksmith and the goldsmith.

At last my three-year contract approached its end and I interviewed my chief to tell him that I did not intend to renew it. He was rather upset. Out of all proportion to my merits he had apparently taken rather a fancy to me and had come to regard me as an ultimate successor to his chair after perhaps fifteen years or so. He thought me very foolish to throw away such a golden future; but I was adamant, though I agreed to stay on another four or five months to give him time to find my successor. This suited me, as it meant another 'cold weather' in India.

And so one April day in 1929 I found myself gazing over the stern of the Italian ship *Aquileia*, watching Bombay recede into the distance and feeling rather sad; for I had enjoyed life to the full in the last three and a half years. But I had no real regrets.

The voyage was luxurious: the food marvellous – even in the second class. The only jarring element was the ubiquitous portrait of a pop-eyed Mussolini glowering at us from all over the ship. At Suez I left the *Aquileia* with a party of friends to motor to Cairo. We were driven across the desert in an open car before dawn, and nearly froze to death. On arrival in Cairo we had to be revived with hot toddies. Then we saw the pyramids of Gizeh in pouring rain – the first wet weather they had experienced there for about three years: after that the citadel and the newly discovered treasures of Tutankhamen. A splendid lunch at Shepherd's Hotel made me feel I was in a very civilised world again. That same hotel was burnt to the ground some thirty years or so later by Egyptian chauvinists. We took train in the evening to Port Said and rejoined the ship for the last lap of the voyage. A day or two later I saw the indescribable beauty of Venice growing out of the sea in the early morning; and there we were, at anchor in the Grand Canal.

After steeping myself for several days in the charms of Venice out of season, with blue skies but cold air and no tourists, I concluded that she had no equal – not even the Taj Mahal. The city seemed to have changed but little since the days of Canaletto, and the absence of motor traffic was pure joy. I drank chocolate at Florian's on the Piazza San Marco in the tradition of the eighteenth century Grand Tour, explored St Marks, the Rialto, Santa Maria della Salute, admired the ancient bronze horses and the Colleoni statue, gazed at the treasures of the Doge's Palace, crossed the Ponte dei Sospire and in fact did all that the visitor is expected to do. I was rather shaken to find mosquito nets round my hotel bed: I had thought I had left such things behind me in India. Forty-one years later I was to revisit Venice. She was still beautiful, but visibly decaying. The Piazza and St Mark's were under water, and pedestrians had to walk on duck-boarding. Tragically, one of the most beautiful cities in the world was slowly sinking into the lagoon.

Then on to Milan and Aïda at La Scala; Locarno for a few days; over the Gothard to Luzern, where I renewed the acquaintance of a Swiss co-apprentice from my Lancashire days; Engelberg; the Rigi; Altdorf. Finally on to Paris for three days where I walked through my shoe leather exploring the city by day, and sat through the seat of my pants in the evening looking at the nudes at the Folies Bergères and feeling rather naughty.

I was met at Victoria station by my mother. My parents had moved into a small Regency house in Bayswater after my sisters and I had left the nest. They seemed like strangers to me. I had never been close to them, and now I knew I never would be. India meant nothing to them, and I was still too young adequately to appreciate their world.

The next four and a half years I put to good use by gaining experience and acquiring qualifications as an engineer, partly in London and partly in the Midlands. At first, reversion to near poverty after the affluence of Bombay life was painful, but it proved to be worthwhile; for in 1931 I landed a moderately well-paid appointment with the Central Electricity Board, which stood me in good stead for better things to come. By 1933 I was becoming restless, for I realised that I was only a small cog in a very large machine. I felt too young to settle down in a staid job waiting for dead men's shoes. Tedium laudamus was not my motto. At a more mature age I came to regard ambition as the enemy of happiness, but for a young man of barely thirty years a certain amount of ambition can serve as fuel to drive him forward and to prevent the premature formation of rust.

Then, like a bolt from the blue, came an offer which I found irresistible. A certain Englishman who had held various appointments in the princely state of Hyderabad was about to retire. Would I be interested in taking over from him the directorship of the Electricity Department? Here, apparently, was the opportunity I was seeking. To be chief of an interesting concern at the age of thirty or thirty-one was something that would never be offered twice. I telegraphed to say I was interested and went to London for an interview at the Hyde Park Hotel with some of the Hyderabad State ministers who were then attending the Round Table Conference on India's future political constitution. They offered me the princely salary of fifteen hundred rupees a month as deputy director, with a promise of more if I should succeed to the directorship. My salary would be tax-free and I would receive a reasonable car allowance. I accepted, bade farewell to my friends and sailed again for India in the P&O ship *The Viceroy of India*. Here, once again, was Chance sending me to India.

III

Pen portrait of a Pooh-Bah

It was into the feudal and outlandish world of Hyderabad that I was now pitched, and it was there that I lived for nearly twelve years in gilded splendour such as I had never known before, have never known since and shall never know again. I was destined to hold certain rather exotic appointments that do not usually fall to the lot of an ordinary engineer like myself; and to explain how this came about it is necessary to go back to the year 1908, when a certain Robert Loraine Gamlen started a train of cause and effect that was eventually to embroil me, although at that time I was a small boy in sailor suits who had heard neither of Gamlen nor of Hyderabad.

Gamlen was an extremely handsome man of unbounded self-confidence and romantic disposition. In his early youth he had fluttered on the fringes of elegant London Society when led by the Marlborough House set in the Naughty Nineties. He was, however, by no means of the idle rich. He had been trained as an electrical engineer when that profession was in its infancy – public electricity supply in Britain made its first appearance in 1878 only – and in his early thirties he took a job in Calcutta. While there, he heard that the Mintmastership of Hyderabad had fallen vacant. By comparison with the social life of Calcutta – a city of pukka (and not so pukka) sahibs – that of Hyderabad seemed to his romantic imagination to hold all the allurements of the court of Harun-al Rashid. He took train, at his own expense, to the Deccan, called on the Nizam's Finance

Minister, Sir James Cassom Walker, and applied for the post of Mintmaster and Superintendent of Stamps.

'And what do you know of minting and printing?' asked Sir James.

'Nothing,' replied Gamlen, 'but I'm an engineer and can soon learn.'.

By a nice combination of sheer cheek and personality Gamlen was taken at his word and appointed. With the job went a magnificent house – a veritable palace in miniature, with a large garden. The splendour of his surroundings and the feudal atmosphere of the State appealed to Gamlen's romantic soul: he fell in love with the place and stayed there for twenty-seven years.

The duties of directing the Mint and Stamps Department were not then particularly arduous, and it was not long before Gamlen found he had time on his hands. Being a man of abundant energy, and by virtue of his early training, he established an Electricity Department with himself as Director. At first this department supplied only the Mint, the Stamps Press, a group of government offices close by, a few large houses in the vicinity and (most important) the Mintmaster's residence (without a meter!). A special cable was also laid to supply the principal royal palace a mile or so away. Within this select area the oil batti gave place to the incandescent bulb and the old-fashioned boy-operated punkah yielded to the rotating electric fan. The virtues of these innovations soon claimed the attention of an ever-widening circle of environs that lay outside the privileged enclave. The electrical distribution system was gradually extended until, within a few years, it had reached the remote corners of the city, which boasted of some three-quarters of a million inhabitants. Anxious to keep up with the times, the British Administration of nearby Secunderabad and the military cantonments was supplied in bulk from the Hydera-bad power house. It was not long before the electrical child had outstripped its Mint parent in complexity, if not in prestige.

To serve the needs of the Mint, the Stamps Press and the new Electricity Department a versatile workshop was required; and this too was set up by Gamlen under his directorship. To improve the economic efficiency of this State Workshop he accepted orders from outside parties, notably the Public Works Department, on a commercial basis. In the course of time the activities of this new organisation covered a very wide range of manufacture, from road rollers to coffee spoons made from ancient coins, and from street lamp standards to vast quantities of fly buttons for the trousers of the Army and Police. Gamlen often described himself as the State Tinker.

As a natural sequel to all these enterprises their creator found it necessary to establish a large and well equipped Technical College of which, of course, he was Principal. This was for the purpose of feeding his other organisations with artisans and foremen.

In addition to all these major activities, Gamlen was appointed Warden of Weights and Measures, Consulting Engineer to the Secunderabad Cantonment Board, Electrical Inspector to the Government of the British Administered Territories and Justice of the Peace. He was made a Governor of the Victoria Memorial Orphanage and at one time became President of the Secunderabad Club. He was also made responsible for decorating the city with bunting and illuminations whenever a viceroy or other illustrious state guest paid a visit to the Nizam.

And so, little by little, Gamlen's empire grew; and with it the number of his enemies grew - for jealousy is certainly no less common a vice in India than elsewhere. When he began to age, the State government decided that never again would one man control so much. Mene and Upharsin, though not Tekel. By 1933 he was sixty-two or sixty-three and had already been given several extensions of office beyond the normal retirement age of fifty-five on grounds of indispensability. Something had to be done. It was therefore decreed that Gamlen should definitely retire in April 1935, that the Mint and Stamps Department should be taken over by an elderly Parsee who had for several years served as Deputy Mintmaster, that the Osmania Central Technical College should pass to its European vice-principal, and that a new man should be imported from Britain to inherit the Electricity Department. The fate of the State Workshop was left undecided for the time being.

Empire-building was by no means Gamlen's sole activity. He was a versatile musician with a pleasing baritone voice and a not inconsiderable gift for playing the piano and violin. His vast drawing room, furnished in the Victorian-Moghul style suggestive of Osborne House, with a plethora of carved blackwood tables and settees from Travancore, palm stands and autographed photographs of Indian nawabs and rajahs in silver frames, was often the setting for chamber music reproduced by such local talent as could be mustered from Hyderabad and nearby Secunderabad. On one great occasion no less a person than Dame Nellie Melba sang in that room.

Be-monocled, immaculately clad in tropical suit by day and in evening dress after sundown, Gamlen made an imposing figure. He was a good conversationalist and raconteur with a gift for aptly quoting from the works of W S Gilbert. His dinner parties, at which he could seat up to twenty-six people at one long table placed indoors in the 'cold weather' or monsoon and on the tennis court in the hot season, were enjoyed by thousands in the course of his long reign. His port wine was invariably served iced – an idiosyncracy that he was well able to carry off – and his brandy was handed round with a jug of hot water with which each guest was expected to rinse out his balloon glass before helping himself.

As an engineer, Gamlen appeared to have been a pupil of the late, and greatly lamented, Mr Heath Robinson. Although somewhat limited technically he had a flair for improvisation. A piece of mechanical equipment held together by wire and made to work by virtue of an improbable assembly of levers, cranks and wheels, held for him a greater appeal than any carefully streamlined contrivance. His economic vision was apt to be clouded by a prejudicial blind spot that enabled him to convince himself that some patently wasteful practice was economical, simply because it had been devised by himself as a masterpiece of unorthodox thinking.

In the early days of Gamlen's régime government procedure was very free and easy. The then reigning Nizam, Mahbub, was as open-handed as his son was close-fisted, and his Prime Minister, Nawab Sir Imam-ul-Mulk, was more concerned with champagne dinners than with the minutiae of administration. Heads of Departments, so long as they did not openly indulge in malpractices, had largely been left to their own devices and had enjoyed a considerable degree of autonomy. Gradually the cold hand of bureaucracy had tightened its grip and Gamlen found himself increasingly subjected to irksome restraints as the style of government slowly changed from the mediaeval towards the modern. An incoming Finance Secretary to the government, after vetoing a request from Gamlen for administrative sanction to some pet project of his, received a letter from him that began with the words 'And there arose a Pharaoh that knew not Joseph'. During the ten years that followed Gamlen's eventual departure from the state, government departments were subjected to increasingly bureaucratic interference from ignorant jacks-in-office: I was to learn from bitter experience the meaning of frustration.

Shortly after my arrival in Hyderabad, the Muses descended upon me and I was inspired to write the following piece of doggerel:-

> A stranger man you ne'er will see
> Than R.L. Gamlen, O.B.E.,
> Who undisputed sway doth hold
> O'er sixteen hundred souls all told
> (And even more than that, they hint)

PEN PORTRAIT OF A POOH-BAH

He sits enthroned within the Mint,
      Pooh-Bah of Hyderabad.

Now you or I might feel content
And e'en consider life well spent
If in this earthly pantomime
We play but one part at a time.
But singularity would bore
And *never* prove sufficient for
      Pooh-Bah of Hyderabad.

And so, to make life many-sided,
Occupations are provided
For our noble O.B.E.
To prove his versatility;
And thus it happens that his fame
Has aptly earned for him the name
      Pooh-Bah of Hyderabad.

Master of the Nizam's Mint,
Exalted stamps he too doth print;
And furthermore in all simplicity
He generates the electricity;
And lest the Rich the Poor should fleece
They made him Justice of the Peace
      To safeguard Hyderabad.

The niceties of education
Exercised a fascination
On his mind, in which pursuit
He built a technical institute
Which now may boast a well earned fame
(I think Osmania is its name):
      It stands in Saifabad.

As Electrical Inspector he
Is given full authority

Of Government to criticise
Contractors' work, expose their lies,
And generally make them fear
The name of this great engineer,
     Pooh-Bah of Hyderabad.

The Military Cantonment Board
Elected him with one accord
Consulting Engineer. His soul
At times assumes a different rôle
In charity (without a wage)
As guardian of an orphanage
     For babes of Hyderabad.

But still he found that boredom irks,
And so he started up a Works
Where craftsmanship of every grade
Is practised with the Master's aid.
He'll make a brooch or build a fleet
With equal ease. You can't defeat
     Pooh-Bah of Hyderabad.

Ex-president of local club;
Well... No. He *doesn't* keep a pub.
But nothing need surprise, because,
For fear he might be bored he was
(Compliant with Exalted pleasures)
Appointed Warden of Weights & Measures
     To the State of Hyderabad.

And if a Viceroy comes in state
To visit the Nizam en fête,
Then who the great occasion meets
By flying bunting in the streets
And makes the city gay to see?
Why! R.L. Gamlen, O.B.E.,
     Pooh-Bah of Hyderabad.

In April, 1935, Gamlen finally left Hyderabad and India. Up to the last he found it difficult to believe that the government would ever really insist on his retirement, and he hoped for yet another extension of service. Being crippled with asthma he went to live at Famagusta in Cyprus where the climate is kinder than in England. Within two or three years he died there.

A curious incident occurred at the time. As an amateur campanologist Gamlen had, many years previously, cast a bell in the foundry of his workshops. He was inordinately proud of this bell, which was hung outside the guardroom at the gate of his house and was struck every hour by one of the military guard. One day, the tone of the bell noticeably changed, adopting a muffled sound. Thinking that a crack might have developed I had the bell examined, but no flaw could be found. Then came the news of Gamlen's death. On the following day the bell resumed its former clarity of tone.

And so departed Robert Loraine Gamlen, one of the last of the British nabobs, a man of great versatility held by some in awe and by many in great affection and respect.

IV

Naib Nazim

After an overnight train journey from Bombay I arrived in Hyderabad in the early morning of 17th November, 1933. Gamlen met me at the station and drove me to his home, the Mint House, where I was icily received by his unmarried sister, Isobel Gamlen. Many years earlier, Mrs Gamlen had parted company from her husband and had returned to live in England, ever since when Isobel had reigned in her stead as Queen of the Mint. Clearly she did not take kindly to the thought of her brother's impending retirement and of her consequent loss of position: she found it difficult to conceal her resentment towards a young man of thirty whom she could only regard as an upstart and usurper. A married daughter of Gamlen was also staying with her father at the time of my arrival.

After a sumptuous breakfast I was taken on an extensive tour of Gamlen's dominions. This occupied all the morning. The Mint and the Stamps Press were subjected only to a cursory examination as these would not be my responsibilities, but the power house, electricity offices and workshops were shown to me in detail with great pride. I was impressed by the extent of my new chief's activities and by the evidence of his unbounded energy and ingenuity, though I was somewhat alarmed by the gim-crackery and untidiness that prevailed. The sight of a cow serenely chewing the cud in the turbine room of the power house, at the same time depositing her visiting cards at random on the tiled floors, rather shocked my ideas of good engineering 'house-keeping' but did not seem to strike my guide as in any way incongruous. The power house building itself had been built, at Gamlen's inspiration, in the saracenic style of architecture, with smoke (and plenty of it) issuing from pseudo minarets. (Any resemblance to the oriental was purely occidental). But this exotic effect was somewhat spoiled by the ruthless demolition of several panels of intricate Moghul tracery to make way for makeshift structural excrescences of rusty corrugated iron to serve some Heath Robinsonian and strictly utilitarian purpose to which the refinements of architectural correctitude had to take second place. Some of the machinery seemed to be so patched and decrepit that nothing short of a miracle could apparently account for the fact that it functioned at all.

In the afternoon I took possession of my desk in a large office room that I was to share with Gamlen. I was left alone to study records and routine documents while Gamlen went to attend a meeting of the Executive Council elsewhere. Suddenly an excited chaprassi rushed into the room wringing his hands and calling out 'Ag! Sahib, Ag!' Now although I had learned a modicum of Urdu in my earlier Bombay days, my vocabulary had become extremely rusty, and the meaning of the word 'Ag' had escaped me. Signing to the chaprassi to keep calm I searched for an English/Urdu dictionary and looked up the word. It meant 'Fire'. Fortunately by the time I had been led to the scene of excitement the fire had been safely extinguished.

Gamlen, his sister and daughter dined out in the evening of my first day in Hyderabad and I had to eat alone in solitary state in his huge dining room, waited upon by a posse of servants. There is nothing like loneliness in strange surroundings in the presence of dumb witnesses for raising doubts as to the wisdom of having taken a step that has led one into such a situation. That night I heard the unmistakable roaring of tigers. This was not so romantic as it sounds. The Zoo was only a quarter of a mile away.

43

My first experience of the absurd rigidity of the Hyderabad Civil Service Regulations was a hard one. The day of my arrival happened to be the first of a series of twelve consecutive public holidays on account of Ramzan. Although the Electricity Department, being regarded as a 'commercial' organisation, enjoyed only three of these holidays, the more leisurely government departments took advantage of them all. As a State civil servant, although I worked continuously from the day of my arrival, I was debarred from earning even *one anna* until the holidays had ended; so I had to wait for twelve days before I became entitled to any salary whatsoever. The most unkindest cut of all was that had I joined service one day earlier I would have been entitled to draw salary immediately. In ignorance of this absurd rule I had dallied a whole day in Bombay to meet old friends.

It had been arranged that I was to live en famille at the Mint House as a paying guest. I was allotted a fair-sized bed-sitter with my own dressing room and bathroom. At the end of each month, Isobel made out her accounts and gave me a bill, the amount of which fluctuated according to the extent of entertainment during the preceding weeks. This would have been quite satisfactory if any of the innumerable guests who flocked to the Mint for dinners, tennis and bridge parties had been of my choosing or if some of them, at least, had credited me with an iota of hospitality. As things were, I was regarded as 'the lodger', placed well below the salt at dinner and was never offered a word of thanks by any of the guests for hospitality partly paid for by me. Tennis parties at the Mint were famed for chicken sandwiches – a curious diet for such occasions – while Isobel's bridge parties (in which I took no part, having an intense dislike of cards) were famous for a different reason. For while Isobel collected her winnings in cash, she paid out her losses with sticks of celery grown in the Mint garden. Celery was a sufficiently rare delicacy in Hyderabad as to be regarded by the hostess, if not by the recipients, as a form of currency (with unspecified rate of exchange).

After a few months of this domestic régime, and after a few minor humiliations inflicted upon me by Isobel, I decided to move my quarters to the Secunderabad Club where I could enjoy a greater degree of social freedom. It was with some apprehension that I announced to Gamlen my intention of doing this, but he took it very well, even expressing surprise that I had endured the situation for so long.

As though to emphasise the fact that Hyderabad was in some ways a few centuries behind the times, the government observed two Muslim calendars. One was the hijri, or lunar calendar dating from the Prophet's flight from Mecca to Medina in 622 AD. All religious festivals and observances were fixed according to this reckoning. The other was the fasli, or solar calendar, used for dating secular events. I arrived in Hyderabad in the year 1353H, or 1343F. It was not very difficult to imagine one was living in the fourteenth century.

A day or two after my arrival at the Mint House I was taken by Gamlen on a calling tour. Visitors' books were provided at the Residency, the Nizam's King Kothi Palace, the palaces of the two young 'official' princes, Flagstaff House (the residence of the British GOC) and at the devdis of the more important and wealthy nawabs and rajahs from the paigah nobles and prime minister downwards. These books had to be signed and visiting cards left. Calling on less exalted folk was simplified by the provision of a rack of miniature posting boxes at the Secunderabad Club, to which 'everyone' belonged. All that was required was to post the correct number of cards through the slots of these boxes and then await a dinner invitation. Could anything be simpler, or more absurd? Bachelors and grass widowers were also expected to call on all the regimental messes, both of the Indian Army and of the British Army in India stationed in the Secunderabad Cantonments. This chore was rewarded by a formal invitation from each colonel to enjoy the privileges of honorary membership of his mess – not that one would have dreamed of dropping in, uninvited, to any mess.

The result of all this calling was a life enriched by banquets, garden parties, balls and mess dinners. It was always my misfortune to be invited to mess dinners during the hottest season, when the agonies of wearing full evening dress with stiff collar and white tie were hard to bear. The discomfort, however, was well worth enduring for the sake of the unique atmosphere that still smacked of pre-Mutiny India – of mess uniforms, shining silver trophies, loyal toasts, the regimental band playing during dinner, the port circulating clockwise and the snuff counter-clockwise, the inevitable invitation from the colonel to the bandmaster to take a glass of port with him at the end of the meal. This Kiplingesque atmosphere prevailed even in the daytime throughout the cantonment area – a conglomeration of small districts such as Trimulgherry, Bowenpalli and Bolarum under the collective name of Secunderabad. The stately porticoed barrack buildings, the smell of horses, the sound of bugles and of crisp commands, the neat beds of cannas, the flagstaffs, the polished brass of the gunners, the British cemetery and the stuccoed 'gothic' garrison churches: all this contributed to an illusion of the permanence of the British Raj. Little seemed to have altered since the early nineteenth century, except the advent of the motor-car – and that was by no means obtrusive. When Gamlen had first gone to Hyderabad he had attended regimental dinners and balls in Bolarum and had made the ten-mile homeward journey by bullock cart, lulled to sleep beneath the stars by the lilting motion and the squeaking of the wheels.

There was a most romantic spot near Bowenpalli near the barracks, occupied at the time of my arrival on the scene by the Baluchi regiment. Close to a banyan tree was a typical Indian well, a deep wide hole in the ground surrounded by a low parapet wall measuring perhaps twelve to fifteen foot square. A few yards away stood a gravestone to mark the burial spot of a young British officer and his charger who had perished there early in the nineteenth century. One night, when the drink had been flowing freely in the mess, the officer had laid a wager that he would jump the well on horseback that very moonlit night. He put himself to the test then and there, but failed to clear the well. Horse and rider were both killed. To visit this eerie spot at full moon while the rest of the world slept was almost enough to make one believe in ghosts.

Another famous spot, also in Bowenpalli, was the regimental mess building that had once housed the famous Sir Ronald Ross, who had traced malaria to the anopheles mosquito in that very building. Ross had been dead only about a year when I first saw this house and the memorial plaque to mark the great discovery.

Since Urdu was the official language of the State (regardless of the fact that some eighty percent of the population could not speak it) it was necessary for me to brush up the very rudimentary knowledge of it that I had acquired in Bombay; the 'Ag' incident had underlined this need. I engaged a venerable white-bearded munshi who, according to universal custom, produced a sheaf of faded testimonials for my inspection. Glancing through them I noticed one signed by a Lieutenant W S Churchill at the turn of the century. In 1933 that ex-officer was in the political doldrums; but I advised the munshi to take particular care of his letter, as it might become quite valuable one day.

Meanwhile, on the assumption that I would be taking charge of the Electricity Department after rather more than a year, I had to study my future job. The physical and 'electrical' geography of the city and environs had to be learned by heart, my fellow departmental officers (all Indians) had to be known and observed, plans had to be tentatively hatched for improvements that in my opinion could be introduced after I was in the saddle, the power plant and its performance had to be carefully studied and the departmental routine mastered. Although I had been imported explicitly with a view to taking charge of the Electricity Department, Gamlen left to me most of

the day-to-day management of the Workshops – an activity by
no means to my taste. The jargon used in government
correspondence was easily picked up, and I soon learned that if I
wanted the contents of a letter to be widely publicised I had only
to mark it 'strictly confidential' – or better still 'secret' – and the
whole world would know of it in no time. One minor problem
bothered me slightly because opinions differed as to its solution.
Should the word 'government' be treated as singular or plural,
and should it be spelt with a small or a capital 'G'? This point
was eventually solved to my satisfaction by a senior British civil
servant whom I had known for some years. 'His Majesty's
Government *are*,' said he. 'Other governments *is*.'

Gamlen's dinners were attended by all castes and creeds –
British, Muslim, Hindu, Parsee and Anglo-Indian. They also
covered a wide range of rank, from the prime minister or British
Resident to junior subalterns and nursing sisters from the
military cantonments. A good cross-section of local society
could therefore be seen at these dinners which, like the much
larger banquets of the State nobility, formed a prominent
feature of Hyderabad life. Bridge, vingt-et-un music and
conversation occupied the guests after dinner.

The Secunderabad Club was the focal centre of the social
life of the British community. Although there were Indian
members, few of them made much use of it. The club was
mostly frequented by the officers of the British and Indian
Army Garrison, the civilian officers of the Nizam's State
Railway who inhabited a separate enclave at Lalaguda two or
three miles away, and the few European state officials – and, of
course, the wives and families of members. The club was well
equipped with swimming pool, library, shop, restaurant, bar,
ballroom, billiard room, squash and tennis courts, stag lounge
and mixed lounge, residential quarters and, above all, the *lawn*.
As in all Indian clubs the lawn was the favoured place for
sipping drinks after sundown, being the coolest spot available.
The library was well stocked. On one occasion Isobel Gamlen

wrote to the Library secretary to complain that one of the books
was obscene. To support her contention she quoted many page
numbers and lines. 'Dear Madam', came the reply, 'You appear
to have studied this book very thoroughly'.

The British Indian community of Secunderabad had an
aptitude for dubbing certain conspicuous characters with
appropriate nicknames. A particularly stout parson was known
as 'Pregnant Percy'; a lady addicted to the bottle was 'Shot-away
Sheila'; while the eloquent sobriquets of two other local ladies
were 'Bed-and-breakfast Betty' and 'The Charpoy Cobra'; and
a chinless lady was referred to as 'The hangman's dilemma'.

A few weeks after my arrival in Hyderabad a five-day state
visit was paid to the Nizam by the Viceroy and Lady
Willingdon. Gamlen was responsible for illuminating the city
and for erecting screens of coconut matting, decorated with
crude paintings of elephants, tigers and improbable flowers, for
the purpose of concealing from the viceregal eye the more sordid
dwellings along the ceremonial routes by which the Willingdons
were to drive through the city. This work kept both him and me
very busy for a month before the great occasion. As a mere Naib
Nazim, or deputy director, I was not eligible for the more
exclusive banquets, but I attended the more democratic garden
parties and even the Residency Ball. I had to wait five years for
the next viceregal visit before being admitted to the 'full works'.

The Residency ball was a very glittering function of civil and
military uniforms, crystal chandeliers and Japanese lanterns in
the gardens – the latter put up under the supervision of Gamlen
and myself. The splendour of the occasion was not quite
matched by the sanitary amenities: the 'gentlemen' was
furnished with an impressive array of chamber pots aligned with
military precision upon a long wooden bench, the height of
which had been calculated to a statistical nicety so that only the
shortest of the guests need stand on tip-toe while none but the
tallest and the least skilful of marksmen would be compelled to
genuflect. I observed a colonial bishop, correctly clad in

episcopal purple, eyeing the arrangements critically, as though to reassure himself that there were indeed thirty-nine articles – no more and no less.

The arrival procession of the Viceroy and Vicereine from the railway station to the Falaknuma Palace, which served as a guesthouse for the viceregal party, passed through the city by the famous Char Minar, a sixteenth century victory memorial of vast proportions. This building had been equipped as a grandstand for government officials and their ladies who wished to view the procession. Gamlen, as one of the élite had to attend the welcoming ceremony at the station and needed his car for this; so I volunteered to transport Isobel Gamlen and her niece to the Char Minar in my car. After dropping my passengers there, I went off to park the car, and on returning I found two ladies ensconced in front seats. It had not occurred to them to keep a seat for their 'chauffeur' who had no choice but to stand at the back.

Somewhat unwisely I had imported into India a long, low sports Lagonda car which I had owned in England and to which I was very attached: I cut quite a dash with it in Hyderabad and Secunderabad. One day I was invited by Lady Chenevix-Trench, the wife of the Honourable Police and Revenue Member of the State Executive Council, to accompany her and her brother to the ancient fortress of Bidar, a stronghold of the Bahmani dynasty of Muslim kings who had ruled the Deccan for two hundred years from the fourteenth to the sixteenth centuries of the Christian era. To show willing – or as some might say, to swank! – I offered to take them in my car. This was accepted, and the three of us set forth early one Friday morning. After some fifty miles we came to a bad patch of road to which the Lagonda, with its very low ground clearance, was ill suited. The crank-case was holed, the oil gushed out, and we came to an ignominious halt. Fortunately a roadside police outpost was not far away, and as Lady Trench's husband was in charge of police affairs we were treated with great deference and invited to make free use of the spartan shelter afforded by the outpost hut. Telephone there was none. We were stranded. This was particularly unfortunate because a civil reception awaited our party at Bidar. After an hour a country bus, bound for Bidar and packed with odorous passengers and a couple of goats came by. We stopped it and sent an appropriate message of apology to the taluqdar of Bidar. Later, another bus came along from the opposite direction, bound for the capital. By this we sent an SOS to Sir Richard Chenevix-Trench. After that there was nothing more we could do but to resign ourselves to a long wait. Eventually, at about four o'clock in the afternoon, when we were half starved and very thirsty, two relief parties arrived more or less simultaneously. From Bidar came the taluqdar with a posse of local notables, who covered us with garlands and prot- estations of esteem and sympathy and regaled us with most welcome curry puffs and sherbet. From Hyderabad came the minister's car with a length of rope, with which my derelict Lagonda was taken in tow. Then followed a nightmare journey over fifty miles of untarred road in a cloud of dust so thick that I could scarcely discern even *my* end of the tow-rope. No warnings of stops or of bends in the road could be given to me. Somehow we made harbour, where my appearance must have inwardly shaken the outward imperturbability of the servants. From head to foot I was white with dust: the only sign of an inner man was a pair of crimson bloodshot eyes. It took hours to clean myself, and days to clean the car. A new crankcase was very soon made in Gamlen's versatile workshop.

By far the most important event to me personally during my sixteen months of naib-nazim-ship was my engagement to be married. The young daughter of a British colonel in the Indian Army, freshly down from Oxford, had accepted for the sake of experience a teaching post in a large Indian girls' school in Hyderabad. She arrived there a couple of months after I did and lived in the school staff bungalow only a few hundred yards from the Mint. We met at a tennis party at the Gamlens, and she wrote to her mother in England to say she had met 'rather a nice old man'. I was thirty. Within a few weeks I took her for a moonlight drive to Golconda in the Lagonda (a happy euphony), and there popped the question. A more romantic setting to a proposal would be hard to imagine. The gaunt hill fortress and the huge mausolea of the Qutb Shahi kings, floodlit by the moon, surpassed the wildest extravaganzas that could have been thought up by Hollywood: the only sound to be heard was the chirruping of myriads of cicadas. After 1934 Golconda became the scene of an annual nocturnal pilgrimage à deux on March 23rd for eleven consecutive years – moon or no moon. We were married in January, 1935, in St Peter's cathedral church, Colombo, and spent a blissful honeymoon in Ceylon and what were then the Dutch East Indies.

When we returned to India we were met at Secunderabad station by a large gathering of Electricity Department officers and employees. We were profusely garlanded and driven to our first home – a freakish building of improbable architecture standing on a high stepped plinth and situated opposite the Secunderabad Club. This curious house, which had an octagonal drawing room, was our home for a few weeks only, during which time I fought a successful skirmish with the Hyderabad government for possession of the Mint House after Gamlen's retirement. In theory, his house should have passed to the new incoming Parsee Mintmaster; but as he was already past retiring age and had a perfectly good home of his own, it was eventually agreed that I should occupy the house provided I paid ten percent of my salary as rent. As the Mint House was about the most splendid home in Hyderabad except for the Residency and the palaces of the 'nawabery', I accepted this arrangement with alacrity, especially as the house was only a few yards from my office. I had, however, no security of tenure. Everything depended upon who would succeed to the Mint-mastership after the Parsee's retirement, which could not be long delayed. However, sufficient unto the day was the evil thereof. I kept my fingers crossed.

The next act of the State government, in their generosity, was to bequeath me the directorship of the State Workshops – without extra salary!

Gradually the day of Gamlen's impending departure approached. I looked forward to it with mixed feelings. The attainment of a senior position at the age of thirty-one, together with the acquisition of a splendid house, were matters for great satisfaction; but the responsibilities were rather formidable to one so inexperienced as myself. The lotus-eating days of my deputy-directorship, during which I had worked hard but had been exempt from making major decisions, were drawing to an end. An interminable series of farewell functions filled Gamlen's last days. He had become a rather embittered man by then. Feeling in honour bound to inform him of certain changes I intended to make after taking charge of the department, I was amazed and disappointed at his obvious and intense anger on hearing of them. If I liked to make a fool of myself that was my affair, was his attitude. What had been a very happy relationship between us for more than a year ended in estrangement. Gamlen was also a very sick man, with acute asthma; and he found the farewell ceremonies with their endless speechifying, garlanding and declaimings in verse very irksome.

Finally the great day came. The railway station was thronged with many hundreds of his employees, servants, friends, ministers and others. Garland after garland was placed round his neck until his tired face was only just discernible in the middle of what looked like a float at the mi-carême carnival at Nice. All of a sudden there was a disturbance, as four coolies made their way through the crowd bearing an immense scale model of the Golden Temple of Trichinopoly, made in pith. It was a parting present from the Stamps Department. The monstrous creation must have measured at least six foot by four foot and could only be squeezed into the railway compartment, already overflowing with luggage, by manoeuvering it sideways.

Poor Gamlen's face was a study. I have often wondered how he disposed of that enormous white elephant, hardly suitable for service as a paperweight or as a chimney-piece ornament in a western home. Osborne House could doubtless have taken it in its stride, but freightage would have been a problem.

I was rather disconcerted to see the army of Gamlen's former employees weeping copiously on all sides.

The day was 3rd April, 1935 AD, or 28th Ardibehisht, 1344 F. I was no longer a naib nazim but a fully fledged Nazim of two government departments. I must confess I felt rather frightened.

V

Nazim, Mahakma Barqi

I need not have been worried by the tears that I had seen shed at Gamlen's departure. The very next day I was approached by a large crowd of employees of the Electricity Department and State Workshop. They were wreathed in smiles and had come to congratulate me on my succession and to assure me of their delight in the change of régime which 'heralded an age of promise', adding further flowery insincerities. I made the conventional and platitudinous speech of self-deprecation and spoke of the difficulty of filling the vacuum in their hearts left by the departure of my predecessor whom they had held in such high regard, as witness the emotion displayed the day before at the station. This was shrugged aside. It appeared that tears at the departure of a senior state officer were a matter of tradition and meant nothing. I then discovered the true object of the deputation: it was to ask for a day's holiday to mark the 'auspicious occasion of my elevation'. I deemed it politic to grant a *half*-day's holiday.

Ten years later I in my turn was seen off at the railway station in the presence of a weeping multitude, and I had not the slightest doubt that my successor in office would be receiving similar protestations of transferred loyalty on the next day, as well as a request for a special holiday! The Indian seems to be capable of turning on his tears as though from a tap.

As Director of HEH The Nizam's Electricity Department I rejoiced in the title of Nazim, Mahakma Barqi. Translated

55

literally this meant that I was the director of the Department of Lightning. It had never been my intention to usurp the prerogative of Jove or Thor, but it seemed that, willy-nilly, I had been set up as a Pretender.

For ten years I strove for the technical and administrative improvement of my first department, sometimes against fearful odds, particularly during the war years. Professionally I was, of course, in a backwater and I knew it; but the experience stood me in good stead in later life and I have never regretted those years – though there were too many of them. The pay, at first, was princely by comparison with what I could have earned in England at that time and at my age; but the real dividend afforded me by the job, and the other jobs that were to follow, was the unique opportunity of witnessing – as it were from a ringside seat – the sunset of a feudal world, now dead as the dodo, and the last years of the two centuries old British Raj. Hyderabad was as different from Bombay as Bombay was from Balham.

One of my first tasks on taking office was to persuade the government to appoint a new deputy director to share some of my burdens. Every one of my departmental officers, both in the Electricity Department and in the State Workshop, was a Hyderabadi. Some of them were good men in their limited way but several had a great propensity for intrigue; a few of them were clearly corrupt. Of the two or three on whose integrity and loyalty I could rely, none had sufficiently wide experience to take a major hand in the direction of either of my two departments. The government, in their inimitable and bureaucratic way, took advantage of my youth and newness in office to cut the offered salary of the deputy director to well below what I had been paid for that post. Ministers and officials to whom I protested took refuge behind 'His Exalted Highness's pleasure'. I was unwilling to force the issue to the point of resignation because, had it been accepted, I feared that my departure from the state at the tender age of thirty-one so soon after taking over

Our temporary woodworking shop. It was needed when the State workshops were bursting at the seams. It produced anything from foundry patterns to furniture. The vigilant foreman sits at his raised desk on the right.

Our machine shop. Note the overhead, old-fashioned belt drives to the individual machines and the foreman's desk in the distance. The workshop would normally have been alive with humanity. Did the photographer clear the area for action?!

Our temporary saw mill at the State Workshops. Apart from our own work we also fulfilled work for other Government Departments.

Our fitting and assembly shop. In the (right) distance is a large mortar mill for the Public Works Department. Hindu, Muslim and Christian workers were employed.

The portico of the
Mintmaster's House.

The author's drawing of the
house, where he spent his early
married life. 23 servants
administered to its needs.

The drawing room
of the house was
cruciform, with a
polished marble
floor. Some of the
furniture was
made in the state
workshops.

An unlikely example of Saracenic architecture—the Hyderabad power station: a folly of the author's predecessor. Coal-fired, it supplied electricity to the whole city and also to the * British administered areas of Secunderabad.

The dumb policeman of Hyderabad, designed by the author and made in the Electricity Department workshops; positioned by the Public Gardens. At night its hands and sleeves lit up, and its eyes blinked by means of a simple electro-magnetic pendulum hidden in its abdomen.

would be interpreted by my professional colleagues in England as failure to hold down the job. To find a really good man at the pittance offered was impossible. Some of the letters I wrote to prospective candidates failed to reach their destination and were undoubtedly intercepted: my Indian staff were certainly aware of my efforts to recruit an outsider. I was reduced to sending my correspondence from the British post office in Secunderabad, from where the chances of a letter's arrival at its destination were higher.

After two or three months I recruited a rather part-worn European of eccentric and unattractive habits, some twenty years my senior in age, whose technical ability was very limited but whose enthusiasm for theosophy and 'phoney' philosophy was unbounded. I will call him Mr 'Y', or rather *Captain* 'Y' as he liked to be called. Unwisely I invited him to stay with us at our home for a few days after his arrival in Hyderabad, until he could find permanent quarters. After the 'few days' had stretched to several weeks he was eventually persuaded to move elsewhere by words far blunter than the broadest of hints. Evidently he had not heard of that excellent proverb to the effect that after three days guests and fish stink.

During those tedious weeks we were treated to endless monologues on all the claptrap of theosophy – karma, nirvana, astral bodies, transmigration and the lot. Hitherto I had associated theosophy with elderly maiden ladies who worshipped at the shrine of Annie Besant, Madame Blavatsky and Colonel Olcott; but I had never met a *man* so completely under the spell of this trinity as Captain 'Y'. The Mecca of theosophy is Adyar, a pleasant suburb of Madras. It was there, I have heard, that a certain guest was invited to a meeting in the early days of the movement. When someone rose to make a spe·ch, an earnest lady whispered in the guest's ear 'That is the famous Colonel Olcott. He was once Asoka, you know'. 'Really?' came the reply, 'And how did you cure him?'

One day Captain 'Y' came to my office and calmly told me had talked for two hours on the previous evening with his wife.

57

As the lady in question was at that time living in Geneva, I remarked that a two-hour trunk call from India must indeed have cost him a fortune. 'Oh!' said he, 'I didn't telephone. This was an *astral* conversation'. Some time afterwards he was bemoaning the fact that he so much wanted to see his wife again but could not afford to take overseas leave. 'That's easily solved', said I. 'You need only take astral leave without incurring the cost of a P&O ticket.'

A year or two later his wife returned to India and, after a respectable lapse of time, produced a baby boy. Captain 'Y' announced this event to me in language typical of himself. 'A fine boy!' he proudly declared. 'Mother and child are both doing well and the milk is flowing freely'.

Not the least attraction of my job was the Mint House that had been allotted to me and which afforded a splendid setting to our early married life. In the language of an estate agent it could have been described as 'a highly desirable residence in the Colonial style, standing in its own grounds (as though it could have stood in any other) and provided with 22 rooms including six bathrooms (h & c), each with "toilet".' The sanitary norm in up-country India in those days was the portable commode, aptly known as the 'thunder-box'. To possess even *one* plumbed WC was a considerable status symbol: to have *six* was positively plutocratic. The drawing room was cruciform in shape and measured sixty feet each way and twenty feet high. Access to the house was by way of an imposing pillared portico with a wide flight of steps adorned with innumerable potted cannas and crotons. Broad verandahs ran across the building, back and front, on both floors. An array of outbuildings provided servants' quarters, kitchen, garage, godowns, stables and a dhobi-ghat. A large and beautiful garden surrounded the house and there were two tennis courts. A blaze of colour was provided by the flaming gulmohr trees, the creeping masses of alamanda, thunbergia, antigone, bignonia and Dutchman's pipe, by potted poinsettias, cannas, hybiscus and by annuals; while the night air was sweetened by the overpowering scent of frangipani and rat-ki-rani (Queen of the night).

To support this stately home no less than twenty-three servants were in attendance. Six of these were gardeners provided by a (sometimes) munificent government. The financial burden of keeping the remaining seventeen at my own expense was not heavy, since the three principal servants – the head boy, the khitmagar and the cook – were paid only thirty-five Hyderabad rupees a month each (£27 a year). Lesser fry earned from £4 to perhaps £12 a year and the total wage bill amounted only to about £175 a year. Theoretically the servants provided their own food out of their wages, but from the rate at which our stores disappeared it was clear that this was at least partly fiction. To those who would talk of 'exploitation' or 'slavery' I can only reply that these wages were paid at the prevailing market rates, that locally produced food was incredibly cheap, that the living conditions in a European household were positively luxurious by comparison with the squalid homes from which the servants came, that any servant was free to leave our service at any time if he wished, and, above all, that the entire staff was undoubtedly contented. A very happy relationship was established between our servants and ourselves. They were always respectful and we treated them with courtesy and insisted that our children always spoke to them politely, with a 'Please' or a 'Thank you'. When, years later, the time came for us to leave Hyderabad, being anxious to find good jobs for the three or four principal servants who had been with us for many years, we tried to use our good offices to find them employment in the Residency where their prestige would be boosted by imposing liveries; but our offer was politely declined. After years in our service, they said, they would never be happy doing domestic work elsewhere. For thirty years after we had left India these servants wrote to us regularly in quaintly worded English, lamenting the vanished past and enquiring affectionately after 'Baba Sahib', and 'Baby Sahiba' after these two children of ours had themselves become parents of families. Then, in quick succession, with one exception they died. The last survivor, as I now write, still writes to us regularly, as do the widow and son of another.

The multiplicity of servants was largely due to an unwritten 'trades unionism' of custom. Each 'boy' would only undertake certain specific duties, and no others. If these duties were sufficiently important he expected to be provided with a 'matey'. Thus the cook, the khitmagar and the dhobi each had an assistant, the car driver had an attendant cleaner, and the head mali was supported by five female malans. A minor member of our domestic community was the dog-boy, whose duty it was to exercise and groom our dog. The only way of ensuring that the dog was properly exercised was to tell the dog boy to deliver an unnecessary 'chit' to some friend a mile or so away; otherwise, the boy and dog would be liable to squat under a tree a hundred yards from home.

Naturally Guen could undertake no domestic chores herself: to have done so would have meant irreparable loss of face! But as châtelaine she had a great time organising the household, a task at which she was extremely efficient. Every morning she would sit at the seat of custom with the keys of the store cupboards as the servants came in to receive their orders for the day. Dirty laundry was handed to the dhobi and newly washed linen was checked and neatly stowed away. Clean dusters were issued against the return of used ones. Soap, polishes and cleaning materials were given out after checking the dates of the last issues. Meals were ordered for the day and the cook's bazaar bill was checked. A modicum of 'perks' was winked at, but brazen pilfering was reprimanded before it became a habit.

The khitmagar and head boy were each issued with a livery, consisting of a long white coat, white trousers, white pagri with a green and yellow band bearing a chrome plated monogram of 'Master's' initials (made in the Mint) and a broad cummerbund of the same colours – all in duplicate, except the monogram. No servant ever appeared before his employers wearing shoes: to have done otherwise would have been a mark of the greatest disrespect. The drawback of this custom was that one could not hear the approach of a servant; and it was difficult sometimes to repress a start of surprise when one of them suddenly materialised from nowhere.

In addition to my own private car I was also provided by the government with a departmental car, together with a uniformed chauffeur.

But our most imposing status symbol was the military guard at the gate of our 'compound'. A platoon and NCO of the Hyderabad Regular State Forces were on duty there, day and night. Their ostensible duty was to guard the Mint, with its treasure, and the person of the Mintmaster. In the early days of our occupancy of the Mint House I was not responsible for the Mint, nor was I the Mintmaster; so I enjoyed this unsolicited honour vicariously. Later, it became mine by right, but that is another story. In point of fact, the chief occupation of the guard was to strike the hours on a large bell – the bell that had behaved so mysteriously when Gamlen died – and to present arms whenever I came or went. This latter courtesy did not extend to Guen when she was unaccompanied by me, as women were considered to be second-class citizens according to Muslim thinking. Later, when our son was still a very small boy, the guard would present arms to *him*.

Our family and domestic staff formed a self-contained community. We baked our own bread, reared our own poultry and geese, grew our own vegetables, oranges, mangoes and bananas, had our own laundry facilities and even our own self-contained water supply system with chlorination and filters. It was all curiously suggestive of an eighteenth century English country squire's home. Household stores such as meat, fish, tea, sugar, coffee and flour were bought from the local bazaar by the cook; while more exotic foods such as New Zealand butter, tinned delicatessen and imported kippers were obtainable from the club shop. Until the War we were supplied with excellent milk from the British Military Dairy in Secunderabad, but supplies to civilians were stopped in about 1940 and we had to rely thereafter on buffalo milk. The buffalo was brought to the side door of our house every day and milked there under Guen's eye, so that the produce could be measured at source before 'the rain got in'. Unfortunately this earthy scene was sometimes marred by the sight (and smell) of a dead calf carried before the mother buffalo to bluff her into extending her lactation period.

Inoculations against plague, cholera, enteric and paratyphoid were frequently necessary. An important statistic known as the 'flea index' was published every week by the Public Health Department. This had something to do with the average number of fleas found on each killed or captured rat and was regarded as a measure of the risk of plague. When the flea index reached some prescribed figure, anti-plague inoculation was recommended. The doctor would then arrive at our house with a stock of vaccine, and the Ceremony of the Needle would follow. The simple Indian is apt to be terrified of the hypodermic syringe. It was therefore necessary for an example to be set by Guen and myself. We would head the queue by being inoculated first in full view of the assembled company (and therefore reaping the benefit of the needle when at its sharpest). By smiling and chatting while this was being done we were supposed to inspire the onlookers with a mite of confidence, so that the entire household in order of precedence would then timidly present their arms and those of their children. As most of the servants were very prolific, some eighty or ninety jabs were necessary, often to the accompaniment of tears.

One of Captain 'Y's' foibles was a strong disapproval of all forms of inoculation. He loved to talk about the 'body beautiful', 'polluting the purity of the blood' by the introduction of 'alien fluids'. When he heard that our children had been vaccinated he tried to lecture me on the wickedness of submitting innocent 'babes' to such evil practices. Impatiently I said that if he failed to have his own children vaccinated in a country like India he was taking a great risk. Sadly, a year or two later their small unvaccinated son caught smallpox and died. The parents quickly abandoned their former principles and got themselves vaccinated.

We did not actually occupy the Mint House until some weeks after Gamlen had left, as the whole place badly needed decorating. A grimy wallpaper of some twenty-seven years' standing was stripped off and the walls were entirely repainted. As with the Forth Bridge, this was no mean operation, and it involved a great deal of scaffolding. The formidable task of curtaining and carpeting such a vast house made us decide at first to occupy some of the rooms only, leaving the others empty. Within two or three years, however, when our children started to appear on the scene and an English 'Nanny' had been imported for their care, we had filled every corner of the house as a gas fills its container. The furniture we bought was by no means valuable – apart from the cost, the climate and insects were hostile to really good furniture. Much of ours was made in the State Workshops to my design. By dint of choosing pleasing curtains, sofa covers and rugs we gradually made for ourselves a cheerful and beautiful home. Our only household possessions of real value were our oriental rugs, which we had started to collect from the days of our engagement. These have since followed us from home to home and are, I am glad to say, still with us, though some of them are rather the worse for wear. Very little of our furniture was bought from Gamlen as his tastes leant rather towards massive and heavily carved Indian pieces. We did, however, buy from him his long dining table and a dresser, both made in his workshops; also a large lampshade that hung in the middle of the huge drawing room. It had been made by Isobel in the saracenic style and was christened by us 'Brighton Pavilion'. It would have looked horrific in any house but the Mint, but it seemed entirely appropriate in that huge room.

The cost of setting up house was alarming; but so great was the rate of inflation during the last few years of our occupation that it proved to have been a good investment.

Pride in our house, tinged with a pardonable measure of vanity, led us to continue the Gamlen tradition of entertaining. This offered none of the difficulties that face the chore-burdened hostess of modern England. It was only necessary to tell the cook, even at short notice, that there would be twenty to dinner, to choose a menu and to await our guests. Food was incredibly cheap except for imported luxuries: pigeons cost 1p each! Far from resenting large parties, our cook would become restive if more than a week or two passed without one; for he was a true culinary artist who liked to have scope for exercising his talents. Some of his creations would have done credit to Claridges, particularly his sweet courses. What was seemingly a miniature grass lawn held in a flat dish and covered with mushrooms and a bird would prove to be a concoction of marshmallow, pistachio nuts and meringue. At one of our dinners the woman next to me was offered fairly late in the meal what she took to be crumbed cutlets, complete with frills, in brown gravy. Thinking this to be a display of vulgar gourmandism she refused it. The 'cutlets' were in fact of ice-cream, the 'crumbs' fragments of walnut, and the 'gravy' was chocolate sauce: even the frills were of the edible kind commonly associated with macaroons.

With two hard tennis courts it was a simple matter to give tennis parties on Fridays, and with whisky at eleven shillings a bottle it was easy also to give drinks parties. Our vast drawing room could accommodate fifty guests or more without a trace of crowding.

Among the legion of guests we entertained over several years in the Mint House, apart from local 'notables' like Prime Ministers and Residents, were Somerset Maugham, Beverly Nichols and Lord (then Sir Walter) Monckton who used to visit Hyderabad to advise the Nizam on constitutional affairs. All this entertaining did not of course exclude the simple pleasure of breakfast or moonlight picnics for just the two of us.

One unfortunate result of our hospitality was that we acquired an unmerited reputation of immense wealth that we did not possess. We were, of course, comfortably off for the time being; but a day of reckoning clearly lay ahead of us when we would have to send our children to school in England, with fees, board and passages to be paid. Our philosophy was to enjoy a glamorous way of life while the going was good; particularly as the cost was so moderate. We estimated that only about one person in every three whom we entertained in our home ever bothered to invite us back: not that entertaining should be a tit-for-tat affair, but this ratio was rather revealing. The fact that we were social 'suckers' was forcibly brought home to us by two incidents.

There was a custom among the British community of giving dinners on Saturday evenings and for the parties to go on afterwards to one of the local cinemas, where British and American films were shown. One day Guen remarked to a woman friend that this custom was very expensive to the host, particularly if – as we did – he had a large number of guests. 'But surely' said the other woman, 'your guests always pay for their own seats? It is always expected, you know'. After that, realising I had made a social gaffe on a few occasions when we had been guests in such circumstances, I invariably offered the host the money for our two cinema seats. Equally invariably was my offer accepted, with well simulated embarrassment. On the other hand, few of *our* Saturday night guests – not even the husband of the woman who had put us wise – ever made such an offer to me.

The other occasion was later, when we had rented a cottage at Ootacamund where Guen and the children could escape from the stifling heat of Hyderabad in the summer months. A party of four, such as Guen, the two children and Nanny, could occupy the whole of a 4-berth first class railway compartment for the twenty-four hour train journey. Alternatively, at very slight extra cost, it was possible to reserve the whole of an 8-berth second class compartment. It was therefore quite customary for two European families to share between them the larger carriage so as to save money and to have more space in which to move about. We discovered that the wife and child of an army captain whom we knew, would be travelling to Ootacamund on the same train as my family; so we suggested they should all share an 8-berth carriage and that as our party was four and theirs two we should pay two-thirds of the cost. The captain's wife said they could not afford this, but they were willing to pay for their own two berths if we would pay for the two unoccupied berths; i.e. they would pay one-quarter but not one-third. Thinking them to be badly off we agreed. *In the train* the captain's wife said that her husband would be retiring from the army in a year's time. Guen remarked that he was very young to retire. 'Oh!' said the other woman, 'Bill has estates in Scotland and a private income of £5000 a year' – a positive fortune in those days.

The Hyderabad climate was very pleasant in the 'cold weather' from October to early March: it escaped the steamy 'second hot weather' of Bombay. In the monsoon season from mid-June to October it was quite tolerable; but it started to stoke up in March, and the months of April, May and early June were sheer torment. Air-conditioning was only just beginning to be known in Bombay, Calcutta and Madras: it was almost unheard of 'up-country', and in any case would have been difficult to install in our house with its huge rooms and many doors and windows. There is no theory more nonsensical than that one becomes 'acclimatised' to heat: it is just the reverse. My first few hot seasons in India, though uncomfortable, could be endured without suffering too acutely; but with every passing year I found the summers harder to bear. Now, at an advanced age, I just dread the few occasions when I still from time to time have to revisit the tropics (unless at high altitudes). In the nineteen-thirties, those who were able to do so took home leave or migrated to the hills during the hot weather: I was seldom able to escape except for short spells.

In Hyderabad we normally slept in all seasons on a wide verandah under mosquito curtains, as a protection against malaria. Only at times of high monsoon winds were we sometimes driven indoors lest we 'took off'. On the hottest nights sleep was very difficult. The most effective remedy was to ensure a state of physical tiredness – I regularly played strenuous squash in the hot weather – and to sprinkle water over the sheets before getting into bed. This last practice was less drastic than it sounds; for the very dry atmosphere, aided by the action of a ceiling fan, effectively drove off the moisture within a few minutes and left the sheets comparatively cool for a short while. The object of the hard exercise and the wetting was to be able to fall asleep quickly before the bedding had had time to heat up again. A minimum night temperature of 90° to 95°F is hard to endure.

I soon discovered various tricks for alleviating the hot weather. One was the very reverse of what one would have expected. Cold baths were to be avoided (not that a really cold bath could be had): a hot shower was far more refreshing. Another was to shut up the house by closing all the window shutters early in the morning so as to trap a houseful of night air and to keep out the furnace-like midday heat. At sundown the house could be opened up again. Office hours during the two hottest months were from 7 am to 1.0 pm. All office windows were covered with khas-khas matting (a kind of rush) that was sprayed with water every hour or so by small boys. This gave a slight fall in temperature and at the same time shut out the intense glare. The worst thing to do in a hot climate is to rely on a fan; for it dries up the eyeballs, causing acute discomfort. Fans are all right in hot *moist* climates like Bombay, but unless one can sweat profusely – and I cannot – they make matters worse in intense heat. In the hot season we always dined out on one of the tennis courts. This brought some relief, but exposed one to the occasional well aimed droppings of bats and birds into the soup.

Once, when spending a night in the jungle at a government guesthouse, we risked sleeping under the stars without nets. The clarity and beauty of the sky was indescribable, but Guen paid the penalty by contracting acute malaria which plagued her for a year or two during the War when it was difficult to get the necessary drugs. Ultimately she was put out of her misery by a kind friend in Bombay whose dealings with the American Forces enabled her to get what was needed. Although there was little malaria in Hyderabad City, an additional reason for sleeping under a net was the avoidance of rats that were liable to run over one's face while one slept.

On the whole the Deccan was a fairly healthy place. The climate was either good or tolerable for about nine months in the year, and it was possible to keep most ills at bay if one did not make too much fuss about avoiding infection. An army couple we knew were incredibly fussy. Once we were sitting in their house in Secunderabad when our hostess suddenly said 'Walter, there's a bluebottle in the room'. Poor Walter had to spend the next ten minutes in full chase, and was not allowed to sit down again until the wretched insect had been well and truly swatted. This same woman insisted on filtering her child's bathwater through muslin. Needless to say, the poor child got enteric: she had been so coddled that she had lost all powers of resistance.

Thunderstorms were rare events except as heralds of the monsoon. After eight or ten weeks of agonising heat the welcome distant rumble of an approaching storm could perhaps be heard, followed by a refreshingly cool breeze. At such times, if in the evening, myriads of flying ants might invade one's house, attracted by the lamps. These creatures look like maggots; their wings being temporary growths loosely attached to their bodies for the purpose of rendering them wind-borne at the time of migration. Once landed, they would shed their wings and crawl all over the house and verandahs in search of new homes. After the coming of the ants the storm would burst and the temperature would fall by several degrees. Then, out would come the frogs. Hopping up the verandah steps they would spread in all directions and enter the house, acting at the same time as selective vacuum cleaners; glutting themselves with the maggot-like ants until they seemed ready to burst, and fastidiously leaving the wings untouched. After the storm the sweeper would have the task of brooming up the wings into great heaps.

Another unwelcome visitor from the insect world was the 'smelly-bug'. He was a very small flying insect that would alight on one's face or neck. Instinctively its host would brush it away, and it would take its revenge by issuing a most repulsive smell, probably borrowed from his friend the skunk. If a smelly-bug lands in the butter there is no remedy but to jettison the lot.

Snakes were occasional visitors, but fortunately not too frequent. I was certainly alarmed when, sitting at breakfast one day on the verandah, a large cobra glided out of the nursery quite close by me and slid away into the garden. Fortunately the children were away in the hills at the time. Although I myself have a very personal and acute snake-phobia, this has evidently not been inherited by my son; for one day when he was only about four he called out to me 'Look Daddy! See what I've found!' He was holding a long snake by the tail with great pride. Trying to hide my agitation I called back 'Those are dirty things. Drop it and see how fast you can run to me'. It worked. The snake was duly killed by the mali and found to be a harmless daman; but it might well not have been.

Although the different communities lived together in the State quite peacefully, a certain amount of care had to be exercised to avoid offending susceptibilities. To a host it was of course essential that no Muslim guest was ever offered pork, ham or bacon, and that no Hindu was offered beef. It has been said that communal peace will come to the Indian subcontinent only when a Muslim and a Hindu will share between them a veal and ham pie.

One one occasion I wanted to construct a new stores building on a piece of waste land on which there was a very small Hindu shrine – a sort of brick and plaster box measuring about three or four feet cubed and daubed with red paint. Although I was told that no one had visited this shrine within living memory I thought it advisable to consult the local Brahmins who, after long consultations among themselves, told me there would be no objection to the shrine being demolished on certain conditions. First, as a 'spirit' dwelt in the shrine a new one would have to be built for him elsewhere. Secondly, the spirit would have to be propitiated by a gift of two hundred rupees to be distributed among the poor. As the cost of meeting these conditions was negligible by comparison with that of the new stores building, and as an ugly incident might have been the result of riding rough-shod over the feelings of the Brahmins, I agreed; though I had little doubts as to who 'the poor' were. A more difficult situation arose when a muezzin set up his headquarters just on the other side of my compound wall and called the Faithful to prayer at five o'clock every morning. As his voice was far from melodious, and as he was situated only sixty feet or so from my bed, my sleep was regularly interrupted. I asked one of my Muslim officers, a very venerable looking old gentleman, to see if he could persuade the muezzin to move elsewhere, but to no avail. For years I suffered from this din every dawn; and when later I was assailed by insomnia, I nearly became demented. There was nowhere out of earshot to where I could move my bed.

Many of the electricity consumers were tardy in settling their monthly bills, and some of the worst offenders were the wealthiest and most influential citizens, not excluding ministers. The only recourse I had against non-payment was to disconnect the consumer and to charge him a reconnection fee after he had squared his account. Failure to enforce this practice would have resulted in running up a huge sum under 'outstanding debtors' in my departmental accounts. Strict enforcement with influential citizens brought me into disfavour and under great pressure from high places. Either way I was in trouble. One of the most irritating features of running the Electricity Department was the constant stream of individual consumers who would call on me personally at my house after office hours, expecting me to sort out their bill troubles. I had to be rather ruthless, or I would have had no privacy at all. As it was, I was virtually on duty for twenty-four hours a day. Living so close to the power house (about 500 yards away) I could detect the slightest change in the pitch of the distant hum of machinery, even in my sleep; and I would be in the turbine house within a few minutes wanting to know what was wrong. Official letters marked 'urgent' or 'secret', and which were usually neither, were constantly being delivered at my house at all hours and had to be opened just in case they really *were* important. I was often woken up at night by the arrival of a cablegram, and every 'fault' on the mains system was immediately reported to me, often in the middle of a meal. It was difficult to break this custom of business intruding into my private life because I *did* want to be informed of any serious trouble whenever it might occur. The difficulty was in training my staff to discriminate between the serious and the trivial. At one stage, when I was at very low ebb from overwork, I gave orders that I was never to be disturbed at night for *any* reason whatsoever; but that led me into trouble when HEH was appraised of a serious fire that involved heavy loss of life. The disaster occurred late one evening, and my Exalted Master was most displeased to learn that I was not on the scene until early next morning; not that the fire had anything to do with my Department, or that I could have done anything about it anyway.

As Director of the State Workshops I had some rather odd tasks to perform. On one occasion two government messengers came into my office with a parcel and a letter from the taluqdar of one of the provincial towns in the State. The letter said 'Dear Sir, I have the honour to send you herewith one *bomb* that was found placed beneath my chair. Kindly have it examined and report. I have the honour to be, Sir, your most obedient and humble servant...' Even as State Tinker I felt this to be rather outside my province, so I attached a chit to the letter and passed it on, together with the 'bomb', to the Principal of the Osmania

71

Technical College, as I knew he had a chemical laboratory –
presumably with facilities for analysis. Within ten minutes
letter and bomb were back on my desk again with the Principal's
regrets. So I repeated the process, sending them on to the
Science Faculty of the Osmania University: they, at any rate had
the advantage of being a few miles away. After an hour or two
back came the letter and bomb with the professor's regrets.
This was becoming a nuisance. At least the wretched thing was
not ticking, or I would have thrown it into the lake. Then I
suddenly remembered there was in the city a public official
designated as the State Analyst (probably for forensic purposes,
but I was no longer fussy). I sent the whole business on to him.
This time my ruse seemed to work. Nothing came back; so I
forgot the incident. Some weeks later I had a letter from the
Public Analyst. 'Sir, with reference to the parcel you sent me on
10th Khurdad, 1345 F, I have the honour to inform you that,
after analysis, the contents of alleged bomb have been identified
as approximately 50% mud and approximately 50% cow-dung. I
have the honour, . . . etc. etc.'

Shortly after taking office I was instructed to make a machan
for the Heir Apparent. Those familiar with tiger shooting will
know that a machan is a tree platform or 'crow's nest' from
which the hunter operates. But that is an ordinary machan
suitable for ordinary mortals. The Heir Apparent wanted a very
special machan for a very special prince unaccustomed to the
plebeian exercise of climbing ladders or trees. Since Nature did
not provide pre-caged tigers that could be safely shot with royal
bullets from outside, then clearly the only safe way of shooting
tigers was to put the royal party in a cage so that the external
tiger could conveniently be shot from between the bars. Being a
royal cage it had to be spacious enough to accommodate not only
the ample person of the Heir Apparent himself, but also several
servants, such comforts as ice-boxes, alcoholic refreshments,
chaises longues, cushions and, above all, a posse of ladies. It had
been the princely wish to visit Europe that summer, but Papa
had said 'No'. So, if shikar was the only alternative to Monte

Carlo, let it at least be shikar de luxe. The construction of this contrivance offered many problems and involved a sectional assembly in situ to simplify transport without the need for special road wagons or of cutting broad swathes through the jungle. In the draft of a routine report to the Viceroy on happenings within the State, a senior member of the Residency staff had written 'The rigours of camp life are to be tempered with the joys of a portable zenana', but unfortunately this masterpiece was censored by his Chief.

VI

Horse nonsense

This point in my narrative has been reached without mention of the horse. My present interest in that animal is virtually nil other than the nostalgic memories he can arouse and the delight I can still take in his appearance. But I am grateful to the horse for having enriched some of my youthful years, and am mindful that he was an essential element in the Indian scene. I owe it to him to turn back a few autobiographical pages to a time when I had been living in Bombay but ten months and when I was able to take my first local leave.

I decided to visit Matheran, a beautiful shady plateau some three thousand feet high, lying between Bombay harbour and the main bluff of the Western Ghats. In former years it had enjoyed some splendour as the official Government hill station, but after being supplanted by Mahableshwar it had settled down to a quiet and peaceful existence. To reach Matheran it was necessary to change at Neral Junction on the main Bombay-Poona line, and to continue the journey in a toy train that puffed and grunted up the steep gradients with the frequent help of rack and pinion: there was no road access beyond a pony track. As the little train climbed higher and higher the air became sweeter and cooler, bringing blissful relief after the sweltering heat of the city.

The plateau is thickly wooded and populated with monkeys and a few panthers. Its edges are precipitous and it is shaped like a star-fish, the points of which command superb views of pink

74

mountains of fantastic shape rising from shimmering plains. The Rugby Hotel, though unpretentious, was then the place to stay at. Meals on the verandah were enlivened by the monkeys who, if you allowed your attention to wander for a careless moment, would snatch the food from your plate. To sleep under a blanket again was a very real joy, and the nocturnal chorus of chirruping insects acted as an effective soporific. Matheran was certainly an excellent place to restore vigour to the jaded city dweller from Bombay.

During my leave I made several new friends, mostly young men of my own age. We amused ourselves by playing tennis, drinking rather more beer than was good for us and by making expeditions to the points of the plateau for picnics, both by day and by moonlight. Apart from walking, the only means of locomotion were the hill ponies, and it was on this holiday that I first developed a taste for riding. The ponies were not of high quality; but those that were not too bovine were definitely equine, and they gave us plenty of fun. An acute awareness of having no brakes made me resolve to master the arts of equitation as soon as possible.

And so, on returning to Bombay, I joined the Bombay Light Horse as a trooper. This regiment was a 'gentlemen's corps' recruited from the European civil population. Amongst its members were Greeks, Germans, Dutchmen, Scandinavians, Frenchmen, Americans, as well of course as Britons. We were a veritable Foreign Legion. The commanding officer in my day was a Colonel Watson, a jovial fellow known as 'Watso', who affected a suitable parade ground temper that was but skin deep. We formed part of the Auxiliary Force of India and were liable to be called up for service at times of civil disorders.

Membership of the Light Horse enabled me to keep a horse of my own at reasonable cost and gave me access to the regimental riding school where we recruits were put through the mill under the tender care of a facetious and mildly sadistic sergeant-major who delighted in sending us over the jumps bareback before we knew one end of a horse from another. At one lesson, when the sergeant-major had called for the jumping pole to be put up, two syces brought in the pole supports and placed them about nine feet apart. They then put one end of the pole on one of the supports and found that the other end was some distance from the other support. After a thoughtful pause, one of the syces said 'Pole too short, Sahib'. At another lesson the sergeant major asked me ''Ow do you tell the sex of an 'orse?' Not knowing anything about horses' teeth, I replied 'By inspecting its anatomy.' 'Oh! indeed,' was the reply, 'And if you meet a young lady with short 'air, do you lift up 'er skirts just to make sure?' Other sergeant-majorly remarks are better left unprinted.

We had a standing camp for several months each year at Santa Cruz, then on the fringe of open country but now engulfed by the city's suburban sprawl and the airport. For two weeks every year we were expected to live under canvas there: at other times the camp served as a sort of country club.

Besides attending riding school and the annual training camp we regularly paraded as a squadron every week on the maidan or on the sea shore to execute the various movements peculiar to the days when cavalry was truly horse-borne. Musketry courses on the Santa Cruz rifle range, sword drill in the Town Hall, an annual mounted sports meeting and a riotous dinner at the Willingdon Club more or less completed the routine of the dilettante cavalryman. All these activities took place at dawn, in the evenings or at week-ends, so that our normal civilian lives remained undisturbed. Naturally we indulged in equestrian sports such as jumping, tent-pegging and tilting the ring. Some thirty-five years later I was told by a friend that at the East India and Sporting Club in St James's Square, where some regimental mess silver is displayed, he had seen my name on a challenge cup. This recorded one of my very few sporting achievements. About the only other one was the winning of a cup for musketry, the credit for which was more attributable to Gordon's gin than to myself. Before the musketry competition I had lunched liberally at the Yacht Club, and when it came to shooting, I either saw one set of sights and two targets or vice versa. Choosing the double target and aiming midway between them I hit the bull nearly every time. The following year, without the help of Mr Gordon, I was less successful. My musketry trophy perished in the 'blitz'.

My first horse had a truncated ear as a result of some accident in earlier life. This did not improve his beauty. I appropriately called him Malchus. Some of my less charitable friends attributed his disfigurement, quite slanderously, to my maladroit swordsmanship. As I gained in proficiency in horsemanship I found Malchus too dull, and exchanged him for a splendid creature named Mickey, a veteran of twenty-three years. Mickey held his head like an aristrocrat and was a superb jumper. Although he did great things for me in jumping contests he was not built for speed and was therefore quite unsuited for tent-pegging. His successor, Nobby, was ideal for this purpose as he could streak through the air like an arrow.

Once Nobby fell sick just when I was training for the annual regimental sports, so Watso kindly lent me an animal called Hick Boo. Taking a lance in one hand I galloped down the course and neatly spiked my peg; but the moment of triumph was short-lived. Hick Boo decided he had had enough for the day and headed towards his stables, some three miles away, without showing the slightest inclination to reduce speed. With a lance in the right hand and only the left hand to manage the reins I was at a disadvantage, and it was of course a point of honour not to throw away the lance. Not until we had galloped right across the rifle range where a musketry exercise was in progress did I at last succeed in bringing the brute under control. That was an anxious moment.

It was a Bombay tradition that whenever a Viceroy, a Presidency Governor or a visiting royalty first arrived in India or departed from the country at the end of his stay, the Bombay Light Horse would form a special escort. These were occasions of great pageantry. A long procession of British and Indian troops would accompany the state carriage through five miles of streets, lined with police and soldiers, from the Gateway of India to Government House. Hundreds of thousands of Indians thronged the route. The Viceregal and Governor's Bodyguards of Rajput or Sikh cavalry were a splendid sight with their magnificent uniforms and trappings. At the core of the procession would be the state carriage. A 'holy umbrella' of cloth of gold would be held by a postillion to protect the royal, viceregal or proconsular cheek from the tropical sun. Close to the carriages, and resplendent in uniforms of white and silver, rode the Bombay Light Horse, imbued with a great sense of pride. The long ride in the hot sun at a ceremonial trot – that is without posting in the stirrups – with drawn swords and in tight tunics could be very tiring; but we would not have missed these pageants for all the world.

In 1928 King Amanullah of Afghanistan made his famous world tour. A friendly Afghanistan was of great importance to the Government of India, perpetually harassed as they were by the turbulent tribesmen of the north-west frontier. It was therefore decided in high places that the King must be impressed by a great show of pomp and circumstance. In Delhi and Karachi he was treated to suitable displays of military might and pageantry; and from Karachi he was taken by sea to Bombay so as to give time for the Viceroy, his Bodyguard and the self-same troops that had been paraded in Delhi to be rushed post haste by rail to Bombay for the purpose of impressing the king yet again after he had landed there. Unfortunately the Viceroy was taken ill in Bombay, and it fell to the governor, Sir Leslie Wilson, to greet the king on board his ship in the harbour. Amanullah decided to take offence and to suspect that the Viceroy's indisposition was 'diplomatic'. As the governor arrived in his launch alongside the king's ship he saw that his august visitor was wearing flannels. Sir Leslie told the king that 10,000 troops were paraded to welcome him and that if the king preferred to wear informal dress the troops would be dismissed. This was not at all to the liking of His Majesty, who sulkily

retired to don his full regalia. During these parleys we were
paraded in the sweltering sun in our tight uniforms and kept
waiting for about two hours entirely in ignorance of the cause of
the delay. Eventually we marched past the Gateway of India
where the king and the governor had taken their stand with their
entourages. As we rode past and gave the royal salute I saw His
Majesty remove his képi in order to scratch the royal scalp. A
photograph appeared on the following day in the local press,
unhappily catching the king with his eyes closed, bearing the
unkind caption 'His Majesty is watching the march past of the
Bombay Light Horse'.

Amanullah continued to sulk for some time on account of the
Viceroy's illness and kept the guests waiting an hour that
evening at the Government House banquet. He continued his
tour and was fêted in Europe by several heads of state, including
King George V. The tour marked the climax of the Afghan
king's short, but ambitious reign. On his return to Kabul he
tried to introduce a number of reforms in the manner of Kemal
Atatürk and to enforce them upon a reluctant and conservative
people. Typical of these reforms was his attempt to change the
sartorial habits of his subjects. When in London, the king had
been so impressed with the bowler hat that he had ordered
several gross of them and tried to compel his male subjects to
adopt them in place of the traditional turban or fez. As the
devout Muslim, in the act of prayer, is expected to touch the
ground with his forehead, the bowler hat was soon found to be
ill-suited to his devotions. A few attempted to please both their
monarch and their Maker by wearing the bowler with the front
of the brim cut away. The king also tried to prohibit the veiling
of women in public.

Within a few weeks Amanullah was in full flight over the
Khyber Pass, to seek asylum in India. A quick succession of
Pretenders followed in the next few weeks, each of which in turn
was sent packing over the Khyber. On the hotel lawn at Pesha-
war could be seen several rival groups of exiles, each
surrounding a figure who insisted on being addressed as 'Your

Majesty'. Then a wild chieftain named Bacha-i-Saqao held the throne precariously for a while until he, in turn, was deposed by the wiser and stronger Zahir Shah, who reigned securely for several years before he fell at the hand of an assassin. Amanullah lapsed into inconspicuous retirement and eventually died in Turkey in 1960, an almost forgotten figure.

Within a couple of years of joining the corps, I found myself proudly wearing the two stripes of a full corporal. No one was more surprised than myself, for I am the least martial of men. Perhaps my ealier training at Osborne and Dartmouth had imbued me with a sense of discipline that helped me to conform with what was expected of a corps member. At a time of real crisis, which fortunately never arose, I would probably have been quite ineffectual; but as a peace-time soldier I could do all that was required of me. I attended parades regularly, joined enthusiastically in all the optional activities of the regiment and became a passable horseman. The Bombay Light Horse was very democratic. As a twenty-four-year old junior engineer I was greatly tickled to find that one of my firm's directors, Sir Alexander Grey, a man twenty years my senior, was a trooper in my section and had to accept orders from me! Shortly after I left Bombay the regiment was amalgamated with the Bombay Light Motor Patrol and the horse gradually became obsolete. Doubtless this was inevitable, as times were rapidly changing, but I am glad to have belonged to the old regiment before all this happened.

During my last 'cold weather' season in Bombay our regiment was invited to send a troop to Baria State to take part in manoeuvres with the Maharajah's army. This made an enjoyable break from the routine of city life, and my firm allowed me a week off duty without debiting my leave account. What could have been fairer? We lived under canvas, but in considerable comfort, and were entertained hospitably by the Maharajah. Not that we were lotus-eating! Every day we were in the saddle from dawn until sundown, covering immense distances and filling our lungs with dust. I found that tepid water from a drinking flask was so repulsive that I succeeded in surviving each day in the hot sun without a drop of liquid passing my lips. It certainly had the effect of whipping up a monumental thirst, which was liberally quenched on returning to camp in the evening.

In that same last season the Light Horse took part in a military tattoo on the Bombay racecourse. We were dressed as a group of wild Arab horsemen and had to descend at full gallop into the middle of a floodlit mock battle, firing off blank cartridges and shouting cries that were meant to be blood-curdling. No case of curdled blood, to the best of my belief, was ever reported.

Early in 1929 civil disorders broke out in the city. The age-old friction between Hindu and Muslim was incited by some minor incident that led to inflamed tempers, blows, counter-blows and eventually bloodshed. Assassinations occurred. The local press did not assist matters by publishing the numbers of dead on both sides like a cricket score, which naturally spurred on the losing community to retaliate in a spirit of one-upmanship. The Auxiliary Force of India was mobilised, and once more the Bombay Light Horse were encamped, this time on the maidan conveniently near the Gymkhana Club. Our duties were not arduous. We patrolled the city and sometimes surrounded a quarter while the police made a house-to-house search for weapons or for known agitators. Although we saw a great deal of damage – broken glass, looted shops and occasionally an abandoned corpse – we saw no actual violence; for the mere presence of mounted men seemed to have a sobering effect out of all proportion to our aggressive capacity!

After a few days order was restored and we were disbanded to resume our normal lives. The governor, Sir Frederick Sykes, held a review of all troops, both regular and auxiliary, who had helped quell the disturbances. Never shall I forget that review. When the day came, Nobby, once again, had gone lame and I was promised another mount. On reporting for duty I was disturbed to find that this mount was none other than my old enemy, Hick Boo. Now Hick Boo was a splendid hunter, but an appalling parade horse. He did not take kindly to rifle buckets and swords, and was allergic to riding in formation. The great moment of the Bombay Light Horse was the gallop past, when the whole squadron charged, line abreast, past the saluting base where the governor stood in immaculate white topi and morning suit, supported by his aides. This manoeuvre is apt to involve a certain amount of jostling. Hick Boo's reaction was to rear up on his hind legs and to cause me to fall out of line. The only possible choice of action was for me to pretend to be one of the sergeant-majors who always took up their position behind the line. Had I gone forward instead of backwards I would have had to masquerade as one of the officers who, of course, rode in front of the line. It seemed less pretentious and more expedient to fall back; and so I galloped across the maidan behind my fellows, to the accompaniment of a picturesque torrent of muttered abuse from the sergeant-majors. My troubles, however, were not over: worse was to follow. When I eventually got back into line after the squadron had taken up its standing position, the governor made his speech and the royal salute was given. By some horrible quirk of chance the band was stationed just behind the Light Horse; and as the drums and brass blared forth the national anthem Hick Boo showed the world that he was no music-lover by bolting across the maidan in full view of the governor, the 'brass-hats', an apoplectic Watso and a host of my fellow club members viewing the ceremony from the verandah of the Gymkhana Club.

From the Bombay Light Horse it was a short and logical step to the Bombay Hunt. The Jackal Club was, in fact, just across the road from the Light Horse camp at Santa Cruz. I rode to hounds enthusiastically for three seasons as one of the 'unspeakable in pursuit of the uneatable'. In this case the uneatable was the jackal. Every Sunday from November to

March we would meet at dawn at some appointed place in Salsette Island to enjoy two or three hours of good sport, rounded off by an al fresco hunt breakfast. The gradual expansion of the suburbs drove the hunt further and further afield until ultimately the Jackal Club migrated to Dombivli on the mainland. This migration was not until after I had left Bombay, but I attended one or two trial days at Dombivli. This meant catching the 'hunt special' train at about 5.0am, which carried the field, the hunters, the pack, the breakfast and the syces from the city to the meet. The results exceeded all expectations, and Santa Cruz, as the seat of the Jackal Club, was thereafter doomed.

During the monsoon the Bombay pack migrated to Poona, and I once hunted with them there. I also hunted at Bangalore a few times when I took a fortnight's leave to stay with a gunner friend and his wife there. These Indian hunts adopted all the conventions and trappings of the British hunting field, such as pink coats and stocks, raising one's hat to the Master and the standard horsy jargon; but the topper was replaced by the topi with the general field: the British were still sunstroke conscious in those days. The Master and huntsmen, however, wore Jorrocks caps.

As my time in Bombay drew to a close, visions of approaching London life led me to spend more and more time in the saddle. My horsy days were nearly brought to an untimely end when I was riding a borrowed mount through a grove of palm trees. This exercise involved a certain amount of quick decision as one cantered through the trees in a sinuous slalom. At one point I found myself confronted by a tree which I thought expedient to pass on the right. The horse favoured passing it on the left. We compromised by hitting it. The next thing I knew was regaining consciousness in a pool of blood and being packed off to hospital in the car of a kindly Scotsman who, by a miracle, was in a shack sufficiently near for him to hear the loud crack of my skull against the stem of the palm tree. A few stitches, an anti-tetanus injection and a week in bed put me right, though I walked in purple pain for a week or so after being discharged from hospital.

At the annual Willingdon Horse Show, a week or two before I sailed for England, I borrowed my old horse Mickey, then aged twenty-five. We succeeded in being the runner-up for the Governor's Cup. Three times Mickey and I were called back to repeat the jumping course before the judges decided in favour of my rival. After that I felt some sympathy with the traditional Indian applicant for a post who would describe himself as a 'failed BA'.

After returning to London I sadly missed my riding. One day I ran into an ex-Light Horse colleague in Piccadilly. Over a drink at the Long Bar at the Trocadero we reminisced and decided to take to the saddle again together, just once or twice. I, at least, could not afford to do so regularly. A successful hack in Richmond Park led us to venture one Sunday morning onto Rotten Row. We hired horses from a livery stable in Exhibition Road and mounted them at Prince's Gate within sight of my grandfather's sculptures round the podium of the Albert Memorial. At that time a lengthy correspondence was being pursued in one of the Sunday papers about young riders in the park being improperly dressed and lacking proper control of their mounts. The chief critic of these lax practices was the elegant Sir Walter Gilbey, who could regularly be seen on Sunday mornings at the fashionable church parade near Hyde Park Corner. Although my friend and I were irreproachably dressed in stock and billycock, I cannot claim that I was in proper control of my horse. We set off at a canter towards the Serpentine bridge and I very soon discovered that my animal had a mouth of iron. Within a few hundred yards it became clear that as far as my mount was concerned my opinions counted for nothing. We passed the Marble Arch at full gallop, which became a stampede by the time we had reached Hyde Park Corner. From the corner of my eye I caught a glimpse of the

immaculate figure of Sir Walter Gilbey, wearing his characteristic Edwardian bowler with upturned brim and with a gardenia
in his buttonhole, leaning on the rail and balefully regarding
me with disapproving eye. As the Albert Memorial hove into
sight I hoped my troubles would soon be over, as the grooms
were waiting at Prince's Gate. But no! My thrice-damned brute
had by now entered into the spirit of the occasion and thought
an encore would be good fun. Off we sped again, faster and yet
faster. I vowed that if I survived this agonising ordeal I would
seek out the tomb of the immortal John Gilpin and lay a
sympathetic wreath on it to the memory of a fellow sufferer.
(Such vows are unfortunately apt to be forgotten, like New Year
resolutions.) By now my hands were bleeding and all strength
had left my arms. My only devout hope was to stay aboard until
my callous mount should slow down through sheer exhaustion.
Once again, near the Achilles statue, I spied Sir Walter and
heard him say 'Great Heavens! Not again?'

When finally we came to a standstill and I was thankfully
standing on terra firma, my companion rather pityingly offered
to exchange mounts – an offer I accepted with alacrity. Within a
minute he was disappearing in a cloud of dust ahead of me!

I never again rode in Rotten Row, but attended for a while the
riding school at St John's Wood barracks on Sunday mornings.
A year or so later, when I was living in Birmingham and had
become rather more prosperous, I decided to sample the
English hunting field. Hiring a mount and the necessary rig (the
latter from Moss Bros) I attended a meet of the North
Warwickshire Hunt at Alcester. We had a glorious day, but I
was astonished to find that manners in the hunting field were
even worse than I had been led to expect. An elegant lady of title
called me a 'bloody bastard' for riding too close to the pack while
another 'county' female roundly abused me when *her* horse
kicked *mine* as we were jostling through a gate. Hunting in
England was far too expensive for me to indulge in, except on
this one occasion which I regarded as a Christmas present to

myself. If I ever had doubts as to the ethics of blood sports I must have pushed them back into my subconscious. For me, the pleasure of hunting lay entirely in the exhilaration of movement and in the feeling of being close to nature. It is astonishing how one will tackle in hot blood a jump before which one would quail in cold blood. I took no interest whatsoever in the kill.

Apart from an occasional hack in the country at week-ends I never rode again until I had returned to India for my second spell there in 1933. In Hyderabad I kept a horse for a year or so and rode over the wild rocky country outside the city, exploring the tombs of the Kings of Golconda and joining some of the Nizam's cavalry officers on expeditions further afield. It was in Hyderabad that I encountered an example of that curious ethical schizophrenia that is apt to afflict certain people of normally upright character and that has endowed the term 'horse-dealing' with its shady overtones. A British colonel of cavalry from near-by Secunderabad, a model of public school and military correctitude in all matters save one – in fact the archetype of 'an officer and a gentlemen' – offered to sell me a horse, ironically named 'Honesty'. He assured me the creature had a clean bill of health; so after trying him out I bought him. Within a week he had gone lame. I took him to the vet, who immediately recognised the animal as an old lag who had been sent to him repeatedly for lameness. The vet told me the horse suffered from some incurable complaint of the hoof, the hock, the spavin or whatever, and was fit only for destruction. I managed to get my money back, but not the vet's fee, and poor Honesty was shot by his former owner.

I had planned to take up polo, but decided that I could not afford to keep polo ponies *and* a wife: I opted for the latter! I even stopped keeping a horse altogether when I discovered that the Nizam's cavalry had horses to spare that needed exercising.

The last horse I ever owned was a fine creature named Veldrum. I let it be known that I would be willing to sell him for five hundred rupees. One day an Indian came to examine the horse on behalf of a certain nawab. I asked him if he were a vet. 'No,' said he, 'I'm an astrologer and I have been commissioned to see whether the horse's markings are "propitious". Apparently they were not, for the nawab showed no further interest. What was more serious, the horse acquired a bad name through this wretched astrologer and I could not find a buyer at all. Finally I *gave* him away, complete with saddle and bridle, to an Englishman in Secunderabad, who played polo with Veldrum for two seasons and then sold him for twelve hundred rupees. By then Veldrum's 'stars' had been forgotten.

Since then I have ridden only spasmodically, and it is now many years since I was last in the saddle. In my time I derived much pleasure from horses, but have never felt any temptation to become 'horsy'. Horsy people can be so tedious. Besides, I cannot subscribe to the sentiment that the horse is an intelligent animal. I maintain he is a very lovable fool.

VII

The noble, the not so noble and the ignoble

In the days of the earlier Nizams the state nobility was more or less confined to the military commanders, the diwans and other close advisers of the Ruler, and their descendants by primogeniture. As in Tudor England the ranks of this privileged class were later swollen by the admission of wealthy merchants and lesser fry until, at the time of the last ruling Nizam, there was a host of nawabs and rajahs of whom only a small minority could, by any stretch of the imagination, be regarded as 'noble'. State titles had become debased currency. In the words of W S Gilbert, 'when everybody is somebody then no one's anybody'. However, in the sunset years of the State there were still a few outstanding families of considerable glitter. Some of them had been honoured by the King-Emperor with knighthoods and other decorations. Several were of immense wealth and owned jagirs of the size of some of the larger English counties. The four Paigah families were such: they were so well entrenched in wealth and position that there was little incentive for them to enter the political arena when prestige and a comfortable life were already theirs without the necessity for strenuous effort. For the most part the paigah families did not therefore feature prominently in public affairs.

One of the most picturesque figures of the ruling class – a Hindu sheep in a herd of Muslim goats, as it were – was His Excellency the Maharajah Sir Kishen Pershad Bahadur, whose

The arrival in 1927 at the Gateway of India in Bombay of King Amanullah of Afghanistan, with the Bombay Light Horse mounted escort marching past, and the Viceregal and Governor's bodyguards in the foreground.

The Bombay Light Horse paraded on the Bombay *maidan* in 1929 at the time of the Hindu-Muslim rioting in the city. The author served as a corporal in this volunteer corps.

full style and titles were almost as impressively long as those of
the Nizam himself. During my first few years in Hyderabad he
held the position of President of the Executive Council and was
commonly, though not strictly accurately known as the Prime
Minister. The Maharajah was a dignified and venerable old
gentleman who always carried a gold-topped walking stick and
was invariably accompanied by his hukka. When he dined with
us at the Mint House he would arrive with two motor cars. The
first would contain himself and an ADC: in the second would be
his hukka with its liveried attendants. A hukka, or hubble-
bubble pipe, requires a certain amount of preparation before
smoking and constant attention while being smoked; hence the
attendants. At dinner, the hukka was placed beneath the table
and the tube was hooked over the old man's knee, so that His
Excellency might draw on it between courses. As the mixture of
tobacco, sugar and spices also contained a measure of opium,
the Maharajah was apt to doze off from time to time during
the meal. An attendant would then dive beneath the table,
ostensibly to adjust the charcoal fire but also to administer a
discreet nudge to his august master. (I too learned to smoke and
enjoy a hukka - without opium! - but it involved too much
trouble to become a regular habit.)

When the Maharajah himself was host at a banquet, his guests
were entertained by such old-fashioned spectacles as firework
displays, sword-swallowers, fire-eaters and jugglers. Once a
year he would invite a large number of guests to witness the
procession of the Nal Sahib. This was a sacred Muslim relic; in
fact, if I remember rightly, a horse-shoe that had belonged to
one of the early Caliphs. It was carried in a casket round the city
in procession, from its normal resting place in the principal
mosque to the quadrangle of the Maharajah's palace, in which a
vast multitude would be assembled. There it was formally
blessed, scattered with flowers and sprinkled with perfumes by
the Maharajah and then carried back to its shrine. Nowhere in
all India, but in Hyderabad, would it have been thinkable that a
sacred Muslim relic should be blessed by a Hindu. The mere

possibility was indicative of the normally peaceful relations that prevailed between the two communities: the custom was in no way considered incongruous. After the blessing ceremony, the Maharajah's guests would each be presented with a bag of small copper coins, which they would scatter like chicken-fodder from a balcony onto the crowd beneath so as to watch the people scrambling for the money. There was indeed an element of vulgarity in such ostentation, but in Hyderabad 'the vilest things became' the Maharajah.

The old man died at a great age in 1940, just when Hitler's hoards were sweeping across Europe.

Reputedly the richest man in the state after HEH was Nawab Salar Jung Bahadur, familiarly known as 'SJ'. His grandfather, known as Salar Jung I, had been diwan to the then Nizam at the time of the Indian Mutiny and had used his considerable influence to persuade his royal master that his bread was buttered on the British side. Some of the princes had wavered between loyalty to the British on the one hand and the temptation to back the mutineers on the other hand so as to create for themselves an opportunity of winning substantial pickings in the free-for-all that would have followed the successful expulsion of the British. The Governor-General is said to have sent an urgent message to the British Resident in Hyderabad – 'If the Nizam goes, all is lost'. Salar Jung I saw to it that the Nizam did *not* 'go'. Queen Victoria invited the diwan to England to express her personal appreciation of his statesmanship.

The grandson, Salar Jung III was a jackdaw. His city palace was a curious mixture of the Wallace collection and a junk shop in the Edgware Road. His jade and his Persian manuscripts, his carpets and his jewelled daggers were superb; but masterpieces and trash were exhibited together higgledy-piggledy. The fact that one particular gold-topped walking stick had been presented to his grandfather by the Prince of Wales (later Edward VII) seemed a slender pretext for a whole room full of hundreds of other walking sticks devoid of any artistic or historic merit. One room was devoted to a collection of busts, but the absence of a competent curator had led to a somewhat surprising association of busts and labels. An admiral with a patch over his eye was described as Socrates; a snub-nosed bearded Greek as Queen Victoria; and a plump but regal lady in a lace bonnet as Lord Nelson. A mechanical blackamoor could be persuaded, by winding a key in the regions of his lumbar vertebrae, to emit from a flute a refrain from a Rossini opera. Stuffed birds in glass cases abounded everywhere; but above all there were chandeliers – hundreds of them, encrusted with grime. Besides his city palace SJ had a large mansion a few miles away that was a rich storehouse of priceless rugs, some of them stacked seven or eight deep for lack of sufficient acreage of floor space. Here he did only a little intimate entertaining: his famous formal lunch parties were always in his city palace.

Never was there such a collector as SJ. His immense wealth and catholicity of tastes made him scorn speculation. He collected anything and everything, from tapestry to toy soldiers, from jade to junk. Nearly every year before the Second World War he would visit Europe and return to India with crate loads of booty. When in Venice he would order quantities of Venetian glass; in Switzerland a gross of cuckoo clocks; in Savile Row a dozen suits; in Budapest cases of Imperial Tokay; and so on, picking upon the speciality of wherever he might be, regardless of intrinsic merit. No wonder his collection was such a motley of taste and trash.

Returning to Hyderabad from Paris one year in the 1930s SJ brought with him a large gilt rococo bed, alleged to have belonged to La Pompadour and covered lavishly with shells, whorls and shocked cherubim. On the journey to India the bed suffered some damage and had to be sent to the workshop for repair. There, beneath the visible splendour was found a quantity of softwood boarding liberally covered with the legend 'Tate & Lyle'.

SJ was the perfect example of a rich but unhappy man. He

was rumoured to have passed through an episode of unrequited love in his youth, and he remained a bachelor all his life. He could have anything that money could buy; but happiness eluded him and he suffered from acute boredom. Once, in the hot weather of 1934, I called upon him personally – not merely in the formal way of signing in the book. He was sitting in a wicker chair in the large quadrangle of his palace, gazing into space, in the silent company of his secretary and his nephew. He gave me a whisky and soda and insisted that I listened to his latest toy, a fully automatic record-changing gramophone newly arrived from London. Such machines were a novelty at the time. The strains of Brahms's Symphony No 1 caused me considerable surprise; but the effect was somewhat spoiled when it was followed by a click, a pause, and a rendering of 'Why did I kiss that gal' on the backside. This was later followed, automatically, by a second instalment of Brahms. Not one of my fellow listeners registered any emotion whatsoever.

SJ was a very good friend of the British, to whom he was extremely hospitable. When the State was invaded in 1948 by the Indian Army he saw the writing on the wall. It spelled the end of his world: nawabery was finished. He died quietly, absorbing large quantities of his famous Napoleon brandy. His treasures are now displayed in a public museum bearing his name; but I have heard that there have been considerable depredations.

Another picturesque nobleman was Nawab Fakhr-ul-Mulk Bahadur who dwelt in a vast palace of horrific architecture perched on a hill overlooking the Hussein Sagar Lake. He too had a great reputation for hospitality. In appearance he resembled the Emperor Franz Josef of Austria-Hungary, with mutton-chop whiskers. When his begam died he built for her on the outskirts of the city a mausoleum in the style, though not on the scale, of the Taj Mahal. He died in the mid-1930s in a somewhat dramatic manner. Feeling unwell, and having a premonition that his end was near, he visited his wife's mausoleum, returned to his palace and gave instructions that he was not to be disturbed for twenty-four hours. They found him dead, seated in a ceremonial chair and decked out in all his court regalia and jewels.

A venerable old gentleman of patriarchal appearance, with long white beard, was Nawab Sir Amin Jung Bahadur. For some years he had served as Private Secretary to HEH and he lived in a mansion a mile or two outside the city. Next to his house stood a rococo library that housed his impressive collection of Persian, Urdu and English books. On the day I left Hyderabad in 1945 he came to see me off at the railway station and presented me with a leather-bound copy of the poems of Iqbal, in Urdu, which I treasure (regrettably unread) to this day as a memento of a grand old man. One of his sons, Hyder Hussein, was a well-mannered young man who was an officer in my Electricity Department.

Another patriarchal old gentleman who looked as though he had walked straight out of the Old Testament and who, as Finance Secretary, was for some time my administrative chief, was Nawab Fakhr Yar Jung Bahadur. He was a very devout Muslim, and had the disconcerting habit of suspending meetings so that he might break off to say his prayers in an adjoining room at the appropriate hours.

The Maharajah was not the only Hindu in high places. Rajah Dharam Karan Bahadur was for a time the minister to whom I was responsible. He was a large portly man who lived in the heart of the city in a palace of icing sugar rococo architecture with hideous modern furnishings. His idiosyncrasy was to make his own liqueurs, with such exotic flavourings as jasmine, fig, partridge and quail; they were not very palatable. There were also two very rich rajahs, brothers, who entertained lavishly in their Hyderabad palaces and kept a racing stable at Poona. The curious thing about them was that the head of the family was debarred by tradition from marrying, and had to *adopt* his heir. It was perhaps less curious that for several generations the estate had passed smoothly from father to son without this custom being broken.

As to the royal family itself, only the two official sons of HEH, and also his brother, Nawab Basalat Jah Bahadur, led social lives that overlapped with local European society. The Heir Apparent, Prince Azam Jah Bahadur (later to become His Highness the Prince of Berar) lived in a pleasant palace known as Bella Vista close to the Hussein Sagar Lake. There, with his statuesque and handsome wife, the Princess Dureshevar, he entertained quite lavishly and invited British guests. His brother, Prince Moazzam Jah Bahadur, then married to the beautiful Princess Niloufer, dwelt in a bogus Gothic mansion in the style of an Oxford college, perched on a rocky hill not far from our house. The uncle of these two brothers, and brother of the Nizam, Prince Basalat Jah Bahadur, lived quite modestly in a pleasant house close to the Mint. He too had a very beautiful wife, the daughter of Brigadier Qadr Yar Jung Bahadur of the Nizam's Regular Forces.

HEH's Chief Wife, Her Exalted Highness the Dhulam Pasha, mother of the two official younger princes, was an eccentric old lady who often drove round the city in a curtained car, preceded by police whistles to clear the traffic (a privilege shared by senior members of the royal family and by the British Resident when on official business). By no stretch of the imagination could this lady's attire be described as smart; but as she was seldom seen in public this was of no great importance. On two occasions her comings and goings touched upon the lives of my family. It was our custom, when our small son was at the perambulator stage, to let him be taken by Nanny to the Zoo every morning. This zoo was in the Public Gardens about half a mile from our house. One day, when Nanny was unwell, we entrusted the child to the care of our very faithful servant Balaram. An hour went by after the expected time of their return, but there was no sign either of Balaram or of the child. We became extremely anxious. Eventually they appeared at full speed, with Balaram in a great state of agitation. Her Exalted Highness had that day visited the Public Gardens, had noticed and apparently taken a fancy to the very fair-haired child and had summoned Balaram to the side of her car to demand who was the father of the child and what price would he be likely to accept for him as a palace mascot! A long argument followed, and at one time it seemed likely that our son might then and there be abducted to the Exalted Zenana – a sort of inverted Entführung. With great presence of mind and tact, Balaram had suggested that the proposition should be put to me so that I might name my price! With that he fled Mintwards.

Years later, in the same Public Gardens, there was an exhibition of Hyderabad arts and crafts. By then we had two children, and Guen had taken them with her to the exhibition. While she was examining some cloth at a stall, she was astonished to see the stallholder seizing several bales of cloth from the counter and throwing them beneath, out of sight. He had spied the approach of the Dhulam Pasha, who had never been known to pay for anything; if she took something from a shop, it was an honour to the shopkeeper. Her EH, sure enough, came up to the stall, spoke to Guen and made flattering comments on the children. By then our son's hair had darkened a few shades, and the Dhulam Pasha did not seem to recognise the baby she had coveted two or three years earlier. She then started grabbing bales of cloth and presenting them to Guen, saying that *this* would make a nice suit for the little boy, *that* a nice frock for the little girl and yet another a suitable dress for Guen herself, until most of the stallholder's stock, except what he had hidden out of sight, was exhausted. Fortunately there was nothing there that Her EH fancied for herself. As she turned to leave, a tense moment occurred when our son said 'Mummy, she hasn't paid for anything!' Guen, well understanding the situation, waited not only until the august lady herself but also her retinue had passed out of sight before she returned all the bales to the stallholder who, by that time, was in tears. He insisted on giving her, without payment, a dress length of material in token of his gratitude for her having saved him from ruin.

There were one or two 'foreign' royalties living in the State in my time. One was the widow of the last Caliph of Islam and Sultan of Turkey, mother of Princess Dureshevar, who lived quietly in her daughter's household. She was entitled to be addressed as 'Your Imperial Highness'. It is interesting to speculate that, had the Caliphate ever been revived, the most legitimate claimant might have been the Nizam's grandson – the present nominal Nizam, Prince Mukharam Jah Bahadur – as he is also the grandson of the last of the Caliphs.

Another 'foreign' royalty was Sirdar Omar Khan, brother of that same King Amanullah of Afghanistan in whose escort I had ridden with the Bombay Light Horse in 1928. He had been given asylum in Hyderabad State, together with a small pension, on condition that he fomented no political intrigues for the restoration of his family's dynasty to the throne of Kabul.

Yet another minor royalty was His Highness the Sultan of Mukalla who has already been mentioned in this narrative as one of the jemadars of HEH's Irregular Forces. He used to entertain to dinners of Arabian cuisine; but I am glad to say I was never embarrassed by the offer of a sheep's eye as the supreme delicacy.

The most influential man in the State during my time was Sir Akbar Hydari. He was not a 'noble', nor even a Hyderabadi, but a Khoja Muslim from Bombay with a high reputation as a financial wizard. When I first came to the State he was the Honourable Finance Minister: later he became President of the Council: finally he left Hyderabad to become a Member of the Viceregal Council in Delhi. He was the first Indian ever to become a Privy Councillor to the King-Emperor. In appearance a bearded tubby little man, and with a propensity for making sententious speeches, he skilfully managed the State's finances and won the confidence of his royal master to the extent of being granted the unique privilege of wearing a fez without a tassel. HEH himself wore a fez with no tassel: lesser Muslim mortals wore fezzes that were always be-tasselled or be-stalked. The tassel-less state was regarded as a mark of supreme honour.

Sir Akbar was supported by a wife of formidable dignity. Lady Hydari was a matriarchal personality who, although observing semi-purdah, was reputed to exert great influence from behind the scenes. Both the Hydaris paid frequent visits to a 'holy mother' at an ashram near Pondicheri to seek her advice, particularly, it was said, before making major decisions.

Hydari liked to ensure that all the male members of his not inconsiderable family were well placed in government positions. Early in my régime he sent for me and pointed out that there were too many Hindu officers in my Departments. This, he said, was dangerous, because the loyalty of the Hindus to their Muslim Ruler could not always be counted upon. I protested that I had seven Hindus and six Muslim officers under me, and that in a state with more than 80% Hindu population this could scarcely be taken as a mark of pro-Hindu bias. Nevertheless, he said, he would like me to take on one of his sons in the Electricity Department; a son who had just returned from England after a training course with the British Thomson Houston Company. As the son was inexperienced, as there was no vacancy, and as I could not 'create' a job without adversely affecting the economy of my Department, I tactlessly said that this would be difficult. From that moment I plummeted in his favour. Later he returned to the attack, but on behalf of another Muslim protegé of very limited brain capacity and unrelated to the Hydari family. This time I was able to oblige; for there was a certain appointment, not falling within my departmental budget, in which it suited me to have a pliable dummy. So at one stroke I found the dummy, satisfied the minister and rose slightly in his favour.

It would be impossible here to mention more than a few of the many other interesting and picturesque Hyderabad personalities and families. There were so many of them; aristocrats and commoners alike.

There were, for instance the Naidus. Mrs Sarojini Naidu was a great personality and a good friend of ours. She was a dedicated politician and feminist, who had taken a prominent part in the Swaraj movement of the Congress Party and in Ghandi's policy of Satyagraha. Her activities had landed her several times in gaol. Although a sworn political enemy of the British, Mrs Naidu bore no personal grudge against individual members of the British community: in fact her house was often filled with British guests whom she entertained at very lively parties. It was said that she really rather liked going to gaol, where she could enjoy every comfort except freedom of movement and where she could receive her friends and even organise her anti-British campaigns. At times of political crisis she would pack her suitcases and await the arrival of the police, welcoming them with a smile when they came to arrest her. Her husband was a charming retired doctor, whose eyesight failed rapidly when he began to age. Her daughters, Lilamini and Padmaja were both highly intelligent and well educated women. The latter became a provincial governor after Independence. The Naidus' son, always known as 'Baba', was a bearded character of left wing political leanings and with a German wife.

An unusual Englishman was Muhammed Marmaduke Pickthall. He had spent his boyhood in Turkey, where he had embraced the Islamic faith. He attained some success as a writer; his best known book being 'Saïd the fisherman'. For a time he held a minor appointment in Hyderabad as warden of a students' hostel and as a professor of Islamic History.

There was one so-called 'nobleman' whose conduct was far from noble. At one time we had a fine golden retriever dog, named Paddy, to whom all our family were devoted. One day

Paddy disappeared, and after reports to the police and offers of rewards had proved abortive we sadly gave him up for lost. Then one day a man called on me and told me he knew where the dog was. When he said that the animal had been stolen by a highly respected nawab I was frankly sceptical. Nevertheless, I asked the police to send an inspector accompanied by one of my servants to make discreet enquiries. On arrival at the nawab's devdi they were greeted by jubilant barking, and Paddy made a bee-line for the servant, wagging his tail with excitement. The nawab's excuse was that he had found the dog wandering and was on the point of making enquiries to trace the owner; but we were informed on good authority that he had been earning stud fees from Paddy.

Perhaps it was this episode that gave Paddy a taste for acquiring a thorough knowledge of the facts of life from personal experience. He developed a habit of wandering at night in search of nocturnal adventure. He would return in the morning with a smile on his face and bags under his eyes. Paddy became a hopeless roué, and I have no doubt that many of the more handsome pariah dogs in the city were sired by him: he was not fussy about his choice of girl friends. Once he arrived home early in the morning, seated like a king in a rickshaw. The rickshaw-wallah claimed, and received, a rupee for his pains. After that, Paddy's disappearances and restorations became a minor industry among the city's rickshaw-wallahs.

One of Gamlen's mantles that had fallen upon me was the governorship of a very large orphanage. I was also a member of its three-man working committee, and we prided ourselves on a well run institution at which some three or four hundred boys and girls were taught some craft or trade and were well cared for while growing up. Many children of the intake were rescued slaves who had been maltreated by their owners. Slavery had never been outlawed by the state government, for fear that legislation would have been followed by the unloading onto the streets of an army of beggars and prostitutes. Many slaves were well treated by their owners, but a few were victims of horrific sadism. One child admitted to the orphanage had been found with its hands bound over live coals for the edification of his master. There was a nasty scandal, before the days when the orphanage had been taken over by a responsible committee, when it was discovered that one of Hyderabad's most respected citizens – a dignified nawab who had been educated in England, graduated at Oxford and knighted, had been using the girls' wing of the orphanage as a brothel.

Apart from the large numbers of well-to-do families who still lived in the style of the eighteenth century, a new upper middle class was appearing in Hyderabad by the 1930s. This was mainly composed of government officials and minor nawabs or rajahs whose ambition was to build for themselves a modern villa on a rocky ridge, called Banjara Hill (renamed Jubilee Hill after HEH's Silver Jubilee in 1937) overlooking the Hussein Sagar Lake and the city. Building operations on this hill involved much blasting and levelling; and many an aspiring builder had to suspend, or perhaps abandon, his activities before even the foundations had been completed, for lack of funds. Many, however, finished their castles-in-the-air, some by virtue of honestly earned resources and others by the fruits of graft: by the 1940s the whole area had the appearance of a newly built holiday settlement on the Costa del Sol. From a look at the natural landscape it would have seemed a miracle to have grown any vegetation there but a cactus bush or babul thorn, but many attractive terraced gardens with elaborate irrigation systems nevertheless made their appearance. One retired government officer installed a crescent-shaped glass-topped dining table with water and concealed illuminations beneath: as one dined one could watch exotic Japanese fish swimming in and out of waving weeds a few inches below one's soup plate. It would be an exaggeration to describe the Jubilee Hill inhabitants as the 'jet set' of Hyderabad society, but their ways were for the most part much more westernised than in the devdis and homes of those who remained in the old city. Open air supper parties and 'parlour games' were de rigeur among the Jubilee Hill community, and an atmosphere of friendly informality was created.

No description of pre-Independence Indian society would be complete without at least passing mention of the 'Heaven-born'. This was the nickname given to the Indian Civil Service, a fine organisation with a great and historical tradition of fair and honest government of hundreds of millions by a mere handful of dedicated men. A justifiable pride in their service was understandable, but it must sadly be recorded that a few of its members gave themselves insufferable airs: hence the sobriquet. The ICS were not very much in evidence in the State. There were one or two 'lent' officers who served for a term in certain key appointments, while the Residency staff were from the Indian Political Service which was partly recruited from the ICS and partly from the Indian Army. On the whole we were very fortunate in the individuals of the ICS who served in Hyderabad State during our time there. Some of them were very good friends of ours; but there were one or two regrettable exceptions who regarded a mere Nazim of tender years – and only an engineer to boot – as beneath their notice.

One of these rare exceptions was holding forth at a state banquet to a lady sitting next to him about the great engineering achievements that had been accomplished in the Nizam's Dominions. (It was apparently possible to admire the *achievements* of engineers so long as one ignored the *achievers*.) After praising the good road and rail systems and a famous dam, he referred to a remarkable railway bridge that spanned one of the great rivers that flowed through the State 'with 52 arches'. At that point, a little man sitting opposite, who had hitherto uttered no word, interrupted. 'Forty-six arches,' said he. The Heaven-born, ruffled at being corrected, said coldly 'I think you are wrong. There are fifty-two arches.' 'Forty-six' was the reply. 'And what, may I ask, makes you so sure?' asked the Heaven-born. 'I built the bloody thing,' replied the little man, who happened to be the Chief Engineer to the Nizam's State Railways.

Late in the War, when petrol rationing was introduced, I found the only alternative to social isolation was to ride a bicycle. Admittedly it was difficult to look dignified on a bicycle when the Guard presented arms to me, but that just could not be helped. One day, Guen, talking to the daughter of the Haughty One, told her how we had been forced to adopt the push-bike as a means of locomotion. 'That's all right for you,' was the reply, 'but we could not possibly ride bicycles because of Daddy's position.'

Another famous service with a deservedly high reputation was the Indian Police, who lent senior British Officers to the State from time to time. Not one of these, whom we knew, gave himself airs: they were delightful people.

Yet another famous service was the Indian Cavalry who were, and are, justly proud of their record. We have counted several Indian Cavalrymen among our close friends; but, as with the ICS, they had a small awkward minority. A very few conceited young subalterns clearly divided British society into four groups – the Cavalry, the rest of the Army, the ICS and the boxwallahs – in descending order of merit. I was once in the bar of the Secunderabad Club with an eminent civilian from Madras who had had an impressive record in the 1914/18 War. Near us a young cavalryman was holding forth about boxwallahs in terms of contempt. I could see my companion's blood pressure rising. When he could take no more he said in a loud voice, 'I've nothing against the Army so long as they remember that I pay for them in peacetime and fight for them in wartime.'

VIII
Il Seraglio

The keeping of women in purdah has of course always been a prevalent custom throughout the Muslim world, and Hyderabad was no exception. In the early years of the twentieth century no well-born Muslim woman would be seen in public; but the State became gradually infected from the West by a movement towards the emancipation of women. It is true that throughout British India and in other princely states high-born Hindu women were also kept in purdah. Outstanding personalities like Mrs Sarojini Naidu made an onslaught against a custom which, they maintained, was degrading to the dignity of women. Mrs Naidu, being herself a Hindu, made some progress with her propaganda among the Hindu community, but had little impact upon the Muslims. The emancipation of women, even among Muslims, received a big push, however, round about 1930 when the two Hyderabad princes married their French-educated and sophisticated Turkish wives, neither of whom would have been content to dwell forever behind the walls of the zenana. There then grew up in Hyderabad a class of women, particularly among the ruling échelons, that observed what was known as semi-purdah; that is to say, they would meet the menfolk of 'respectable' Indian families if well chaperoned, and also European men, but would not appear in crowds or even drive through the streets except behind darkened or curtained car windows. As an Englishman I thus was able to meet many Muslim women in the presence of their husbands; but there were also many Indian men whom I knew well but whose wives I could never meet, though Guen could know them.

My first close encounter with purdah was when Nawab Lutf-ud-Dowlah, a paigah nobleman, asked me to call on him shortly after I had been appointed Director of the Electricity Department: he wanted to discuss the bringing of power supply to one of his farms outside the city. After we had settled our business he invited me to drink tea with him in a large room in the company of one or two male members of his family and household. As the nawab spoke no English, the conversation was in Urdu, which I found a great strain. Suddenly he asked me how many children I had. I had then been married only a few months: I replied, quite truthfully, that I had none. This statement seemed to tickle the nawab, who laughed immoderately. To my consternation I also heard a wave of tittering from above. Glancing upwards I saw a gallery running round the room, curtained off with bamboo screens through which our tea-party could be observed from the other side without any clear vision in the opposite direction. The ladies of the zenana had heard every word uttered and had shared the nawab's amusement at what must have been considered either as impotence or celibacy on my part.

In Indian cinemas the balcony was reserved for women and children only, who viewed the film through a veil curtain while the men sat below. In 1941 a disastrous fire broke out in one of these cinemas. So great was the inhibition amongst the women against being seen in public that many were burnt to death rather than face the 'shame' of escaping with the crowd. The Commission of Enquiry set up afterwards, of which I was a member, had to interview several purdah lady survivors for evidence: the examination had to be conducted through curtains.

Muslim law allows a man to have as many as four wives – one on and three in the wash, as it were – but most of the more eminent Hyderabadis produced only one before the outer world. Nevertheless, Guen once escorted two wives of the same husband at some official gathering. The husband was a very sophisticated and well educated man. One of his wives was for the bedroom: the other, a former Girton girl, for intellectual companionship.

At a large reception at the palace of a wealthy rajah our host received his guests and introduced them to two be-saried ladies standing by his side as 'the senior rani and the junior rani'. The junior rani was very glamorous, and I could not help feeling sorry for the older woman who, by comparison, appeared at a distinct disadvantage. This was a case of a Hindu adopting a Muslim custom.

Guen met one or two European women living in full purdah. They had met their husbands when they had been University students in Britain. Tales of the Glamorous Orient had lured more than one Lancashire landlady's daughter from the fogs of Manchester to virtual captivity in Hyderabad: by then it was too late to put the clock back.

When Lady Hydari died during the War, a vast crowd of sympathisers went to Sir Akbar's house to offer their condolences, as was the custom. Guen and I went also. We were separated on arrival and the men filed past the widower to mumble words of sympathy. The women had a more gruesome experience: they were taken to view the remains of Lady Hydari laid out in state and surrounded by huge blocks of ice as a concession to the climate. The air was heavily scented with flowers and a chorus of mourning women maintained a moaning lament in the best Roman ululatory tradition.

The custom of purdah had, of course, been practised also in mediaeval Europe, especially when knights went to the crusades leaving their wives locked up in chastity belts – even though often, no doubt, Love laughed at Locksmiths. A curious relic of this segregation of the sexes impressed me when I was a schoolboy. My mother sometimes took my sisters and myself on Sunday mornings to the Temple Church off Fleet Street to hear the music and the preaching of Dr Barnes, then Master of the Temple and later Bishop of Birmingham. It gave my young heart a thrill when I was always led to a cushioned seat in the main body of the church among all the barristers and other male members of the congregation, while my mother and sisters had to be content with hard benches at the side.

A story is told of a famous Vicereine who gave a purdah party to the distinguished ladies of New Delhi. In the middle of the proceedings an unseasonable rainstorm broke. A new and very young British ADC, fearing the wrath that might result from a viceregal wetting, rushed in upon the scene with an umbrella. No fox among chickens could have caused greater pandemonium. The excited and outraged ladies clucked hither and thither, fearful for their chastity. The situation was saved by a dignified begam who mounted a chair and declaimed in a loud voice 'Ladies, be calm! It is only one of Her Excellency's eunuchs'.

IX

High days and holidays, Indian style

The Indian calendar is profusely marked with public holidays, most of them having a religious significance. In a land of Hindus, Muslims, Christians and Parsees this is not altogether surprising, particularly when religious piety is strongly reinforced by a congenital reluctance to work. Thus, for the most part, each sect not only celebrates the holy days laid down for observance by the hierarchy of its own faith, but is happy to cash in on those demanded by the devotees of other creeds.

The Muslim holidays were the most numerous in Hyderabad, as would be expected in a country with a Muhammedan ruling class. The observance of Muharram and Ramzan covered a whole month each, of which several days were marked on both occasions by government holidays: it was in this way that I had lost twelve days' salary on my arrival in the State. In an enlightened Muslim land in which freedom of worship was an article of political faith, it was a foregone conclusion that the principal religious holidays of *all* creeds were celebrated by the closure of offices. Thus, most government departments were inaccessible for perhaps a quarter of the year. This happy state of affairs, however, applied only to those departments that *spent* revenue. 'Commercial' departments such as the Electricity Department, which *earned* revenue were strictly rationed in holidays. But although I personally was unable to enjoy the same privileges of idleness as most of my fellow civil servants, I nevertheless felt the impact in various ways of the innumerable public holidays celebrated by others.

Christians were allowed to absent themselves from their offices on Sunday mornings for the purpose of worshipping; and although my Goanese and other Christian staff could be found nowhere in their Sabbath morning, I myself could not conscientiously pretend to be a worshipper. Sundays for me were therefore indistinguishable from other working days.

A feature of *all* Indian festivals, indeed of all comings and goings of any significance whatsoever, is the *garland*. On the slenderest of excuses a sweet-smelling garland of marigolds, frangipani, jasmine and other flowers would be placed round one's neck: and if the occasion warranted the presentation of garlands from several sources one would be almost suffocated by the overpowering scent and weighed down by their bulk. In the centre of Hyderabad City, close to the Char Minar, could be seen rows of garland weavers: their handiwork must have been one of the State's major industries. If one were unlucky one might, when being garlanded, have a daub of red or orange dye placed on the forehead just above the eyebrows, at the same time receiving a liberal wetting from a silver dispenser of rose-water. On very special occasions one might receive *everlasting* garlands made, not of flowers, but of gold and silver thread.

The Hindu festival of Divali, which I had known in my Bombay days, was the one that intruded most prominently into my professional responsibilities; for it imposed a fearful burden on the power supply system that had to provide the electricity for the thousands of lights that transformed the city into a fairyland. It was a worrying time; and I was always to be found in the power house during the peak load hours, anxiously watching the instruments, while extra staff manned the substations throughout the city. The most beautiful part of the illuminations, however, owed nothing to electricity but to the old-fashioned oil lamp. There was one street in particular, leading to the Chowmahalla Palace, bounded by high walls covered with thousands of small flickering lamps.

The month of Ramzan (or Ramadan, as it is sometimes known in other Muhammedan countries) was, and is, observed by the Muslims by fasting from dawn to twilight every day for the whole month. This meant rising very early and absorbing enough food and water to sustain the faithful throughout the day. As soon as the sun had dipped below the horizon in the evening, the firing of a gun signalled that a hearty meal could be taken unsinfully. As the lunar Hijri calendar slipped back every solar year by eleven days, Ramzan could occur at any season; and when it fell during the hot weather it was not uncommon for the devout to faint in the daytime for lack of food and water. The end of the month was marked by the feast of Id-ul-Fitr, which began as soon as the firing of a gun announced that the new moon had officially been seen by the mullahs. This was a great holiday, when Muslims would visit the houses of their friends, of whatever faith, to exchange good wishes. Throughout the day a stream of Muhammedans would call on me, stand about a pace away, and bow from the waist as though with intent to butt me in the stomach. I was then expected to place a pontifical hand on the back of my visitor's head and utter the words 'Id Mubarak', which mean 'auspicious festival'. The same procedure was observed at another Muslim holiday, Bakr Id.

Nawab Salar Jung Bahadur was in the habit of giving intimate curry suppers at his 'small' country mansion at Sarunagar, outside the city, during the month of Ramzan, when his guests broke fast with him after sundown. Those of us who had not fasted during the day found it difficult to compete with the appetites of the orthodox.

The Hindu festival of Holi was an occasion for the foreigner to keep off the streets. It was then the practice of the Hindu populace to throw coloured dye powders at one another, all in a spirit of friendly horseplay. But to return home apparently clad in Joseph's coat would not have been a pleasant experience; so it was best avoided.

One of the most colourful festivals of the Hindu calendar, with the possible exception of Divali, was Dasserah. It was then the custom, even as now observed in certain Christian communities, for the tools of trade to be blessed by the priests. The smith's hammer and anvil, the farmer's plough and rake, the soldier's weapons, the merchant's books, the fisherman's nets – all these and many other occupational implements were blessed by the Brahmins. The custom even extended to the machines of modern industry. The boilers and turbines in the power house were decked out in flowers: so were the presses and crucibles in the Mint.

Although Dasserah is celebrated throughout India, nowhere was it observed more magnificently than in the City of Mysore. Visitors from far and wide would travel to see this splendid spectacle; and this Guen and I did in October, 1935. The city itself was decked out with thousands of lights every night, as at Divali, during the festival which lasted about a week. Even the outline of the massive Chamundi Hill, which dominates the city, was picked out in lights. Every day there were durbars attended by the Maharajah of Mysore, an enlightened ruler of simple personal tastes who led a quiet unostentatious life during most of the year but who did not grudge the populace an occasional display of the splendid pageantry that was expected of him. At these durbars the state coaches, the royal elephants and horses, the military arms and all the trappings of the Maharajah's court and authority were paraded and garlanded before the Ruler. The elephants and horses were trained to 'salaam' the prince as they passed the royal box. Torchlight parades, garden parties, processions through the city and banquets given by Their Highnesses the Yuvarajah and Rajkumar (the brother and nephew of the Maharajah) helped to enliven the week's festivities. To have visited India without witnessing the Mysore Dasserah would indeed have been a great mistake.

While in Mysore we met Sir C V Rahman, the first Indian to be honoured with a fellowship of the Royal Society as an eminent physicist. He showed me over his laboratories and I was surprised to find that he was apparently far more interested in the irridescence of pretty seashells than in the more obscure mysteries of the universe: he had a whole laboratory full of these shells. Lady Rahman took Guen and me to visit the Krishnarajahsagar Lake, a beauty spot not very far from the city.

We had a curious experience in Mysore as a result of a courtesy call I felt obliged to make on my opposite number, the Chief Electrical Engineer of Mysore State, an Indian who had recently taken over from his American predecessor. He was most friendly and suggested that I would wish to visit the hydroelectric power station at Sivasamudram on the Cauvery River. He said he would send a car with one of his senior engineers to act as escort to collect Guen and myself from our hotel, from where we would be driven to Sivasamudram through pleasant countryside. There a guesthouse would be put at Guen's disposal while I would be shown over the power plant. After that we were to have lunch and drive back to Mysore. Everything went according to plan and we had a pleasant and interesting day, after which I again called on the Chief Engineer to thank him for the VIP treatment he had so kindly accorded to us, and to take my leave. A few weeks later, in Hyderabad, I received a bill, covering the hire of a taxi with waiting time, the cost of three lunches, the rent of the guesthouse for four hours and the services of one senior engineer for a whole day. I sent a cheque with a rather frigidly worded letter to say that if I had known I was under financial obligation I would have settled my debt before leaving Mysore. Two weeks later I had a further bill for eight annas (about 3p), for clearing my cheque across the state boundaries!

Dasserah in Hyderabad was an occasion I rather dreaded, for I was required to make a sort of royal progress from boiler house to turbine room, from carpenter's shop to foundry, and so on throughout my small empire, receiving the full treatment of garland, daub and rosewater at each stopping place and being expected to make a speech every time. To vary one's platitudes in eight or ten speeches strained my almost non-existent powers of oratory to the limit. Once, during the War, I had just finished my last boring Dasserah speech when a peon came to announce the arrival of some British military officers who wanted to see me. Before I had had time to divest myself of a load of garlands or to wash the dye from my forehead the military visitors appeared. They were a group of top brass, one general and a clutch of staff colonels, who wished to discuss the possibility of certain munitions being made in my workshops. Seldom have I felt more foolish, having to greet my visitors, mostly new to India and unversed in its strange customs, decked out like a sort of floral Laocoon.

Of all the holidays Christmas was the most memorable. It was observed not only by the Europeans and Indian Christians but also to some extent by the non-Christian Indians, especially the Muslims. The exchange of Christmas cards became a nightmare. Every year we received between four and five hundred cards, and we made a point of acknowledging every single one either in kind or by means of a brief note of thanks. Our first few Christmas Days were ruined for us by an endless ceremonial that filled most of the morning and could not be avoided without giving offence. Later we let it be known that the 25th December itself was to be a quiet family occasion without disturbance and that our more public activities would be performed on Boxing Day.

The activities started immediately after breakfast, when a vast assembly of our household servants and their families approached the steps of our house. Our twenty-three servants somehow accounted for some four or five times as many souls. In order of domestic precedence each servant came forward, grinning from ear to ear, to wish us happiness and to garland us. Each had to be rewarded in cash, and every child given a bag of sweets. At the second Christmas of our married life we noticed that the size of the crowd had visibly swollen. The cook, who had presented three children to us the previous year, had now miraculously claimed fatherhood to five, only one of which was a baby in arms. Similar phenomena occurred with other servants, and we soon ran out of sweets. Henceforward we kept a register of the number of children claimed by each servant. Although the numbers increased regularly at a rate of one child per year per servant, we managed in this way to keep some sort of vague control over the scale of largesse without having to pray every year for a repetition of the miracle of the loaves and fishes.

After the servants came the office peons from every government department with which I was in any way connected – not only those of which I was in charge but also departments with which I had dealings, such as the Finance Office. Each delegation was led by an elaborately liveried jemadar who added to our already heavy burden of garlands and then stepped back with a coy expression on his face, expectantly waiting for a suitable handout of bakhshish. Even the chaprassis from the royal palace came for their share of the loot although they had done nothing whatsoever for me during the preceding year. It was advisable to propitiate them, for they could exercise a form of blackmail: these humble menials could wield considerable power by delaying files from reaching the Nizam – for instance I could not take even one day's leave without Exalted sanction. So they too had to be paid Danegeld every Christmas.

The next to arrive were all the officers and many of the employees of my own departments. Mercifully this involved no further handouts of bakhshish. But each had to be shaken by the hand and thanked for their good wishes, and enquiries had to be made as to the health of their wives and dependents. Our stock of garlands continued to rise: even our children were garlanded, though not to quite the same extent as Guen and myself.

Not all European officers in the State had to undergo such a pressing and expensive ordeal, but the custom at the Mint House had been established by, or at least with the cheerful concurrence of, my predecessor Gamlen, who had thoroughly enjoyed playing the part of an old-time Nabob. When my turn came it was virtually impossible to turn the clock back.

My greatest embarrassment at Christmas was caused by Indians who tried to give me expensive presents, often with ulterior motives. A bowl of oranges from a donor's garden was all very well, but a pearl necklace for my wife was another matter! Refusals had to be firm, but they always led to tears, to protestations of affection and respect, and sometimes to assertions that I had offered insult. It was all very unpleasant. The worst offenders were the electrical contractors who hoped to be given contracts for illuminating the city on state occasions, or for wiring a new public building. I once came across from my office to my house at breakfast time to find the children shouting with delight at the sight of a working model railway set out on the verandah. My rejection of this expensive gift subjected me to an assault of tears on two fronts – from the contractor and from my children.

Our house was always profusely decorated every Christmas with paper chains, Chinese lanterns and the usual baublery. As the Norwegian spruce will not grow in Southern India we had to be content with an ersatz Christmas tree, though it looked quite like the real thing with the help of the usual tinsel, glass ornaments, cotton wool 'snow' and fairy lights. Although the climate was not conventionally seasonable in the Christmas card sense, it was at least at the coolest time of year, and darkness fell rather earlier.

We always gave a Children's Party near Christmas time. This involved the borrowing of an elephant and a camel from one of the nawabs. To reach the Mint House from their stables the elephants had to pass through the most congested part of the city, and to give the necessary headroom I had to arrange for some of the street lights to be raised by a few feet. In December 1938, the last Christmas season before the War, we really let ourselves go for the children's party. In addition to the usual elephant and camel rides we laid on an elaborate entertainment that had to be rehearsed to a precise minute-to-minute programme like a military operation – with synchronized watches! It went off perfectly. One hundred and sixty children, parents and friends came. After the usual feast, with crackers and paper streamers, came the first excitement. It was a huge Humpty Dumpty made by placing an earthenware chatti upside down into the mouth of a larger one and plastering the 'waist' so that the whole looked like a vast egg. This had previously been filled with bags of sweets. It was provided with home-made stuffed arms and legs and a painted face. He was pushed over the parapet of our front porch and shattered on the ground: a general scramble then ensued for his 'innards'. At dusk, Santa Claus suddenly appeared high up on the roof of the house with his reindeer sleigh. The reindeer's head had been cut out of plywood and hinged from a bolt fixed to the inner side of the roof parapet, so that by manipulating the reins the head could be made to nod up and down. Another piece of plywood represented the curved front of the sleigh, while the swag was a collection of cushions placed beneath a dustsheet on a couple of stools and nicely visible over the top of the parapet. Meanwhile the 'dog-boy', concealed behind the parapet, was busy jangling bells and letting off crackers to make Santa Claus's whip more convincing. The whole effect was most realistic against the evening sky. Santa Claus invited the children to go inside the house and sit on the floor of the large drawing room. The door that led from this room onto the back verandah had been rigged up to look like a big chimney, behind which a roaring fire seemed to be blazing. This was a contrivance of canvas, ribbons, concealed lights and electric fans that gave a most convincing impression of a real fire. It was a trick I had already tried out for 'beacons' during the viceregal visit of 1933. The dramatic moment came when Santa Claus descended the chimney in his conventional uniform with white beard, wearing my riding boots (three sizes too large for him) and carrying a giant illuminated stocking filled with booty. I had arranged a contrivance of platform and pulleys for this pantomime scene. All went well except for a rather jerky descent, punctuated by exclamations (not entirely sotto voce) from Santa Claus of 'Not so fast, you bloody fool!' Safely on terra firma and uninjured either by the hazards of his descent or of the 'fire', Santa Claus distributed presents to every child in the room.

Unbeknown to me the local press were present on that occasion, and our efforts were rewarded by the following literary gem that appeared in the local newspaper, the Hyderabad Bulletin:-

TREATS FOR THE CHILDREN

Joy rides on a camel and on an elephant, delightful presents and dainty refreshments, these were some of the items on the programme of amusements to which tiny tots were treated to their hearts' content at the Christmas Tree and Treat for children organised by Mr and Mrs Armstead at their residence on Saturday evening. About 160 guests were present, prominent among whom were Nawab and Begam Mehdi Yar Jung Bahadur, members of the Wali-ud-Dowlah family, Major and Mrs Challen, Lt Col R F D McGregor, Major and Mrs Gordon, Captain and Mrs Dawson, Captain Stewart and Mr and Mrs Morris. They were all received by Mrs and Mr Armstead, and as befitting the occasion the kiddies came in for much fondling. An item of unusual interest to the children was the elephant ride. In spite of their unwillingness to go near the animal, they were loathe (sic) to part from the fun which the rides provided them. When the gong was sounded, the guests adjourned to tea to a lawn at the rear of the building which was tastefully decorated. Special tables were arranged for the children. After tea, Humpty Dumpty, placed on the terrace, was pushed down by Mr Armstead, and a happy smile lit up the children when they found numerous presents for them in the shattered egg. An excited chase for Father Christmas followed, and the children in right earnest took up the hunt after the personage in great demand just now. Finally he was discovered on the chimney with his reindeer sleigh, and after much cajoling he agreed to come down. The children rushed into the hall, which, with decorations and the Christmas Tree and egg head and fire, claimed the gaze of the children. Father Christmas, after coming down from the sky, as it were, promised to give them presents. A sprite was next conjured up with whose assistance Father Christmas caused a beautifully decorated stocking, lit with tiny electric bulbs, to appear from the sky. It contained numerous presents to the young ones. Father Christmas then gave away the prizes to the kiddies amidst much merriment, after which the happy function terminated, and the guests, one and all, departed with smiles wreathing their faces in remembrance of the innocent pranks of the tots and their catching joviality.

There was a curious little incident after this party. One of the small boys, the son of a British major, received as his present a jigsaw puzzle. A day or two later we had a letter of complaint from his mother to say that a piece of the puzzle was missing!

During the War we could not of course repeat the lavishness of that 1938 party, but we always managed to find a conjuror or a puppet show with which to amuse the children.

At a New Year Eve party, for adults this time, a friend of mine and I had spent some hours making a fire balloon. Neither of us knew anything about fire balloons except that a hole in the top was necessary and the whole contraption should be as light as possible. So we made a framework of split bamboo strips, covered it with coloured tissue paper, and suspended from it with wire a sort of 'birdsnest' of straw soaked in paraffin wax. The climax of the party was to be the release of the balloon from the tennis court. The guests assembled on the steps at the back of the house, the 'birdsnest' was kindled, and my friend and I, standing on chairs, held the balloon and waited apprehensively. I frankly expected either a conflagration or a non-take-off. But after a minute or two we felt a slight upward pressure and let go

117

our hold. Slowly and majestically the balloon rose, to much applause. The moment of triumph soon turned to alarm; for as soon as the balloon had cleared the height of the house and trees it was caught by a breeze and carried towards the Mint, apparently falling slowly. Now I knew that in the Mint quadrangle, quite inaccessible at night without an elaborate system of keys held by various people then at their homes scattered about the city, was a large consignment of wooden packing cases containing tens of thousands of paper currency notes newly arrived from the Security Press. I had a ghastly vision of the whole treasure going up in flames; but mercifully the breeze carried the balloon up and away. It finally fell to earth in flames at Golconda, some six or seven miles away. The local papers were full next day of eye-witnesses' accounts of a fiery object from outer space. What could it portend?

In the early part of 1937 Hyderabad went very gay on the occasion of the Silver Jubilee celebrations to commemorate the first twenty-five years of the Nizam's reign. I had a busy time serving on a committee for the preparation of an exhibition, the planning of a programme for the celebrations and for the decoration and illumination of the city. At one of the committee meetings an item on the agenda was to choose an artist for a mass group portrait of HEH surrounded by his nobles. The committee solemnly debated the rival merits of Mr Rajah Din Dayal, a local photographer of repute, and Mr Richard Sickert, RA. The vote went to Mr Rajah Din Dayal on the grounds of supporting local talent. I do not remember ever seeing the finished picture.

A special Durbar Hall was built as a Jubilee Memorial, the city was lit up in a big way, and banquets and junketings abounded. One of the Jubilee durbars was devoted to the presentation of caskets to HEH. He sat on a raised throne while representative groups from various communities within the State made their speeches of congratulations and expressions of loyalty and presented him with ornate caskets containing replicas of the speeches printed on silk. Their royal master examined each casket critically, demanding assurance that each was *really* made of gold, and not merely plated. During the speeches the august recipient sat busily picking the royal nose.

At another durbar medals were distributed. I managed to collect one. It now reposes – regrettably without companions – in a cabinet in my house.

An odd custom observed in Hyderabad, and for all I know elsewhere in India too, was the presentation of a complete meal to a distant 'guest'. Many times I have been visited by a group of servants bearing dishes of curry and rice and other delicacies, covered with gold-embroidered cloth, together with a note of good wishes and the Urdu equivalent of bon appetit from an Indian who may have been living some miles away. This hospitable alternative to an invitation to attend a dinner in person has much to commend it. Usually these 'meals on heels' were sent on occasions of a family wedding or perhaps at some religious festival.

A commoner custom, much observed also in British India, was to send a dish of fruit, often grown in the garden of the donor. The wife of an incoming Residency staff member once received such a gift shortly after her arrival in Hyderabad. Attached to the gift was a scrubby note saying 'With compliments. MOAK'. The lady dutifully sat down then and there to compose a letter of thanks, beginning 'Dear Mr Moak'. Fortunately her husband returned home in time to explain that MOAK was none other than Mir Osman Ali Khan – His Exalted Highness himself.

X

Pooh-Bah The Second

The first two years of my directorship of the Electricity Department and State Workshops passed fairly peacefully, though I had my share of troubles. Being a new broom, I found plenty to sweep away; so I was kept very busy. One of the consequences of reforms is the inevitable making of a few enemies; and I have no doubt that I upset some of the more conservative of my colleagues and subordinates who had come to regard Gamlen's ways as Holy Writ. To mollify some of my more difficult staff I encouraged their social activities and gave them amenities they had hitherto lacked, such as a recreation hall and tennis courts. The senior staff members of the Electricity Department formed a social club called the 'Bijliwallahs' Association'. Guen and I had to attend their tea parties, and conversely had to invite them all to our home once a year. These rather sticky occasions helped to oil the wheels of smooth administration to some extent.

As 1937 drew nigh, a dormant anxiety began to gnaw. The elderly Parsee who had inherited the Mintmastership from Gamlen was about to retire at last. In all probability his successor would want to turn me out of the Mint House on which we had spent so much and in which we had made ourselves so comfortable. At about the same time a major decision had to be faced. Should I be content to remain in a professional backwater, gradually losing contact with my colleagues in Britain; or should I cut my losses and return home

The Rt Hon Sir Akbar Hydari, Honourable Finance Minister to The Government of Hyderabad in the 1930s, then President of The Nizam's Executive Council, and later a member of the Viceroy's Council. The first Indian appointed to the King-Emperor's Privy Council.

Newab Salar Jung Bahadur III, son and grandson of former Prime Ministers of Hyderabad State; himself Prime Minister for one year. A great collector of works of art.

His Excellency The Nawab of Chattari, President of The Nizam's Executive Council later in the Second World War.
(Photos: Raja Deen Dayal)

An example of public illuminations: the entrance gate to Khilwat Mubarak Palace.

Hyderabad's Char Minar in its full glory for a Viceregal visit – a building which features prominently on the State's coinage. Some idea of the scale of this 16th century memorial is gained from the lesser buildings nearby.

at (almost certainly) a much lower salary, for the sake of the future? I decided that to have held down my job as chief for only two years was not sufficient, and that it would be good policy to stay on in Hyderabad for another three years or so. Anything more than about seven years in all, spent in the State, could, I felt, spell stagnation. It was fortunate I could not see into the future.

I therefore called on the Finance Minister, Sir Akbar Hydari, and asked if he was sufficiently satisfied with my services to grant me a further three-year contract. When he said 'Yes', I promptly cashed in by saying I would accept such a contract only on condition that my salary was increased by one-third. Again he agreed, and I inwardly kicked myself for not having demanded more. Having negotiated that hurdle I called again on Sir Akbar about a month later. This time I offered to take on the duties of the Mintmaster and Superintendent of Stamps without extra salary in exchange for continued occupancy of the Mint House rent-free. At that time the Mint more or less ran itself, and the Mintmaster's duties were largely of a routine nature. I therefore felt that if my proposal were accepted I, as well as the government, would be getting a good bargain, for I would be saving ten percent of my salary as rent. Again Sir Akbar agreed. A few years later I came to realise that my 'bargain' was by no means as satisfactory as I then thought, but at that time I was delighted. I had secured a marvellous home without the risk of being ejected at any time. I signed a new agreement which entitled me to 'one further return sea passage between England and India'. This, I thought, would be my last Hyderabad agreement, for I was determined to return to Europe for good after it had expired, if only because of the problems of our children's education.

The best laid schemes o' mice an' men...

And so it came about that the wheel had almost come full circle. With the exception of the Osmania Technical Institute, Gamlen's empire had been reconstituted and had fallen to my lot. My new designations were Mintmaster, Superintendent of

Stamps, Director of HEH The Nizam's Electricity Department, Director of HEH The Nizam's State Workshops, Warden of Weights and Measures and Currency Officer. To all these offices were added some others of minor importance, a few of which brought me in modest fees, such as Electrical Inspector to the British Administered Territories within the State, Consulting Electrical Engineer to HEH The Nizam's State Railways, Consulting Engineer to the Azam Jahi and Osman Shahi Cotton Mills at Warangal and Gulbarga, Director of the Deccan Pottery Works, Technical Adviser to the State Broadcasting Department, Governor and Working Committee Member of the Victoria Memorial Orphanage for all of which I was paid the equivalent of £20 a month. The duties of these secondary appointments, some of which had not been held by Gamlen, were not onerous. In the case of the Broadcasting Department, which was managed by an efficient but temperamental Irishman, my appointment as Technical adviser was bitterly resented – quite justly, since I knew not the first thing about broadcasting. However, as the appointment was honorary and as my advice, fortunately, was never once sought, my title remained no more than a piece of paper. I was also made responsible for examining and reporting upon patent applications of a scientific nature. Many hours were wasted in wading through hopeful claims of those who were convinced that they had discovered the secrets of perpetual motion. Finally I inherited Gamlen's responsibilities for illuminating and decorating the city on the occasions of viceregal and other state visits and public celebrations, and I was coopted onto many government-appointed committees.

If in this narrative I have hitherto stressed the social aspects of state life, let it not be thought that life was all junketing and idle pleasure. Far from it! The popular vision of the British civilian reclining in a chaise longue on his verandah, sipping chota pegs beneath a punkah, bossing his servants about and doing little else is a gross misconception. In point of fact I have seldom worked harder in my life than in Hyderabad. During my

period of overlap with Gamlen, when I had been Deputy
Director only, I had indeed enjoyed a certain amount of leisure;
but after my predecessor had left, and particularly after I came
into my full Pooh-Bah-ship, my nose was kept very much to
the grindstone for the rest of my days in Hyderabad. Both
Saturdays and Sundays were full working days in the Muslim
ruled state; and although Friday was the official sabbath it was
only that day that afforded me the opportunity for getting down
to serious planning unhampered by the constant interruptions
of routine work. Generally I worked six and a half days a week
with eight hours or more on every full day.

One of the curious consequences of my multifarious
appointments was that I was constantly having to write letters to
myself. The Director of the Electricity Department would write
to the Mintmaster to remind him that the last electricity bill was
still outstanding. The Mintmaster would reply giving assurance
that the account would be settled within 48 hours. The
Superintendent of Stamps would write to the Director of the
State Workshops to ask that a perforating machine might be
repaired, while the Director of the State Workshops would
place a written order with the Superintendent of Stamps for a
supply of printed billheads. Sometimes I would write quite
acrimonious letters to myself. Correspondence of this sort was
constantly being put before me for signature, and I was assured
by my babus that they were all necessary if the departmental
records were to be kept in order.

To this Gilbertian situation I sometimes dreamed of adding
yet another improbable appointment which, alas, never
materialised. Hyderabad State was completely landlocked, and
all its imports had to pass through British India. HEH's
Customs Department levied an octroi of 5% ad valorem on all
imports (except on government purchases) and this had to be
paid even on the freight costs from the coast – a matter that
caused some resentment among Hyderabadis. At one time there
was talk of giving HEH a 'free port', or even a corridor à la
polonaise to the coast. If ever this should happen, I thought, it

would surely be apposite for me, as an ex-naval cadet, to apply for the post of Lord High Admiral to the Exalted Navy!

During the War I was introduced to a British brigadier by some humorist who listed my appointments, ending with Warden of Weights and Measures. 'I can beat that', said the brigadier. 'You are talking to the ex-Admiral of the Sea of Galilee'. Apparently, as an army captain he had been responsible for transporting supplies across the Sea of Galilee during General Allenby's campaign. He had applied for, and was granted, the title of Admiral of the Sea of Galilee with permission to fly the white ensign!

Thus, in the twenty-sixth year of the reign of Nizam-ul-Mulk VII did I become a sort of Pooh-Bah The Second. I was now legitimately entitled to the military guard at my gate.

Before assuming my new duties in the Mint and Stamps Departments I returned to Europe to enjoy the only home leave I was able to take during my twelve years' service in the State. Guen and I spent six weeks in England and a further six weeks on the Continent. As Hitler had by now become more than a cloud on the horizon we thought it advisable to explore parts of Eastern Europe before they became inaccessible.

XI

Halli Sicca

Of all the sovereign powers enjoyed by the Nizam, the right to mint his own money was one of those he most prized. Seven other States also had this right in theory; these were Jodhpur, Gwalior, Dungarpur, Travancore, Maler Kotla, Patiala and Junagadh. All seven produced small quantities of coin, mainly for ceremonial purposes, but Hyderabad alone possessed a fully equipped mint devoted to the production of the entire coinage requirements of the State. In all other princely states, British Indian currency was the only legal tender. To serve the needs of some seventeen or eighteen million subjects of the Nizam, immense quantities of coin and paper currency were needed, and a mint of no mean size had to be maintained.

The right to strike their own coins had for long been a highly valued privilege of the Nizams of Hyderabad, but until the middle of the nineteenth century theirs was not the only mint in the State. Several private mints were also maintained by powerful noblemen and even by wealthy merchants on payment of licence fees to the royal exchequer. These noblemen or merchants, as well as the Nizams, struck their own names or initials upon their coins in addition to that of the Emperor who in those days reigned in Delhi. The prevalence of private mints, however, resulted in a multiplicity of alloys and weights and often to the shameless debasement of the precious metal content. Gresham's Law ruled. These evils became so pronounced that in 1857, during the reign of Nawab Nazir-ud-

Dowlah, the fourth Nizam, all private mints were abolished throughout his Dominions on the advice of his Diwan, Nawab Sir Salar Jung Bahadur the First. Thereafter the Nizam's royal mint became the only authorised institution of its kind in the land. From that same year the public were permitted to bring their own bullion or ornaments to the mint for conversion into coin on payment of 'seignorage', a minting fee charged at the rate of two rupees per single gold coin or per hundred silver coins. But this practice was stopped in 1901, partly on account of assay difficulties and partly to concentrate all minting profits into the hands of the Nizam's government.

It was also in 1857, after what the British call 'The Mutiny' and the Indians call 'The Independence Movement', that the name of the Delhi Emperor ceased to appear on the Hyderabad coins, since with the dissolution of the Moghul Empire the nominal allegiance owed to Delhi by the Deccan was severed. The new Hyderabad coins were named 'Halli Sicca', which simply means 'current coin', and this name persisted for ninety years to distinguish the Nizam's from the British Indian currency. (The irreverent often used to refer to the Hyderabad State Forces as 'The Halli Sicca Army').

The halli sicca coins have always borne the dynastic title of the ruling house – Nizam-ul-Mulk, Asaf Jah Bahadur – together with the *initial* of the reigning Nizam. The currency was also often referred to in terms that linked it with the ruler of the time: thus during the reign of the last ruling Nizam it was called Osmania Sicca, while during the rule of his father it was called Mahbubia Sicca.

Until 1895 the coins were struck in a very primitive manner; but though the craftsmanship was crude the results were most pleasing to the eye. Some of these old coins are still to be found in the former Dominions of the Nizams, often in the form of bracelets or other ornaments. Machinery was first introduced in 1895 and in 1903 the Hyderabad Mint was thoroughly modernised on the lines of the European mints. A new design of

Deccan coin appeared in that year, embodying as the central
feature of the gold and silver series the famous Char Minar
building that dominates the old city. These coins were of very
fine quality, and the golden ashrafi (now worth £80-£90 in
gold content only) was particularly beautiful, being about half as
large again as the British sovereign. Until 1942 there were
twelve denominations of coin – four gold, four silver, one cupro-
nickel and three bronze.

The gold coins were not used as normal currency, as their
value fluctuated in terms of the price of gold bullion. When I
first took charge of the Mint an ashrafi was valued at about forty
rupees: by the time I left Hyderabad its value had soared to well
over one hundred rupees. Gold coins were used for ceremonial
purposes only. At weddings and births they were traditionally
offered as presents: they were also often made into jewellery.
But it was for the ancient custom of nazar that they were chiefly
in demand. For centuries it had been the custom of Indian
princes to hold an annual durbar, or court reception, to which
they would invite their noblemen, courtiers, state officials and
the more prosperous local merchants. The guests would file past
their royal host, make obeisance and present him with a number
of coins. This form of cash tribute, known as nazar, was
doubtless resented by many but was regarded by the more
philosophical as a form of income tax. The amount of nazar was
fixed by strict protocol and varied with the rank of the victim.
An offering of five coins, of which at least *one* must be gold, was
the bare minimum with which the humblest of state officials
could get away; but a diwan or prime minister was expected to
give as many as eleven golden ashrafis. By the twentieth century
the presentation of nazar had, in most of the princely states,
become a mere symbolic ceremony at which the money was
placed upon a silk handkerchief and held in both hands, palms
upwards, shown by the subject in token of his allegiance, and
touched by the Ruler in acknowledgement. The subject then
backed away from the princely presence, bowing, and as soon as

127

he was decently out of sight he pocketed his own coins. No one can complain of such a harmless and picturesque ceremony. I myself have seen this done in Mysore. In Hyderabad, however, the Nizam preferred the substance to the shadow of this ancient custom: the booty was collected in sacks! Since it was supposed to be an honour to be admitted into the princely presence, no word of thanks was considered to be necessary, but after the ceremony the company would be regaled with sherbet and sandwiches. On the principle that if a thing is worth doing at all it is worth doing thoroughly, the income level that qualified a government official for the doubtful honour of presenting nazar was lowered so as to swell the numbers of donors, while the frequency of the occasion was extended to include several public holidays instead of being merely limited, as in earlier days, to the royal birthday.

In 1918 the state currency was expanded by the introduction of paper treasury notes. At first these were printed in England by the well known firm of security printers, Messrs Waterlow & Sons; and some of them were the subject of a curious incident that caused acute embarrassment to the Nizam's government.

In 1922 the P&O ship *Egypt* collided with another vessel off Ushant and sank. She was carrying a valuable cargo of gold bullion, and several attempts were made to salvage this. In 1932 an Italian salvage vessel succeeded in recovering some strong boxes from the bed of the ocean out of the ship's strongroom*. These boxes were suspiciously light in weight and, to the disgust of the salvors, were found to contain not gold, but Hyderabad currency notes en route from Waterlows to India. It so happened that a consignment of 165,000 currency notes of various denominations, of total face value of Rs5,125,000 had gone to the bottom of the sea with the *Egypt*. As the notes were *unsigned*, they were valueless as currency; for in those days the

---

* An interesting account of the salvage operations can be read in The *Egypt's* Gold by David Scott (Penguin).

signature of the Hon Finance Minister was overprinted on all currency notes in the Hyderabad Mint after their arrival from England. Waterlows had insured the consignment for £2,000 only, being the cost of the paper, printing and packing: the insurance company had settled the claim, and the Hyderabad government had ordered a replacement stock from the printers. These replacement notes were given the same serial numbers as had been allotted to the original (lost) notes, but in a slightly different type to show they were duplicates. The replacement notes had duly been safely received in Hyderabad and put into circulation; and the *Egypt* affair had been regarded as closed – until 1932.

By international law the salvors are entitled to fees based on the value of the recovered cargo; the fees being payable by the owners of the cargo – in this case the underwriters who had paid up the insurance claim. The salvage company was of course primarily interested in recovering the gold from the ship's strongrooms, but they had wasted valuable time and effort in raising a cargo of notes that were technically valueless. Since salvage operations are very costly, they felt entitled to some compensation. The underwriters were naturally disinterested: it mattered not to them whether the salvors kept the recovered notes in lieu of compensation. But the Hyderabad government could not contemplate with equanimity the prospect of genuine, but 'uncurrent' paper money being held by anyone but themselves. They wished to have the notes destroyed. Negotiations were opened between the government and the salvage company and a long process of bargaining began. The salvors meanwhile undertook to keep the recovered notes in their safe custody pending a settlement.

On 17th August, 1932, the *Times of India* published an alarmist article to say that some of the salvaged notes were being smuggled into Hyderabad State and that their encashment was being refused by the banks and treasuries in Hyderabad. The Hyderabad press took up the scare and the government published a vigorous denial. A few months later, however, two notes, identified as part of the salvaged cargo, were presented at an Indian bank. These were traced to the lady friend of one of the officers who had attended the salvage operations: she said she had been given the notes as *souvenirs*. This, though irregular, seemed fairly innocuous; but shortly afterwards other salvaged notes were found in circulation. The importation of the notes had been prohibited by the Government of India, who were supporting the State government in this affair; but it is of course not easy to enforce such an embargo. During the next few years, while negotiations dragged on, more and more illicit notes were discovered in the State and even in Paris. Once or twice there was something verging on panic in the local bazaars of the State, lest the halli sicca paper currency should not be honoured by the government. The detection of unsigned notes of high denomination is fairly easy, as these are carefully examined whenever they change hands; but who troubles to look for the signature on a five- or ten-rupee note? If a dozen or so unsigned notes of low denomination are recovered, the probability is that hundreds or thousands are in circulation. It was clearly evident that the salvage company were failing to honour their undertaking to release none of the salvaged notes until after a settlement had been reached.

Litigation in the Italian courts eventually produced a judgment in favour of Hyderabad, with a ruling that fixed the indemnity to the salvors at 60,000 lire. But the salvors still refused to surrender the notes and lodged an appeal in the Italian courts. This was later quashed; but meanwhile a new complication, smacking of the novels of Edgar Wallace, had arisen – and this was during my régime as Mintmaster. A solicitor in Austria wrote to me to say that some of the recovered notes had come into his possession, and he claimed to have knowledge of an unscrupulous gang of international crooks who had acquired the bulk of the salvaged cargo and intended to flood the Hyderabad market with them after overprinting the forged signature of the Finance Minister. I reported the matter to the Finance Department and to the London solicitors of the

State government, and meanwhile I challenged the Austrian solicitor to quote the serial numbers of the notes in his possession. This he failed to do; and from that moment he discreetly faded out of the affair.

Ultimately in 1939, seventeen years after the notes had been printed and after seven years of protracted negotiations and litigation, the salvage company surrendered about 128,000 notes, claiming that the remaining 37,000 pieces were still at the bottom of the sea. The Nizam's government paid a pro rata indemnity of 46,727 lire and remained haunted by anxiety concerning the true whereabouts of the missing 37,000 notes. The surrendered notes were burned before witnesses of both parties. For several years after that, unsigned notes were occasionally discovered in the Hyderabad banks, and no one can yet say how many had been illegally released. The question has now of course become one of academic interest only, except to collectors, as halli sicca is no longer current.

Anxiety over the *Egypt* affair and the shadow of approaching war led the State government to end their contract with Waterlows. It was thought safer to have the notes printed in future in India, and the business was transferred to the Government of India Security Press at Nasik. Later during the War the pressure of need for currency became so acute that small denomination notes were printed in the State itself.

Another sovereign privilege of the Nizams was the right to print their own stamps – not only for postage but also for raising revenue in other ways. Close by the Mint was the Stamps Security Press where large quantities of postage, revenue and judicial stamps, cheque forms, stamped postcards and envelopes, etc. were printed. The stamps were of unsurpassed quality, being printed by the costly intaglio process with the design raised above the surface of the paper by using line-engraved blocks. The Stamps Press supplied the needs not only of the Nizam's government but also of the British Administered

Territories within the State and for the paigahs and jagirs that were entitled to have their own stamps.

Philatelists caused me a certain amount of nuisance; and the morals of some of them (as with certain horse-dealers) were distinctly elastic where their hobby was concerned. I was approached by more than one stamp collector, men of impeccable character in other spheres, in attempts to persuade me to let through the odd sheet or two of 'imperforates' or other freak productions that could acquire mysteriously inflated values in the philatelic world. One collector told me had a very rare pair of Hyderabad stamps printed 'tête-bêche', that is to say with one stamp upside down relative to its fellow. I assured him that our method of printing was such as to preclude all possibility of any such freak being produced. When he showed me his specimen we discovered, under a powerful magnifying glass, that it was a skilled forgery: the two stamps had been placed with their perforations exactly matching, tip to tip, and lightly glued.

In accordance with Muslim custom neither stamps nor coins bore a likeness of the ruler. Instead, they were embellished with pictures of public buildings or with Persian inscriptions that bore witness to the Moghul origin of the Principality. A device made much use of was the toghra, or royal monogram in decorative Persian caligraphy. The avoidance of portraiture was partly a matter of religious belief and partly due to a curious conception of lèse majesté: for it was argued that discarded letters would be liable to suffer the indignities of the waste-paper basket or worse, and it would never do for the royal portrait to be treated with contumely. This attitude had led to a strange incident shortly after I had first arrived in the State on the occasion of Lord and Lady Willingdon's state visit. As part of the process of beautifying the city for the official processions, a vast new cast iron lamppost of saracenic design had been made in the State Workshop and erected at an important road junction in the city. Gamlen had been immensely proud of this creation.

The design incorporated, in the middle of each side of a square base, a bas relief replica of the dastar-i-mubarak, or royal crown of Hyderabad. The day before the Viceroy's arrival a local Urdu newspaper printed an indignant article pointing out that the august symbol of royal dignity, being placed only a few inches above the ground, would become the hydraulic target of every passing dog. As a result of an urgent command from the palace a party of blacksmiths was sent post-haste to work all night chipping off the threatened emblem with hammer and chisel and replacing it with an innocuous set of rosettes, hastily cast in the foundry and less sensitive to canine caprice.

The art of counterfeit was a trade by no means neglected in Hyderabad. Fairly large quantities of forged coins and notes were discovered by our tellers, and others were sent from time to time to the Mint from the city and district treasuries and banks. Some efforts were crude: others highly skilful. A forged ten-rupee note, with all the whorls and squiggles faithfully copied by hand in ink particularly impressed me. Although it must have taken the forger days of meticulous care it could have been detected by anyone of normal vision in daylight; but when passed at night to a railway booking clerk by the dim light of a paraffin lamp at a wayside station, it had escaped attention. The forger had worked very hard for such a modest reward. Coins were often cast in lead – a cheap metal in those days – using a genuine rupee as a pattern; but here again, the reward seemed small in relation to the effort. I effectively stopped this form of roguery by introducing a countersunk 'security edge' to the coins, which increased a hundredfold the difficulties of casting reproductions. This system I copied from the British Indian Mints.

For the benefit of posterity I set up a showcase of skilful counterfeits, both coin and paper. I often wonder what has now become of it.

Money making was not the only business of the Mint.

Weights and measures had to be tested and certified; much engraving had to be done in the making of seals, dies, medals and badges. Gold and silver plating was another activity.

The birth of our daughter introduced a novel feature into the routine of the Bullion Department. Once a week a small procession, composed of Guen, Nanny holding the baby, our three-year-old son, the Bullion Superintendent and his Assistant made its way from our house to the Mint Treasury, where the baby was solemnly placed in the scales normally reserved for the weighing of gold. The weight was measured in tolas (one tola being 172½ grains) and recorded on a chit that was then brought to me. After some complicated arithmetic I translated this vital statistic into pounds avoirdupois and reported back to Guen.

When I first took charge of the Mint and Stamps Department I, like Gamlen in 1908, knew absolutely nothing whatsoever about minting and printing. My main preoccupation for the first few months was to conceal from my subordinates my abysmal ignorance. On the theory that the best way of learning a subject is to write about it, I set about writing two massive tomes known as the Hyderabad Mint Manual and the Hyderabad Stamps Manual. These described the functions, technical processes and security systems of both departments, recorded the relevant government enactments relating to currency, laid down the duties of each staff member and included historical notes. By the time I had finished these works I knew more or less everything that was necessary, and had devised many improvements, particularly in the security system. These books were printed and bound in the Stamps Department press, and only twenty-five copies of each were issued. They were sent to ministers, officers of the Mint and Stamps Department and the Library of the Osmania University. In 1984 a copy of each exchanged hands at Christie's at £1250 for the pair.

During my régime I proposed two major reforms: one was adopted, the other not. The adopted reform was the establishment of our own Assay Department, in the charge of a qualified metallurgical chemist. This enabled us to avoid the very heavy fees that we had had to pay in past years to His Majesty's Mint in Bombay, to whom all our 'musters' and 'pyxes' had been sent for assay. The unadopted proposal was a detailed plan for decimalising the currency. This covered the gradual withdrawal from circulation of certain denominations of coin and the issue of new ones without affecting the rupee piece, the gold coins or the paper currency. I secured the enthusiastic support of Sir Akbar Hydari by suggesting to him that the State could lead British India in a worthwhile reform; but the diehards in the government were too much even for him: the scheme was stillborn. Nevertheless, India eventually *did* 'go decimal'. In view of the *furore* when Britain decimalised her coinage in 1970, the failure of my plan perhaps saved me from much unpopularity.

A mint is really nothing more than a specialised factory, executing orders issued by the Finance Ministry. Nevertheless, it has a popular appeal that other factories lack. The Royal Mint, when close to the Tower of London, drew millions of visitors and has a glamour of its own, enhanced by the fact that England's greatest man of science was once Mintmaster to His Majesty King Charles II. Certainly my tenure of office in the Hyderabad Mintmastership brought me more prestige than my far more onerous (at least in the early years) duties in the Electricity Department. The Hyderabad Mint has, in its small way, been closely bound up with the romantic history of the Deccan and has served its princely masters well.

XII

Feastings and Farces

Social junketings of all kinds were dear to the heart of the Hyderabadi: scarcely a week would pass without a banquet or garden party. Some of these functions could be very impressive, with their glittering façade of exotic titles, uniforms, colourful saris and jewels. The austerity of the Ruler was in marked contrast with the lavish munificence of some of his nobles and other wealthy subjects. Sherbet and sandwiches at the princely palace, but champagne and caviare in the mansions of his ministers. Torchlit avenues lined with the turbaned lancers of a private army, formal be-fountained Moghul gardens, painted pillared pavilions, decayed palaces of icing-sugar baroque architecture: these would often form the fabulous settings of fabulous feasts. Sword-swallowers, nauch girls, fire-eaters, conjurors and firework displays would sometimes follow as after-dinner entertainment.

A gathering of two or three hundred guests would be quite usual at a state banquet or at a private dinner given by a nobleman or high officer of state. These dinners followed a regular pattern. After a formal reception by the host at the end of a red carpet lined with potted cannas and crotons, the guests would be served with cocktails (or tomato juice if the host should be one of the rare abstainers) while the band played selections from 'The Gondoliers' or 'The Arcadians'. A fanfare would perhaps then signify the arrival of the Prime Minister, or 'God bless the Nizam' would herald the approach of HEH or of one of

136

the Princes of the Blood. Dinner would later be announced somewhat incongruously by the playing of 'The Roast Beef of Old England' as a harbinger of the muttons and chicken curries to follow. Owing to a rigid 'warrant of precedence' the habitué was apt to find himself sitting next, or close, to the same people at table at nearly every dinner, which tended to make conversation rather heavy going. Seating was never arranged so that people of common interests might sit next to one another: seniority was the only criterion. I well remember when the British Association under the leadership of Sir James Jeans, the astronomer, paid a formal visit to Hyderabad just before the War and a banquet was given in their honour. I found myself sitting opposite the famous astronomer-physicist-philosopher, Sir Arthur Eddington. Next to him was a very senior member of the Indian Civil Service, to whom science meant not a thing. Likewise, Indian affairs meant little to Sir Arthur; so I could see that conversation between the two men did not exactly flow with ease. At one stage I heard Sir Arthur mention the name of Einstein, to which the eminent member of the ICS said that he could not appreciate 'all this modern sculpture'. The incident brought to my mind a libellous limerick I had then but recently heard:

> I don't like the family Stein.
> There's Gertrude, there's Ep and there's Ein.
> Gert's writings are punk,
> Ep's statues are junk,
> And nobody understands Ein.

The menus of Hyderabad banquets were often arduous. The conventional sequence of European dishes would be extended by the insertion of a formidable curry, though relieved at half-time with a sorbet and Russian cigarette to provide the persevering with a second wind. Wines would usually be plentiful (but not when the host was Sir Akbar Hydari, who was a rabid teetotaller) and punch à la romaine would often add an interesting touch to the alcoholic accompaniment to these feasts. For the abstemious there was always water of doubtful provenance issuing from Evian bottles – so much more suitable than Vichy, as Evian water is practically tasteless.

The government was capable of official entertaining in the grand style, though in rather less exotic fashion than some of the more eccentric and ostentatious noblemen. There was even a special Amerah Department that acted as the official catering organisation for the government and was responsible for state banquets and the arrangements for house-keeping at the official guest-houses.

When a Viceroy or visiting Royalty was present we would dine off gold plate, for the lustre of which I, as Mintmaster, was responsible. This plate was normally packed away in a strong room in one of the royal palaces, and only saw the light of day once every few years when a guest of sufficient eminence was to be entertained. When the time for refurbishing arrived, the plate being too precious to be sent to the Mint, the Mint (like Muhammed and the mountain) had to come to the plate. A group of artisans, supervised by the Bullion Superintendent and provided with electro-plating and buffing equipment, would be despatched to the palace to impart new sparkle to these tarnished treasures behind locked doors and under the watchful eyes of picked police and palace officials.

Owing to the prevalence of purdah the men would greatly outnumber the women at all large social gatherings. The Indian men would wear the dastar – the traditional head-dress of Hyderabad – and the sherwani, a long tunic, usually of white or dark blue according to the season, but sometimes of flowery brocade. If royalty or the Prime Minister were present they would also wear the baghloos, or gilded belt. The Nizam himself would affect a shabby edition of the same uniform except that his dastar would be of the royal colour, yellow, and surmounted by a turrah – a sort of gilded gemsebart or shaving brush that lent the whole head-dress, when seen from the front, an appearance suggestive of a pineapple. This be-turrah'd dastar of yellow hue, was the dastar-i-mubarak – the auspicious turban, or 'crown' – to be worn only by the Nizam, his brother or by his two official sons. European men usually wore full evening dress or, on suitable occasions and if entitled to them, service uniforms.

The most colourful element would be provided by the saris of the relatively few Indian womenfolk. Those of the Hindus were usually of darkish colours with broad borders: those of the Muslims, light of colour and diaphanous of texture: those of the Parsees, rich and tinselly. A great deal of rather flamboyant but decorative jewellery would be displayed.

Although the garden party is a well established Indian institution it has some of the overtones of the English equivalent – the garden fête at the squire's hall: the marquee, the potted evergreens, the red carpet, the brass band, sofas for the eminent, hard chairs for the lesser fry, curled up sandwiches, sticky cakes, flies, tea or tepid 'iced' coffee. The garden party in Hyderabad was a more democratic and less lustrous form of entertainment than the banquet. The qualifications for receiving an invitation were less stringent and therefore extended downwards into less rarified social levels. Indian weddings, after the official marriage ceremony, often involved a garden party for the guests. The degree of sophistication of these parties varied with that of the 'westernisation' of the hosts. It was not unknown to arrive at what one had expected to be a tea-party and find that it was more in the nature of a supper-party, in which case one could find oneself squatting on the ground and eating curry with one's fingers off banana leaves that served as plates. Eating in this manner was subject to a code of 'table' manners: only three fingers should be used for picking up slushy curries – a most uncomfortable art. Slices of water melon covered in flies offered a not very enticing dessert; so that after admiring the display of fairy lights that decorated the garden and were switched on at sundown, the European guests would make tracks for home and the enterovioform tablets as rapidly as possible.

Indian sweetmeats were often served wrapped in silver, or even gold, foil; and one was expected to eat the entire parcel, foil and all. The noble metals were believed to have a beneficial effect on the digestive organs. Certainly I never was any the worse from this practice.

But despite the glister all was not gold beneath the surface at the more exclusive junketings in Hyderabad. A veneer of social graces sometimes failed to conceal the under-currents of petty jealousies in matters of precedence, the self-importance of the pompous, the superficiality and hollowness of the whole social fabric. As soon as a minister or senior government official retired from service, he virtually disappeared altogether from the social scene unless he were a high-ranking nobleman in his own right. The delight of the newcomer in all the colour of the many social functions was, after a while, apt to give way to boredom, though this boredom was sometimes relieved by amusing bathos. The sight of a minor rajah washing his dentures in his finger bowl may have detracted from the dignity, but enhanced the enjoyment, of an otherwise dull evening. On one occasion a flying fox, flitting over the heads of the dining guests in a baradari, or open-sided pavilion, selected me as his target with singular spitefulness and unerring precision: in the manner of the Nazi dive-bombing technique he relieved himself all over my white shirt front. By comparison with the cow, any minor shortcomings in the fire power of the flying fox is amply offset by his superior marksmanship.

After one banquet in a huge marquee by the side of the Osmansagar Lake I happened to stroll behind the scenes, where I saw the son of a well known nawab filling a suitcase with bottles of whisky that had been provided for the guests but which, thanks to over-generous catering, were still unconsumed.

A state visit to the Nizam by HH The Maharajah of Bikaner, a fine looking man with a splendid voice, was celebrated by a suitable banquet complete with gold plate. Early in the meal a host of servants, each bearing a champagne bottle, approached the tables: they were spread out in a proportion of about one servant to every four or five guests. At a signal from the major domo all the corks were simultaneously drawn, the intention being to produce a sort of feu de joie. Now in his younger days HEH had invested not only in bullion and jewels but also in a few thousand bottles of 1911 champagne, in the belief that they would appreciate in value. After the passage of some thirty years in dubious storage conditions this champagne had become no better than it should have been; so the mass cork-drawing ceremony occurred in dead silence. A dark brown liquid with black floccules not unlike tea-leaves was poured into the glasses of the guests. That, alas! was all we were offered to drink on that occasion.

At times a dignified gathering would degenerate into sheer farce. I well remember one dinner party at the Residency at which a self-important guest arrived very late. Being rather punctilious in such matters the Resident asked him if he had mistaken the time shown on the invitation card. The Self-Important One retorted that a man in his position should not be expected to arrive until at least fifteen minutes after lesser mortals. This nettled the Resident into making a sharp rejoinder which reduced the wife of the Self-Important One to tears. Although one other guest was still missing the Resident was in no frame of mind to wait any longer, so the party adjourned to the dining room. The missing guest was a lady school teacher of rather shy disposition. When eventually she arrived she tried to creep unobtrusively into her place at the dining table. Unfortunately she skidded on a tiger skin rug and crashed heavily to the floor, at the same time catching her foot in the electric flex and plunging the room into darkness. The shocked silence was relieved only by the stifled sobs of the wife of the rebuked Self-Important One.

Then again, when Lord Tennyson's cricket team visited Hyderabad, one of the paigah nobles, himself a keen cricketer, gave a large banquet in his private palace. This palace was heavily furnished in the mid-Victorian style, with the crystal legs of the billiard table encased in 'decent' clothing and with an abundance of horsehair upholstered chairs. The banqueting hall had not been used for several years, so the major domo of the household had decided that the somewhat shabby chair seats could do with a coat of varnish. The banquet went splendidly until the time came for the loyal toasts to the King-Emperor and to the Nizam. As everyone rose to his or her feet there was a sickening but eloquent sound. Some of the ladies had altogether parted company from a vital area of their dresses. There was a great rending of hearts and garments.

On two dreadful occasions disaster overtook hospitality in my own house. The first was when our guests included Sir Akbar and Lady Hydari shortly after he had become Prime Minister. Despite the Hydaris' orthodox Muslim views on alcohol we did not feel obliged to inflict his lofty principles upon our other guests, so a table of alcoholic drinks had therefore been set out unobtrusively in a corner of the drawing room. Our other guests included a certain nawab who was a government minister at that time and his begam; also several British military officers and their wives. One of these officers was a major, new to the ways of Indian States. When the Hydaris arrived, two Mint chaprassis, resplendent in uniforms of cloth of gold, stepped forward to open the car door and to make suitable obeisance. From this, the major gathered that the new arrivals were people of importance though he had no notion as to who they were. When he was introduced, he therefore made what he mistakenly believed to be a court bow; but instead of flexing only his neck he bowed from the hips, pushing his posterior backwards and sending the array of alcoholic drinks flying in all directions. To this day I can see the bottle of curacao gurgling its sticky contents over one of our best Bokhara rugs. The disapproving attention of the Hydaris was at once focussed upon the offending bottles whose presence we had hoped to keep discreetly inconspicuous.

At that time we owned a high spirited spaniel puppy and had

given strict instructions that he was to be kept tied up in the background during the dinner party. The upsetting of the drinks had created a disturbance, diverting the attention of the servants, including the dog boy, to the clearing up of the mess. Infected by the general excitement and profiting by the preoccupation of his warden, the puppy made good his escape and rushed, yelping with exuberance, into the assembly of guests — his paws skidding over the polished marble floor as he tried to change direction. With a whoop of glee he took a flying leap into the lap of the begam, a lady who regarded a dog as a contaminant. She uttered a piercing scream.

These alarums and excursions were hardly conducive to a successful evening. The unhappy major, quite unnerved by the situation he had created, found it quite impossible to do anything right during the rest of the evening. He upset the salt, dropped a fork, and betrayed his utter demoralisation in various ways. Towards the end of the meal came the usual ceremony of Passing Round the Port. This involved a sort of 'knight's move' to bypass Sir Akbar who could not be expected to handle the container of a corrupt liquid. By an oversight I had neglected to remove the stopper from the decanter before passing it round. When the port reached the major he picked it up, not by the neck but by the stopper. Instead of coming away, the stopper unfortunately held, but only until the decanter was a few inches above the table. Stopper and decanter then parted company in mid-air, the one flying upwards with the major's hand tensed to carry a weight no longer there, the other to smash a dessert plate and to hurl its sinful contents into the beautifully be-saried lap of Lady Hydari. For the second time in a single evening one of our lady guests screamed. The party was not an unqualified success.

Our other disastrous evening was on 3rd September, 1939. About ten days earlier we had issued dinner invitations to a number of people for that evening. Although by then it had become abundantly clear that Hitler was up to no good we could not have foreseen that we had chosen the fatal day. Our guests included a German doctor, his wife and niece, the Superintendent of the Secunderabad Police and half a dozen others. The Germans had been well liked and were known to our other guests. I had been privately informed that if war broke out all enemy alien men were to be interned but the women were to remain free. On 1st September Hitler struck at Poland and it became obvious that Britain would become involved within a matter of hours. At about six o'clock in the evening of September 3rd we heard over the wireless that the die had been cast. Fifteen minutes later the Police Superintendent sent a message that he regretted he would not be able to attend our party. This did not surprise me, as I knew he would be rounding up the small pathetic colony of 'enemy aliens', mostly harmless refugees, in his territory. What did surprise me was that no other cancellations came, not even from our German guests who, we felt, might have felt embarrassed by the turn of events.

And so the party took place, under a cloud of gloom. The Germans seemed in no way awkward and we were determined to show that our detestation of the Nazi régime would not influence our personal feelings towards individual German friends. We had not bargained, however, for the jingoism of a certain colonel, who was one of our guests. This colonel, until a few hours earlier, had protested friendship for the German doctor: but as soon as he arrived at our house it became clear from his manner that he thought we should have forbidden our house to enemy aliens. The atmosphere was very tense, and although everyone else strove gallantly to restrict the conversation to safe topics, the colonel was full of bombast. He declared that the Allies would destroy the German cities and wipe the Fatherland from the face of Europe. News had just come through that the German liner *Bremen* was in the Atlantic, homeward bound from the States. 'I hope we sink her,' said the colonel.

'Would it not be better,' replied the doctor mildly, 'to capture her as a prize?' (One up to the enemy alien, thought we.)

Towards the end of dinner a servant brought me a visiting

card bearing the name of an Indian police officer with a message that he wished to see me urgently. I made my excuses and went out to speak to him.

'I have come to arrest the doctor,' said the police officer.

'If I undertake to hand him over to you in two hours,' I replied, 'will you spare us from an embarrassing scene?'

Alas! No. The police officer explained that he had to have all male Germans in Hyderabad safely under lock and key without delay. The Black Maria was standing there at my porch with armed constables in attendance. In vain did I plead with him.

Returning to the dining room I asked the doctor to come out with me. 'I am sorry, Doctor,' I said as soon as we were alone, 'but a police officer has called to ask you to accompany him at once to Headquarters.' The doctor clicked his heels. 'I am ready,' said he, and marched briskly out of the house. 'One minute!' I called out, 'Do you not first wish to speak to your wife?' He had not thought of that, but agreed on second thoughts that he should see her before leaving.

Back into the dining room went I, where I sensed mounting tension in the air. I told the doctor's wife that her husband would like to have a word with her outside. After she had left the room, I told her frankly what had happened. Her reaction was typically feminine. 'It is all the fault of Mrs K,' she said and burst into tears. (Mrs K was a social enemy of hers who could scarcely be held directly responsible either for the mad actions of the German Chancellor or for the protective measures of the British or Indian State Police.) Having no handkerchief to staunch her tears, she asked me to fetch her bag which she had left in the dining room. Back I went, to find that the pitch of conversation had risen by about an octave. Returning with the bag, I witnessed an emotional farewell between husband and wife. The doctor was then taken away in the Black Maria and the wife declared she would return home at once.

'What about your niece?' I asked. Yes, she would take her niece with her. Yet again I had to return to the highly charged atmosphere of the dining room and told the niece that her aunt wished to speak to her. The two women departed weeping after I had done my futile best to comfort them.

For the fifth time I rejoined my guests and told them the whole story. The colonel was clearly highly delighted. We did not invite him to our house again.

One of the most hospitable of Hyderabad's nobility was Nawab Salar Jung (SJ), whose foibles have already been described in this book. His favourite form of entertaining was the lunch party, at which his guests would be received on arrival at his palace by his court chamberlain wielding a silvered ceremonial rod. The prudent guest was well advised to fast for twenty-four hours beforehand. Although it was hard to contend with anything but the lightest of lunches in such a hot climate, at SJ's it was expected of one to do justice to a seven-course meal including one of his famous curries, which almost rivalled a Javanese rijstafel in sheer bulk. Guen and I must have lunched with the nawab some dozens of times and we soon learned from experience to nibble at the first few courses so as to be able to cope with the curry. Several dishes of different grades of rice would form the basis of this course, and an endless sequence of interesting and highly spiced mixtures would be offered until one's plate could scarcely, with decency, hold more. Lest this elaborate synthesis should still lack flavour, an assortment of chutnies, papadams and chapattis, cocoa-nut, chopped tomatoes, and a host of unidentifiable objects would be pressed upon one.

These lunch parties were usually given for twenty or thirty guests in a long and rather dingy hall where the appetite was not even neglected in the mural decorations which had for their motif still life panels of dead game and fruit. We ate and drank from the choicest china and glass, all emblazoned with the nawab's cypher. Alcoholic refreshment was neglected no more than food.

At one of SJ's lunches Guen sat next to a well known prince from another state. His Highness, overcome by his host's hospitality, became both amorous and sleepy at the same time. He kept placing his head on her shoulder, uttering protestations of love alternating with belches and snores. All that Guen could think of saying was 'Not now, Your Highness, not now'! From where I was sitting I could not see what was happening; but when she told me afterwards of her ordeal I pointed out that her choice of words had not been too wise, for they held a hint of promise that I hoped was not intended! Matters had not been made easier for Guen by the presence of the Resident's wife who was sitting directly opposite her and directing eloquent glances at her that said 'Don't you dare to let the side down!'

SJ's lunches, which usually lasted for an hour and a half, were invariably followed by a grand tour of his 'treasures'. Almost every visitor of importance who came to the State was invited to lunch by SJ. Barbara Hutton, the Woolworth heiress, was there in the late 1930s with her husband of that era, Count von Rewentlow. She was laden with jewellery seeking, no doubt, to impress her host whose wealth was reputed to rival her own. After lunch SJ whispered to me: 'She's wearing 34 lakhs worth of jewellery.' I asked him how he could know so precisely. 'You see that man over there,' came the reply. 'He's my jeweller and he has valued her for me!' I had never before come across such an on-the-spot-while-you-wait appraisal of a guest. SJ seemed to think it quite normal. Afterwards he brought out his most prized pieces of jade and such special treasures as the jewelled dagger of the Emperor Auranzeb. *He* seemed to be worried lest his American guest were insufficiently impressed: *she* seemed unhappy because she could not bid for what she saw. An anxious time was had by both. Meanwhile I too was having an uneasy time. The Count, on being introduced to me, showed interest on learning that I was the Mintmaster. He told me he was a numismatist, but that he collected *gold* coins only. Would it be possible for him to acquire a set of Hyderabad gold coins? I promised to send him the coins that very afternoon to the guesthouse. He thanked me, and then as an afterthought asked if I would allow him to pay for them. After missing a heartbeat I

147

said 'Well, if you really insist; by all means.' Had the Count accepted the coins as a gift, I personally would have had to foot a very substantial bill.

The last banquet we attended in the State was given, late in the War, in honour of Lord Wavell, the last but one of the Viceroys. Lord Wavell, very correctly, had let it be known that he wanted no lavish entertaining in wartime. This was difficult to reconcile with the State's reputation for ostentation at the times of viceregal visits. As a compromise we were treated to an Austerity Banquet. The uniforms, the gold plate, the chandeliers, the liveried servants were all there, but the meal consisted of watery soup and boiled mutton only. The elaborate epergnes, instead of groaning beneath a cornucopia of exotic fruits as on previous viceregal occasions, each held a handful of boiled sweets made in Madras and wrapped in paper. After the meal a very few of the two or three hundred guests were called up to meet the Viceroy or Vicereine. After four or five women had been presented to Lord Wavell, a voice boomed out 'Mrs Armstead'. Guen, surprised out of her wits, was led up to The Presence, curtsied – thereby laddering one of her last surviving pairs of stockings – and was invited to be seated. Lord Wavell, who was a keen lover of poetry, had read a book of poems that Guen had published: he wanted to meet her. The next day, at some 'war-work' gathering of the local womenfolk, Guen overheard several catty remarks such as 'I can't think why *she* was presented when So-and-So wasn't'. Guen never let on.

XIII

Fakirs and fire-walkers

To see is to believe; or so we are told. Certainly until I had seen with my own eyes I had discounted the many tales I had heard of fakirs and sadhus who make a habit of doing revolting things to themselves for no apparent reason unless it be for their spiritual enlightenment. Sword-swallowers, fire-eaters and eccentrics who seemingly thrive on a diet of razor blades, nitric acid and broken glass can sometimes be seen at a British circus; but stranger sights are to be seen in Asia and Africa.

Nevertheless, my first sight of a sadhu sitting on a bed of nails was somewhat disappointing. The 'nails' were not merely blunt but well rounded, and the holy man had prudently inserted a moth-eaten pillow between his backside and his instrument of torture. He must have been very uncomfortable, but certainly not in agony. For a handsome wager I would have changed places with him for an hour. I was assured that the sadhu was, for all his filthy appearance, a highly educated man and a remarkable linguist, though he had not spoken for several years. It was impressive to see a man being silent in seven languages.

It was a greater shock when, some years later and quite by chance, I saw an almost naked man walking along a street in Secunderabad with porcupine quills piercing his eyeballs. This was not my idea of fun: anything to do with eyeballs turns my stomach. I could never endure 'King Lear' on that account. An eye is a most useful, and sometimes highly decorative, organ so long as it is not treated as a 'vile jelly'.

149

An Indian host would sometimes entertain his guests after dinner with a conjuring performance. The enjoyment was often marred by some particularly repugnant 'turn'. I well remember a dinner party given by the Kotwal, or Chief of the Hyderabad City Police. A conjuror, after producing a five-foot snake apparently from nowhere, quite deliberately bit off, chewed and swallowed the wretched creature's head, leaving the remaining 4ft-8in to writhe convulsively on the floor. Once again – not my idea of fun. Most of the European guests turned green and left the party as hastily as politeness would permit.

This same Kotwal told me that his wife had once had a dream in which a 'monster' had appeared and claimed the life of her son. The monster said he would make his claim three times. Her husband tried to reassure her that it meant nothing. A few weeks later his wife said she had had the same dream, in which the second claim was made. When, after a third dream of this nature, she told her husband that she had received the last warning the poor woman was nearly demented and the husband also became very worried. They called the doctor, who could find nothing whatsoever wrong with the boy's health. The next day he was dead. The Kotwal was a good friend of mine and I think I knew him well. He did not strike me as a man given to inventing tall stories; and I had the feeling that he was speaking the truth.

Burial alive, so long as I am not the victim, does not affect me as do maltreated eyeballs and snakes. I have seen a young man lie down in an open grave with a handkerchief placed over his face and an electric bell-push in his hand. Several stalwart coolies then shovelled earth on top of him until the grave was filled. Many anxious minutes (I think it was about twelve to fifteen) passed before the ringing of the bell signified that our young friend had wearied of subterranean life. The coolies then reversed their former labours and exhumed him as quickly as possible. From his upturned eyeballs he appeared to be in a trance; but after a few violent gasps he recovered fully. The handkerchief was but an innocent concession to his natural objection to having earth in his eyes, mouth and nose. I witnessed this from only a few feet away, and would swear that no air could have reached him while he had been buried.

An eccentric Indian whom I knew slightly said that a woman in Hyderabad could practise levitation. I said I would like to see a demonstration; so he brought the woman to our house. As she must have weighed over two hundred pounds I eagerly looked forward to seeing such a massive weight suspended in space, particularly as I had been brought up to have implicit faith in Newton's Laws. We gave her tea and food, and she ate with a hearty appetite. To my great disappointment she then announced that she was in no mood for levitation that day, so I was cheated of a remarkable sight. The whole exercise seemed to have been for the purpose of winning a free meal.

When offered the chance of seeing a troupe of fakirs perform its horrid repertoire I was torn between squeamishness and curiosity. Curiosity won; and I found myself sitting in a garden crowded with unwashed humanity with a very small sprinkling of British officers from Secunderabad. A small space had been cleared, in which sat five or six ferocious looking men with filthy matted hair. They wore practically no clothing. After a long wait, some drums started to beat and one of the fakirs jumped to his feet jangling a metal ring on which hung a number of burnished steel implements that were something midway between large kitchen skewers and marline spikes. Selecting one of these spikes he suddenly plunged it into his eye, deftly whipping it out from its socket so that it resembled some macabre olive on an out-sized cocktail stick. A young army subaltern sitting near me promptly fainted: he must have shared my feelings about eyeballs. I nearly joined him in oblivion but somehow managed to retain consciousness. Meanwhile our performer had pushed another skewer through his abdomen and had been joined by his confrères who vied with one another in the exercise of their skills in self-inflicted butchery, piercing their thighs, arms and stomachs: they even appeared to drive spikes into their skulls, though to this I could not swear, as the lushness of growth of their filthy locks made it difficult to be quite sure. One of them cut off the tip of his tongue and, after proudly displaying the ghastly morsel of meat to the crowd, replaced it. It seemed to weld itself onto the parent flesh without difficulty. The star turn of the evening was given by one of the troupe who, after placing the tip of a skewer by the side of his Adam's Apple, pressed it slowly through his neck. Viewing this from one side I was horrified to see the back of his neck distend until it was suddenly punctured by the point of the skewer which had passed right through. We were invited to inspect this at close quarters to assure ourselves there was no deception, and I actually prodded the skin and the skewer to convince myself I was not dreaming. After withdrawal, the spike was slightly bent from the force that had been exerted upon it.

The most curious feature of this loathesome masochistic orgy was the absence of blood. Apart from a small red bead which did appear on the neck of the star performer, the whole show was entirely anaemic. Nothing but a dent remained after the skewers had been pulled out. Those eyes that had not been carelessly left lying about cheeks had rolled upwards to give the impression of a state of trance. There was nothing to show that any pain was suffered.

One of my friends in the audience was a major in the RAMC. He affected to be unimpressed and explained it all away by saying that is was only a question of skilfully avoiding the capillary blood vessels. I was unimpressed by his unimpressibility.

Nothing would have induced me to witness this repulsive spectacle willingly a second time, but a year or two later I was a guest at one of SJ's lunch parties. After treating us to the usual gargantuan meal he laid on the same troupe of fakirs by way of light postprandial entertainment. It was not a very good digestive, but an excellent emetic. This time it was a senior British police officer, who had often faced death unflinchingly, who fainted. The ladies of the party, however, showed no signs of distress, thereby confirming my belief that the female of the

A group of blank-cutting presses at the Mint. After cutting the blanks were annealed and then sent to the coining presses, each of which struck about 100 coins a minute.

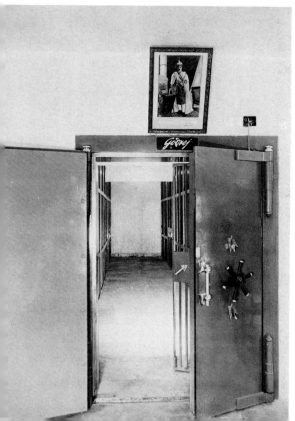

Entrance to a group of all-steel strongrooms at the Mint. It required eighteen keys to gain access to the bullion!

Inside one of the Mint strongrooms. Each bag contained 2000 rupees. Gold was kept in the safes. Silver bars can be seen in the strongroom beyond.

A single day's output at the Mint – 700,000 rupees! These were then packed in bags of 2000 after counting by weighment.

species is tougher, as well as deadlier, than the male.

I was not always content to be a mere spectator at such strange goings-on. It was in 1928 that I first walked through fire. With three other young men I found myself in the thick of a vast multitude in the Tardeo district of Bombay. In the middle of an open space was a trench some four or five feet wide and perhaps twenty-five feet in length. The trench had been filled with faggots that had been kindled and burnt down to a fairly even bed of red-hot embers. A wizened old man sat nearby in deep meditation, whilst a ceaseless rythmical beating of drums and gongs formed an obligato to the weird scene. Suddenly the drum beat changed, the old man raised his voice in exhortation and the crowd surged through the fiery trench - *bare-footed*. Even women in the most diaphanous and inflammable of saris passed through the burning fiery furnace unscathed. Approaching the trench it was necessary to shield one's face against the intense radiant heat from the embers. My compatriots and I decided to risk it but, feeling we were probably more earthbound than our Indian brethren who had clearly worked themselves into a state of enthusiasm, we thought it prudent to graduate by stages. First we went through the fire in shoes, suffering no more than a stifling sensation from the fierce heat beneath us. Then we removed our shoes and went through in our socks. Finally we too went through barefoot. Admittedly we did not dawdle - in fact we almost sprinted - but to our great surprise we found ourselves intact, without burns or blisters. The embers were certainly hot to our feet - extremely hot - but the passage was not much more painful than walking on sunscorched tropical sands before taking a sea bathe. Suddenly the old man, who had meanwhile been uttering incantations in a high quavering voice, gave forth a long wail, and his musicians worked themselves up to a climax of sound. The crowd ran screaming from the fire. Evidently the protection afforded by the old man's incantations had ceased to be effective, so the people deemed it wise to escape while the going was good. The

153

show was over. My friends and I returned to our chummeries to boast of our strange experience.

Eight years later I was invited to a fire-walking party by the Director-General of Police in Hyderabad. Every year, during the month of Moharram, fire-walking was practised in a village that lay a short distance away from the city. The police were concerned with keeping order in an atmosphere highly charged with religious fervour. The ceremony was not due to take place until about an hour before dawn, so our host had laid on a full night's entertainment for us. First we dined at his house – about twelve of us – and then we went on to the cinema. After that we all drove to the police station in the village where the spectacle was to be seen. Everything had been very well organised: we were given seats on a first floor balcony commanding a clear view of the proceedings, and regaled with whisky and sandwiches. Below us was the multitude, milling round a huge blazing bonfire. The inevitable beating of drums and gongs was kept up monotonously, inducing after a while, with the help of the whisky, an overpowering somnolence. At dinner I had rashly confessed to having walked through fire on a previous occasion, thereby placing myself under a moral obligation to prove it by a repeat performance. As the night wore on I became sleepier and sleepier and wished only to be in my bed: but there was no escape. The moment eventually came when the bonfire embers were raked into the trench that had been dug beforehand, the 'musicians' worked up to a steady crescendo, a white clad figure started his incantations and the crowd swept through the fire. I had to rouse myself to follow suit. I remember noticing that a relatively darkish path had been trampled into the embers by the hundreds of feet that had preceded mine: on either side of this path the fire glowed more fiercely. As an old campaigner I chose the hotter, less frequented path and took the plunge, barefoot. A shock of excruciating pain threw me off balance and I nearly fell headlong into the fire. Fortunately I righted myself and made the far 'shore'. It was a point of honour to return through the fire to one's starting point, as I had noticed that all my fellow fools had made the double trip. Somehow I made the return journey and found myself nursing the soles of my feet which by then were rapidly swelling to the size of footballs, and removing some glowing pieces of charcoal that had thoughtlessly lodged themselves between my toes. How I ever managed to drive my car back to the Mint House I do not know: nevertheless I somehow did so. For several days I hobbled about in carpet slippers with the aid of a stick. Ultimately the balloon-like blisters were drained, and I peeled off the soles of my feet like two pieces of tough leather to reveal new pink skin beneath.

In Bombay, sceptical and apprehensive, I had passed through the fire unscathed. In Hyderabad, confident and calm, I came to grief. Perhaps the explanation lay in the accumulation of eight more years of sinful living between the two episodes; but I am inclined to believe it was simply because the second fire was a damned sight hotter than the first.

My advice to those who have the opportunity of fire-walking is 'DON'T'.

I have seen: I have felt: I believe in *some* of the strange things that can happen in India. But I also know that things can go badly wrong.

XIV

Thieves break through and steal

The concentration in one place of about 150 million rupees' worth of treasure was a standing temptation to the hundreds of workers in the Mint and Stamps Department and to professional burglars from outside: an elaborate system of security was necessary. Accurate counts and weighments were made at the end of each workshift, and if any shortage were detected no man was allowed to leave the premises until it had been accounted for. Substantial cash deposits or 'fidelity bonds' were taken from the heads of each sub-department and from the tellers. All strongrooms were provided with multiple lock control and the Mint had its own police force under the direct authority of the Mintmaster. Workers were searched on leaving the premises and surprise audits were taken from time to time. An electrified wire, known as the 'trap' and fixed close to the eaves of the building discouraged cat burglars, and an armed military guard protected the whole area during the nights and on holidays.

The vigilance of the tellers was checked by a very simple device. To keep them 'on their toes' one or two notes would be deliberately removed from occasional bundles of a hundred; so that if a teller failed to detect the shortage it suggested that he was lazily passing all bundles as correct without taking the trouble to count them properly.

When I first took charge of the Mint I expressed concern at the so-called strongrooms which were built only of bricks and mortar, though they were provided with steel doors and heavy double mortice locks. But the Finance Office had shrugged off my fears, arguing that the Mint as a whole was so well protected that the likelihood of any internal strongroom being forced was infinitesimal.

Various petty pilferings were attempted from time to time but were always detected. Some of the Mint workers exercised ingenuity in concealing coin about their persons, but the searchers were equal to their task. The Criminal Investigation Department occasionally planted a spy amongst the work people and more than once this led to detection and arrest. One man, suspected of removing gold, was subjected to X-ray tests which revealed that he had swallowed his booty. A salutary dose of castor oil formed a logical conclusion to that affair.

There was one nightmarish possibility that sometimes haunted me, and which could have effectively defeated every precaution devised for the safety of the treasure: this was the formation of an unholy alliance between the Bullion Superintendent, the Head Melter and the Superintendent of the Mint Police. A conspiracy between these three could have bled the Mint of a fortune between audit checks: and had the Chief Auditor joined the consortium there would have been virtually no limit to what might have been got away with. A judicious distribution of these key appointments between the Muslim, Hindu, Christian and Parsee communities offered the best chances of protection against such a hideous disaster which fortunately never materialised.

In 1937 the first and only serious burglary during my régime occurred. The thief, who was a teller in the Mint Treasury, showed remarkable ingenuity and foresight. A large stock of treasury notes was being counted over a period of two or three working days before being packed into wooden boxes for transfer to the government central treasury in the city. The boxes were provided with padlocks, and at the end of each working day they were locked up in one of the strongrooms.

Circumstances played into the thief's hands in that it so happened that repairs were being done to the roof at the time, and also the work of counting the notes was interrupted by a public holiday that lasted three consecutive days. Furthermore, in a fit of economic zeal, the military Chief of Staff had recently reduced the strength of the armed guard, despite my protestations; so that the premises were guarded only at night: during the daytime on holidays they were quite deserted.

On the last working day before the holiday the thief absented himself from duty on grounds of ill health. Doubtless with the connivance of an accomplice, he mingled with the contractors' men who were repairing the roof. The electric 'trap' had, of course, to be switched off while this work was in progress. No sooner was he on the roof than the thief concealed himself in a gutter and lay low until the field was clear for him. At the end of the day the roof contractor's men were withdrawn and checked by roll-call, the 'trap' was switched on again and the Mint was closed down for the holidays – with the thief on the roof *inside* the live 'trap'. When all was quiet, he had but to lift a few roof tiles and drop onto a pile of sacks he had thoughtfully left in a corner of the treasury floor to break his fall. Once inside the Mint he had three days in which to get down to business, suspending his activities only at night when the armed guard would be patrolling outside the building. Beneath the same pile of sacks our foresighted friend had also concealed a crowbar, and with this he set to work making a breach in the brick wall of the strongroom. To prize open the wooden boxes containing the notes was a simple matter, and by the end of the second day he had relieved the treasury of Rs60,000 in ten-rupee notes, wisely eschewing those of higher denomination despite their greater relative portability. The pile of sacks served also as a comfortable bed for him during the nocturnal hours of enforced inactivity.

His plans for leaving the building had been laid with as much care as those for entering it, and he rightly reckoned that his best chances of escape lay through the annealing department furnaces, fed with metal from *within* the Mint and with fuel from *without*. The stoking chamber was a mere recess in the outer wall of the building; access to this recess being by way of three doors. At the end of each working day two of these doors would be bolted from the inside and the third padlocked and sealed from the outside. This arrangement effectively barred *entry* into the Mint, but no one had ever given serious thought to the matter of egress. By the third day of the thief's activity the furnaces had cooled sufficiently for him to wriggle through one of them from the metal-loading end to the stoking bay. His journey through the annealing furnace must have been uncomfortable, but not very difficult. On emerging from the furnace chamber into the stoking bay all he had to do was to lift the bolt of one of the doors and walk out as free as air, with sixty thousand rupees concealed in his dhoti.

When the Mint reopened after the holidays the hue and cry was raised. The culprit rather foolishly failed to report for work, thereby focussing suspicion onto himself. But it was human frailty in a more extreme form that led eventually to his undoing: for he decided to celebrate his new-gotten wealth by getting royally drunk. Whilst in his cups he felt an irresistable subconscious urge to revisit the scene of his crime. He lurched into a guard at night, and on being roughly handled for his carelessness let fall Rs59,890 of notes from the folds of his garments. The lesson cost the government only Rs110, which was all the thief had been able to convert into alcohol in the space of a few days.

I got my burglar-proof strongrooms and the armed guard was restored to full strength. Meanwhile my unwitting benefactor found ample time in which to ponder upon the fickleness of fate in one of His Exalted Highness's goals.

The security of the treasure was a matter that extended beyond the precincts of the Mint. For escorting it to the government treasuries it was accompanied, by ancient tradition, neither by police nor by regular soldiers, but by the Arab guards from the Irregular Forces wearing exotic and picturesque uniforms. These were the Maisaram Guards referred to earlier.

In 1942, when the Japanese were at the threshold of India apparently poised for invasion, I advised the government to scatter the treasure lest a well aimed air attack should destroy not only the Mint but also the fiduciary value of the entire state currency. The Arab guard was insufficient for this task, so wagon-loads of cash – Rs135 millions worth – were sent to the various district treasuries under military and police escort. A year or so later, when the danger had passed, most of this treasure returned to the capital.

XV

'For which act of kindness...'

For more than two hundred years the English language has served as a lingua franca throughout the Indian sub-continent. Considering that to them it is a foreign tongue, it is a matter of amazement and admiration that the Indians and Pakistanis have such a fluent command of it, albeit that their own rather picturesque version of it is unique. They speak it with a distinctive and rather endearing intonation and have difficulties with certain combinations of consonants, just as the Western tongue can seldom master the subtle range of consonants – particularly the gutterals – that have entered the Urdu language by way of Arabia and Persia. Such minor imperfections of speech are negligible by comparison with the lamentable grammar and excruciating mispronunciations of the average European who flatters himself that he speaks fluent 'Hindustani' – a non-existent language anyway. Any amusement I have derived from the linguistic quaintnesses of the Indians is totally without malice; for I know only too well that I myself have dwelt in a glasshouse.

A knowledge of English used to be regarded as a status symbol, and it was not uncommon for two Indians, conversing together in their own vernacular, to break into English and raise the pitch of their voices on seeing a European approach within hearing range. This technique would sometimes be adopted by those of slender qualifications, as when one Indian was heard to say to his companion 'How are you my friend I hope?' The other, not being quite capable of attaining such a high linguistic standard, replied 'Oh, yes!'

A similar dialogue is alleged to have been heard as follows:-
'How do you my friend?'
'I am so-so.'
'I am also.'

Some oddities of expression are the natural outcome of the lack of an exact equivalent of a word in the other language. The word 'too' in the sense of 'excessively' is an example; for in Hindi and in Urdu it is synonymous with 'very'. This was forcibly illustrated to me when an Indian, clearly wishing to be polite, told me that my son was 'too much like his father'. Other common expressions used by Indians are just not *English* English, such as 'to wish' used in the sense of 'to greet'. 'I met my friend and wished him'. Another fault, no less logical than the French equivalent is 'You are writing one letter, isn't it?'

Among Anglo-Indians there was often to be found a curiously misplaced sensitivity about their mixed blood. Many of them would go to great lengths to pretend they were one-hundred percent British. Even if their complexion might be deceptive their speech usually gave them away. They liked to talk of England as 'home' and to imply that they had first hand knowledge of that country, even though they had almost certainly never ventured beyond the shores of India. One Anglo-Indian, boasting of his knowledge of England, was asked how he liked London. 'I do not know London well,' he said. 'The train did not istop there.'

The Indian's vocabulary is often immense, though textbook words such as 'furlong' are in regular colloquial use, while nuances are sometimes missed. 'He is one very important gentleman. He has a finger in every tart'. I once walked into an office in Bombay and asked a clerk whether a Mr So-and-so were in. His reply was oddly euphemistic. 'Sir, he has gone to commit nuisance'.

Quaintness of expression was sometimes found in quite high circles, as when I had occasion to write to one of the Hyderabad ministers to ask him to raise a certain matter at the next meeting of the State Executive Council. The minister replied with laudable brevity – 'Dear Armstead, I will set balls rolling'.

The use of the verb 'to be' in the Biblical sense ('Rachel weeping for her children because they *are* not') is by no means regarded as archaic in India. A story is told of an Englishman in a train at Victoria Terminus, Bombay, while an Indian fellow passenger was negotiating a sale through the window with an orange vendor on the platform. Before agreement had been reached as to prices the train started to pull out of the station and the vendor was compelled to conduct his business in accelerating motion as the train gathered speed. His concentration on the matter in hand was so intense that when he reached the end of the platform the ground apparently disappeared from beneath his feet and the unfortunate fellow landed on his face with his wares scattered about him. The other party to the unconcluded contract turned to the Englishman and said with an expressive gesture 'He thought the platform *was*, no doubt'.

I heard of one occasion where it was an Englishman who was guilty of using unnecessarily flowery speech. He was the president of a certain professional association whose members planned to give a garden party. Anxious to have Mr Rajah-gopalacharya, the Prime Minister of Madras, as the guest of honour, the Englishman called on him in person and expressed the hope that the Prime Minister 'would grace the occasion with his august and honourable presence despite the many calls which so eminent a personality would doubtless have upon his time'. The Prime Minister replied, 'My dear Mr –, need you be quite so oriental?'

Fruitful sources of masterpieces were advertisements, public notices and menus. Here are a few samples:-

Notice outside a barber's shop	'Gentlemen's throats cut daily'

Notice in a hotel bedroom	'The drinking water in this hotel has been passed personally by the manager'
Printer's advertisement	Diaries for sale! Decently bound Rs2/-. Indecently bound Rs1/8.
Butcher's advertisement	'Mr – kills himself every day'.
Carrier's advertisement	'We will send your luggage in all directions'.
Stained glass merchant's advertisement	'Painted widows make the best memorials'
From a menu in a Bombay restaurant	'Assorted tarts for your pleasure'.

Indian logic is sometimes rather devious. The Secretary of my old Bombay firm was a Parsee, rejoicing in the name of Pestonji Dhanjibhai Mahalakshmiwallah. (He had the burdensome task of signing all the company's cheques and important documents: his signature occupied two lines!) Pestonji was a keen spiritualist. In 1930 I unexpectedly ran into him in London on the traffic island at the top of the Haymarket. We exchanged polite enquiries, and he told me that although he had another six weeks of leave due to him he was returning to Bombay the very next day. I said I hoped there was no unhappy reason for his having to cut his leave short, and he explained that he had recently attended a séance at which he had received a message from a 'departed friend' warning him that if he did not go back at once to India he would assuredly die of double p-neumonia – the 'p' was not silent. Later I heard from friends in Bombay that he was telling all the sceptics 'See! I have *not* died of double p-neumonia. Is this not proof?'

At a school examination, in which the pupils were asked to give the meanings of certain English words, one of the boys had defined 'novice' as 'a nun confined in a monastery'. The examiner wrote in the margin 'One curious misconception'. The comment of the headmaster on seeing this was 'A clerical error, I presume'.

Although not relevant to India, it would not perhaps be out of place here to mention a sentence included in some notes which I saw on the back of a map of Mexico for the guidance of American motorists visiting the country. A rather childish gimmick of some of the young, rich, flashy Mexicans is to equip their sports cars with a horn that plays the well known refrain 'Colonel Bogey'. The notice on the map admonished the foreigner 'not to commit obscenities with the horn'.

The chief fount of babu-English is the letter of petition. The Indian believes in the creed 'Ask, and it shall be given unto you', and his society has long been firmly established on a foundation of nepotism. Any European in a position of even minor authority is constantly badgered to use his influence for the advancement of relatives whom he has almost certainy never met. Whatever objections there may be to this system, it has certainly enriched life with some gems of expression.

The written petition, which must be only too familiar to anyone who has been in India for more than five minutes, is an established institution from which the professional letter-writer does a thriving trade. It is, or certainly was, a common sight to see the scribe, with his semi-literate or illiterate client, squatting in the bazaar and concocting some masterpiece. It may be from a babu requesting a job for his son or nephew, from a servant asking for a loan for his daughter's wedding, from a peon asking for extra leave, or from a young man seeking employment for himself.

The letter of petition follows a form as stylised as that of a classical symphony, each movement consisting of a theme and variations. The standard opening is 'Honoured Sir, I beg to lay before you these few lines for Your Honour's kind and sympathetic consideration'. Then follows the request, with a wealth of circumstantial argument and a catalogue of the virtues and qualifications of the would-be beneficiary. The applicant may have 'studied up to matriculation standard' or even be the proverbial 'failed BA', and will certainly have come from 'a most respectable family'. He will also have taken 'a keen interest in sports at school'. This last qualification is calculated to melt the heart of any Briton, though the effect is often spoiled when the sports are specified as badminton and ping-pong. The next section of the letter is a direct appeal to the sympathy of the reader and usually contains an inventory of the petitioner's dependants whom he cannot possibly support and who must assuredly starve if his request be not granted. The normal finale is with these words, or some variant of them . . . 'For which act of kindness I shall ever pray to Almighty God for Your Honour's long life and prosperity'. A more abrupt alternative to this last 'movement' was once in vogue . . . 'Kindly do the needful and oblidge (sic)', but this seems to have been more or less discarded later, probably because it was apt to promote what the Americans would call 'sales resistance'.

The usual technique is for the suppliant to present his letter and to wait at a discreet distance, with much salaaming and wheedling smiles whenever the reader glances in his direction.

I have personally received many pearls of babu-English and have seen others (some no doubt apocryphal) that have been circulated in the clubs of Bombay. One woman, writing to her late husband's employers to ask for a pension, described herself as 'a poor wanton widow' and went on to say that her husband had 'died as per doctor's orders at 10.24pm on Wednesday, 7th inst.' Then there was the classic from the clerk who claimed that he had to support a large family 'of whom by God's misfortune the feminine gender predominates – three adults and six adultresses'.

A friend of mine in Cawnpore had a letter from an applicant who hopefully tried to display his erudition by misquoting Milton. 'The hungry sheep look up and are fed up'. Once I was approached by an ex-employee of the Mint who wished to be re-engaged on the staff, saying 'I now return like the dove to Noah's ark, which is none other than Your Honour's kind and sympathetic heart'. Another of my employees left during the War to take up a more lucrative job as a stores clerk at the military arsenal at Kirkee. Wanting some favour of me he wrote to remind me that he was 'risking life and limb for King-Emperor and Country'. The palm should perhaps go to this one... 'For which act of kindness I shall ever pray to the Lord Jesus Christ whom Your Honour so closely resembles'.

There was always a great readiness to invoke the Deity in Indian writings and utterances. A story is related of the small British garrison at the remote outpost of Gilgit in the Himalayas. A regimental clerk approached the CO to ask for leave to enable him to visit his wife and new-born baby in Rawalpindi. 'But,' said the CO, 'you have been in Gilgit for more than a year without your wife.' 'Sir,' came the reply, 'With the help of Almighty God and my younger brother all things are possible.'

The following letter is alleged to have been sent to the Bombay Gas Company:

'Honoured Sir,
    I am sorry to give you the troubles but my wife does not like the gas from the front as the house smells from the leek. My wife has preference for gas from the behind because if smells are to smell they remain outside my residence. I thank you from before and hope you will gratify my wife's wish with the gas bringing from behind.
                    Yours truly... '

An Indian guest, making a suitable after-dinner speech, is alleged to have spoken as follows:-

'Ladies and Gentlemen, I have the honour to thank you one and all from my heart's bottom. Yes indeed, and from my wife's bottom too'.

167

A Hindu is reported to have described his adventures on a railway journey as follows:-

'At – istation the train istopped and I alighted to attend to my ablutions and to call of nature. When in compromising posture the guard suddenly blew on whistle very wigorously. So taking lota in one hand and dhoti in other I ran wery fast to catch train, showing all my shockings to female passengers. It was great embarrassment which I could not conceal'.

When I first knew India a personal servant was considered indispensable for every European bachelor. It was expected that the servant would protect his master from being robbed by others so long as he himself were permitted to get away with a modicum of petty pilfering. A wise master shut his eyes to a good deal but periodically read the riot act if he felt that things were getting out of hand. The chief source of unofficial income for the servant was the buying of petty stores such as soap, shoe polish, dusters and so on. From time to time a grubby chit would be presented to the master, showing an account for alleged purchases. The frequency with which shoe polish costs were claimed was quite unrealistic, even though the price per tin might not be too outrageous: a stock of empty tins was always produced as circumstantial evidence of need. A young Englishman, fresh from Home, was once presented with his first 'bill' which included a mysterious item ... 'pepper for horse – 6 annas'. As the young man kept no horse, and as he thought in any case that an equine diet of pepper seemed unusual, he questioned his 'boy'. The servant went all coy and seemed to suffer from a language barrier: so the master took the bill to his office and asked a babu to speak to his servant and to unravel the mystery. A day or two later the babu appeared wreathed in smiles. 'Sir, it is one spelling error,' he said. 'It should not be "pepper for horse" but it is "paper for arse" that he means.'
The sayings and doings of Indian servants could sometimes

be most entertaining. *Punch* once published an illustrated joke by the incomparable Charles Graves, of an Englishwoman interviewing an Indian servant applying for a job. The mistress asked his name, and the servant, with an expression of sublime coyness, said 'My real name is Muhammed Abdullah, but my last Memsahib she call me by pet name – Barabas.'

A mistress, on a visit of inspection to her kitchen, was horrified to see the cook straining the soup through one of her husband's socks. She reprimanded the cook, who ingenuously replied 'But, Memsahib, I not using Sahib's *clean* sock.'

My Norwegian friend, George, having endured for a few days a servant who showed himself to be an incorrigible rogue, dismissed him with a testimonial... 'To whom it may concern. If – should apply to you for a berth, I strongly recommend that you give him one: as wide a one as possible'.

A European hostess, wishing to impress her guests with an unusual menu, arranged to give them a boar's head. Before the meal she gave her khitmagar strict instructions as to how it should be served. 'When you bring it into the dining room,' she said, 'don't forget to place a tomato between the teeth.' At dinner, the boar's head was triumphantly borne in by the khitmagar, whose wide open jaws held a large tomato.

There is an anecdote concerning a railway staff dance at which a shy young Anglo-Indian boy asked a Hindu girl for the pleasure of a dance. The reply was... *'Dancing* ki bat thik hai, lekin *pleasure* ke waste mujhko Mama se puchhna chahiye'. This is not improved by translation, but for the benefit of those having no knowledge of Urdu it amounts to... *'Dancing* is quite all right, but for *pleasure* I must ask Mama'.

Finally I quote the following entry from an Indian country doctor's logbook:-

```
2.30am ... Patient in low degree
3.00am ... Patient in the sink
3.30am ... Patient on the flit
3.45am ... Patient flut
```

XVI

Deccan Digressions

The Nizam's Dominions, excluding Berar, were squarish in shape and the diagonal from the north-west to the south-east corner was nearly five hundred miles in length. This vast area covered a wide variety of landscape and included some interesting antiquities. The central part, for some miles round the capital, was strewn with huge boulders; some of them balancing precariously on others. The effect of this scenery, usually very sparse in vegetation, was extremely wild: somehow one would not have been surprised to encounter at any moment a Walkyrie perched on a rock. The simple villagers accounted for the boulders by a legend of two tribes of giants, one of which dwelt in Ceylon and the other in the Deccan. When these tribes made war they hurled boulders at one another. As the Ceylon landscape does not feature similar heaps of rocks it must be concluded that the Deccani giants' missiles fell short of their mark or wide into the sea.

Elsewhere the Deccan scenery was gentle, with paddy fields, small lakes, prickly pear and other cactus-like growths and pleasant groves of mango, tamarind and various other trees. The lakes, or 'tanks' as they were more generally known, were nearly all artificial, formed by throwing up long low earthen dams, or *bunds*, to catch the monsoon rains and use them as a source of irrigation during the dry months. In this type of landscape, which generally appears to be fairly flat, great ingenuity has been exercised in exploiting slight differences of level so as to gather the maximum possible catchment with the minimum of earthworks. Peaceful scenery of this kind is to be seen throughout the length and breadth of India. It is peppered with large open wells to give water supply to the thousands of small villages all over the country. The creak of teams of oxen drawing water from these wells by means of a rope, pulley and goatskin bucket is a familiar sound of the countryside. One's first impression of this landscape is that it is deserted except for occasional groups of workers in the paddy fields: but we found from experience that no sooner had we driven our car across the sunburnt earth to choose a shady grove of trees well off the road as a suitable spot for a picnic, with no one but Nature as witness, within a matter of minutes little groups of staring peasants would collect and watch us by the hour. Privacy was hard to find, even in the depths of the country: there was always some village within a mile or so of almost anywhere. The villages themselves, smelling of cattle, goats and hot dust, had the appearance of picturesque ruins and consisted of a group of mud-walled hovels, a tiny Hindu temple or Muslim mosque, and a shabby flag flying on a bamboo pole to mark the seat of the headman. This open Indian countryside had a peculiar beauty of its own and, particularly at sunset, gave an impression of unchanging eternity. I learned to know it well by the best of all possible means – on horseback.

Parts of the State were covered with thick forest jungle, in which tiger and panther abounded. Monkeys could be seen sporting on the road or jumping from tree to tree; the babies clinging to the underside of their mothers. The trees were not very large and consisted mainly of rather stunted teak, relieved by vivid splashes of scarlet in the right season, from the 'flame of the forest'.

Apart from the numerous small 'tanks' to be found all over the countryside, there were several large reservoirs that were major engineering achievements. The Nizamsagar, some seventy miles from the capital, has a dam about two miles long and supplies irrigation waters to 430 square miles of land. Only a few miles outside Hyderabad City the two rivers, Musi and Isa (Moses and Jesus) have been dammed to form the Osmansagar and Himayatsagar lakes which give water supply to the capital. Both these lakes have pleasant gardens beneath their dams and are popular with the city-dwellers for short excursions. There is a small, but interesting, dam close to the city called Mir Alam Sagar. Built in the eighteenth century by French engineers, this dam is of the multiple-arch construction – a pioneer design in those days. Another popular dam and lake is at Pocharam, not far from Nizamsagar, where two excellent guesthouses provide ideal settings for a short holiday. It was at Pocharam that Guen caught malaria by sleeping without a mosquito net.

Travel in the Deccan in the days of the Nizams was fairly rough. Although there was quite a good network of roads and railways there was an almost total absence of hotels except for three or four in the capital and Secunderabad. As distances were great, the traveller was catered for by dak bungalows, or state-owned rest-houses. With a few exceptions these were very primitive, but at least they provided shelter, bedsteads and a caretaker who could rustle up a scraggy chicken, eggs and a few other ingredients for a simple meal. The wise traveller carried his own small stock of food and drink, and also an icebox that could serve its purpose for a day or two.

Several great rivers flowed through, or along the borders of, the State; the most famous being the Godaveri which, to the Hindus, had a sacred connotation second only to the Ganges. Immensely long bridges for road and rail spanned these rivers at strategic points, while elsewhere road crossings were provided by causeways. During the hot months the beds of these great rivers were almost dry; but during the monsoon, when they were in spate, many of the causeways were impassable. The waters of the State had great hydro power potential, which was much discussed in my day but never actually harnessed until later. The potential demand for electricity was then too small to justify the huge expenditure involved.

The ruined city of Golconda, only about six miles outside the capital, is an incredibly beautiful and romantic place. Once the diamond market of Asia, the Amsterdam of the East, Golconda became a symbol of riches and of international fame. It is surrounded by several miles of massive stone walls, pierced in two or three places by gates with labyrinthine approaches that could effectively slow down a storming party, hinder the use of battering rams, and provide neat pockets into which boiling oil could conveniently be poured from above onto the heads of invaders. Massive timber doorways in these gates are furnished with huge iron spikes to discourage the use of elephants from bursting them open. Lodged in one of the high fortress walls can still be seen one of the Emperor Auranzeb's cannon-balls, a relic of the great decisive battle in which Tana Shah, the last of the Golconda Kings, was defeated, and after which the Deccan became part of the Imperial Moghul Dominions. Within the city there is a large 'tank', some hundred yards square or so, apocryphally reputed to have been filled with asses' milk for the bathing of the Qutb Shahi queens and their ladies. A hill, rising in the middle of the city, is surmounted by the Balar Hissar, or citadel. Outside the city walls is a large group of vast mausolea in the Moghul style, in which the ancient Muslim kings of the Deccan and some of their queens and diwans are entombed. In my day the city was practically deserted except for a few squatters. The road leading westwards from Golconda passes between two small hills, each having a building on the summit. It is said that two ladies of the court, each seeking the favours of one of the Deccan kings, once lived in these houses and passed much of their time in shouting abuse at one another across the narrow valley.

By far the most famous archeological treasures of the Nizam's Dominions were the caves of Ellora and Ajanta in the north-west corner of the State. At Ellora, temples and monasteries have been carved out of the living rock by Buddhists, Brahmins and Jains. They date from the fifth to the ninth centuries AD.

The intricacies of the carvings and their massive size are most impressive. Huge elephants, lions and other creatures and elaborately carved pillars have been formed by cutting away the virgin rock from around them. At Ajanta, the splendid setting of the twenty-nine caves carved out of the rocky horse-shoe shaped cliff first strikes the eye of the visitor: within these caves is a rich treasure of unique early Buddhist frescoes and carvings. It is of interest to record that after the decline of Buddhism in India in the seventh century of the Christian era, the Ajanta caves became lost to the world, and their entrances were overgrown with vegetation that concealed them from sight. The existence of one of the greatest art treasures in Asia remained unknown until, quite by accident, they were stumbled upon by a party of British troops on manoeuvres in 1819. Some splendid restoration work has since been carried out, and the caves and frescoes have now been restored to their former splendour.

In Muslim architectural treasures the Nizam's Dominions were also very rich. The fortress of Bidar, the famous Masjid of Gulbarga, the Char Minar and Jama Masjid in Hyderabad City, the Chand Minar and fortress at Daulatabad, Rabia Daurani's tomb at Aurangabad (a rather inferior copy of the Taj Mahal) are but a few examples.

At Nander there is a Sikh colony. I was once invited to attend a Sikh religious ceremony in the gurudwar there. The Sikhs hold it as a sign of reverence to remove one's shoes and to cover the head when entering a place of worship. If the headgear is a turban and the shoes are sandals this custom seems both natural and dignified; but a European wearing a topi in a sacred place, and carrying his shoes and socks in his hand feels distinctly out of place.

When approaching the town of Medak one is surprised to see what looks like a cathedral rising out of the landscape. It is in fact a very large Christian church, built in conventional Victorian Gothic, worthy of the late Edmund Street, RA. Nearby is a big seminary for training Indian Christian clergy. Medak was, and for all I know may still be, a most important

Christian missionary centre: another was the leper colony at Dichpalli where the inmates, though not a pretty sight, were well cared for.

From the economic aspect one of the most important small towns in the State was Singareni, where there were large collieries. This was the most important coalfield in India south of Bengal. It was staffed by a small colony of Europeans, mostly Scotsmen, and situated in an area of well timbered jungle. Some years ago the hierarchy of the Anglican Church decided that India, as it then was, was too large to be administered efficiently by the few dioceses into which the country was divided; so they decided to create a new diocese to be centred more or less equidistantly from Bombay, Madras and Calcutta. The obvious choice for the new diocesan centre would have been Singareni. It is said that the Scots General Manager of the collieries, who had long been regarded as the senior citizen of that area, did not take kindly to the idea of a new bishop who would take social precedence over himself: he declared that if there was to be a Bishop of Singareni then *he*, and no one else, should be the bishop. To avoid an awkward situation the centre of the new diocese was fixed at a tiny village called Dornakal which possessed the sole merit of being situated at a railway junction. So it came about that the bishopric of Dornakal was created and a cathedral was built in the middle of nowhere. This cathedral was a 'political', or perhaps 'oecumenical', building. Cruciform in plan, with Hindu columns and Muslim minarets, it was intended to serve as an invitation to men of all creeds to worship within its walls.

Of arts and crafts only a few were peculiar to Hyderabad State. At Bidar they made the famous Bidri-ware – plates, vases, boxes and so forth – of black metal with a delicate inlay of silver wire. When mellowed with age, Bidri-ware could sometimes be very decorative. A rather rough quality of brocade known as himru was an excellent material for ladies' evening dresses, while at Nirmal a small group of craftsmen kept alive a tradition of making chessmen and playing cards in painted wood or papier maché. The Nirmal colours were rather crude but some of the products were interesting. The Moghul playing cards were circular and consisted of eight suits of twelve cards each, making a pack of ninety-six. I never discovered how the game was played, but I have a pack in my possession.

XVII

Nineveh and Tyre

Although Hyderabad lacked the spectacular pageantry of some of the Hindu states, with their richly caparisoned elephants, there were certain occasions that called for stiff, formal ceremonies.

One such occasion was the kharita durbar, held whenever there was an important official transaction between the Viceroy and the Nizam. The arrival of a new British Resident was always marked by one of these durbars, held in one of HEH's many palaces, called Chowmahala. This word literally means 'Four Palaces', and indeed it was formed by four separate buildings surrounding a square garden laid out in the formal Persian style. Chowmahala was reserved for ceremonial only: it was never used as a residential palace. At a kharita durbar the Nizam and the Resident would be seated side by side on 'thrones' placed on a raised dais at one end of a long hall, down each side of which would be placed twenty-five chairs. On one side sat twenty-five representatives of the British Raj – the senior Residency staff, the General Officer commanding the British and Indian armed forces in Secunderabad, and a few of the most senior military officers. Facing them, on the other side of the hall, sat twenty-five representatives of the State government – Members of the Executive Council and senior Heads of Departments. The kharita, or official missive from the Viceroy, would be handed by the Residency Secretary to the Nizam's Political Secretary, and passed on by him to the Nizam's Political Minister who would then read the kharita out loud. HEH would make a suitable acknowledgement, compliments would be exchanged and the whole ceremony concluded in a matter of minutes. Just before the gathering broke up, liveried palace servants would enter the hall carrying silver pan-boxes on trays. Pan is a mixture of nuts, usually including the very tough betel nut, wrapped up in a green leaf and silver foil, and with lime and spices added. The whole package can be chewed by those who can take it, silver foil and all; but at the durbar it was intended to be a symbolic offering only, to be declined with a gracious nod of thanks. This custom served the interests of economy; for the same silver boxes could be used again on the next occasion, and the palace servants could eat the pan. However, it sometimes happened that in ignorance of the correct étiquette the representatives of the British Raj accepted what was offered them and sturdily resisted the efforts of the palace servants to recover the boxes after the ceremony: the silver boxes made interesting souvenirs. Unfortunately for me, pan was offered only to the 'visiting team' (the British). As I had to sit with the 'home team' I never succeeded in acquiring a silver box.

The Berar Treaty was the occasion of a kharita durbar. This was a political transaction worthy of W S Gilbert. Until some time during the nineteenth century the province of Berar, which supported some three or four million inhabitants, had formed part of the Nizam's Dominions: but in exchange for certain services rendered to the State the British Indian Government had annexed the Berar territories and absorbed them into what used to be the Central Provinces. This had long been a thorn in the flesh of HEH who had been agitating for years for the return of Berar to his Dominions. So after years of negotiations a treaty was drawn up whereby the Nizam was to be the nominal sovereign of Berar, his Heir Apparent was to have the style and title of His Highness the Prince of Berar (after the manner of the Princes of Wales), the Union Jack and the Nizam's flag were to be flown side by side throughout Berar whenever there should be occasion for flag-flying at all, HEH and the Governor of the

178

Central Provinces were to exchange official state visits, BUT the territories would continue to be administered by the Governor of the Central Provinces. Face was thus saved on both sides. The Central Provinces Administration continued to function exactly as before; HEH's titles were to become even more extensive, in that he would now be the Nizam of Hyderabad and Berar; HEH could lay claim to another three or four million 'subjects'; and Prince Azam Jah Bahadur was to become a 'Highness' and entitled to a royal salute of guns.

I was present at the kharita durbar that formally ratified this treaty: it was marred by a lamentable incident. The Honourable Political Member of the Nizam's Executive Council *dropped* the kharita in his nervousness. It was a pity that H M Bateman could not have been present, for I was immediately reminded of his famous *Punch* cartoon 'The guardsman who dropped it'. The faux-pas was followed instantly by an exalted rebuke ... 'Clumsy, clumsy, clumsy! Pick it up, pick it up, pick it up!'

In the days of my predecessor, European state officers wore morning suits and white topis on all ceremonial occasions unless their office entitled them to a military, police or ICS uniform. All Indian civil state officers had to wear the Hyderabad Civil Service uniform. Shortly after I took office, HEH decreed by firman-i-mubarak that in future his civilian European officers who were required to attend durbars, viceregal welcomes or other important ceremonial occasions should *all* wear uniform and carry swords. Only five or six of us were affected by this decree, but we rather resented being put to considerable expense for the sake of rare functions. The uniform itself, very similar to the ICS outfit, with its gold epaulettes, spiked white topi and gilded spurs, was quite costly; but the *sword* was a far more expensive item. I therefore came to the rescue with the resources of the Mint and State Workshops. From the Nizam's State Railways I bought some scrap wagon tyre steel, a particularly tough metal: this I had heated and rolled into strips in the Mint. From these strips were cut the sword blades. Sheet

179

metal scabbards concealed their humble origin beneath a veneer of gold plating, while a block of composition 'ivory', such as is used for the manufacture of cheap billiard balls, served to form part of the hilt. For the metal part of the hilt I borrowed a British Civil Service sword as a pattern, from which a number of brass castings were made and subsequently gold-plated. Although these bore the outdated cypher of King Edward VII, such an anachronism was unlikely to catch the exalted eye. The sword knots and belts of gold braid had to be obtained from a military tailor, but the Mint-made swords passed muster. They cost sixty-five rupees each, as against some three hundred rupees charged for the genuine article. I have treasured my own sword ever since, despite its yellowing hilt. It bears my monogram on its blade (engraved by one of the Mint die-makers) and would be quite useless even for carving the Sunday joint; but it is decorative and it revives old memories for me. Unmerited attention was drawn to it many years later when I went to live for some years in the United States. During part of my absence abroad I was fortunate in letting my house in Richmond upon Thames to Field Marshal Lord Slim. As part of the letting process, an inventory of the contents of the house was drawn up. This was submitted by the valuers in a bound volume, on the cover of which was printed... 'Inventory of furniture and furnishings, china, glass...linen, etc. and CEREMONIAL SWORD'. Why this one humble item should have been singled out for individual mention was never clear to me, but that its presence should have been highlighted in this manner for the benefit of a famous field marshal whose experienced eye must undoubtedly have seen through its counterfeit origin struck me as unnecessary, to say the least.

'When I first put this uniform on' was on the occasion of the state visit of the Viceroy, Lord Linlithgow. Somehow I managed to get into my car, but the operation was rather like the construction of a model ship in a bottle. I could not wear my topi, for the spike would have pierced the roof of the car; so it had to be handed to me after I was seated, and carried. The tightness of the uniform trousers scarcely permitted any flexing of the knees; so I had to be threaded into position with the utmost care. All this manoeuvering was successfully carried out in the comparative privacy of my garden with the help of Guen and the servants; but my disembarkation at the railway station before the public gaze was another matter. Ranks of splendidly attired Indian lancers, military bands, police and a large gathering of notables were already assembled there to welcome the Viceroy, and incidentally to witness my discomfiture, in addition to thousands of the Great Unwashed who had collected to see the fun. To climb out of a closed car with dignity, with one hand carrying a topi and the other a sword, while *both* hands are more urgently needed to lever oneself from the seat, with almost rigid knees and with spiked spurs that caught up with everything, was no mean feat. Somehow or other the operation was carried out successfully and I was surprised to find myself in one piece, upright but rather flustered, in my proper place for the viceregal reception ceremony. From where I stood I was somewhat comforted by watching the antics of others, who arrived after me, getting out of their cars.

After the Viceroy and his suite had disembarked from their special train and had been received on the red carpet by the Nizam, the two princes and the Resident, they drove in procession past cheering crowds through the city to Falaknuma Palace. This building, beautifully situated on a hill overlooking the city, was always used as a guest-house for illustrious visitors. Its grand staircase was lined with portraits of all the viceroys and governors-general since Clive. I had noticed, when I had first seen this staircase just before Lord Willingdon's state visit to Hyderabad, that there was space for only four more viceregal portraits, including that of Lord Willingdon. This was to prove just sufficient.

The depositing of the viceregal party at Falaknuma Palace was by no means the end of the official welcome: the ceremony of mizaj-i-sherif had then to be performed. HEH drove back to his own palace, King Kothi, waited there for fifteen minutes and returned all the way to Falaknuma to enquire after the viceregal health. Satisfied on this point he again drove back to King Kothi. The Viceroy gave HEH twenty minutes' start, followed him to King Kothi for the purpose of returning the call and to enquire after the exalted health, and then retired back to Falaknuma. By that time it was generally assumed that everyone concerned was entirely satisfied as to the health of everyone else, and the shuttle service was discontinued. This curious and ancient ceremony gave the crowds the opportunity of seeing both the Viceroy and the Nizam several times.

In bygone days at the Moghul court, the method of greeting one another was to bow and raise the right hand to the forehead a number of times proportional to the rank of the person greeted. This custom had been adopted in Hyderabad at the times of the early Nizams. The number of hand oscillations had originally been decreed by strict protocol, but over the years with an ever-widening circle of nawabs, rajahs and officials it had all become too complicated for anyone to remember who was entitled to what. The custom degenerated to a series of up-and-down hand movements of ever-decreasing amplitude so that no one could say precisely how many salaams they had received. In this way susceptibilities were suitably protected. When greeting HEH, however, so many oscillations were made that if the Nizam had tried to count them he would have abandoned the attempt through sheer boredom long before they had ceased. Europeans were not expected to indulge in this modified form of kow-tow: a sharp flexure of the cervical vertebrae was sufficient.

A visit to the Mint was often included in the itinerary of important visitors to the State. The sight of showers of money seemed to hold a fascination even for the very wealthy. As I was often given very short notice of the arrival of some illustrious visitor I always kept in stock a roll of red carpet long enough to stretch the length of the corridor from the main entrance of the Mint to the inner quadrangle. My own garden was raided on these occasions so that a suitable avenue of potted evergreens and cannas could set off the carpet to advantage.

On one occasion I was given an hour's warning to receive His Highness the Maharajah of Kapurthala. This was short notice; but fortunately the occasion did not call for full dress uniform as the prince's visit was strictly informal. There was just time enough to deck out the corridor, to enable me to don my morning suit and white topi, and to warn all the working departments to tidy up and look industrious. A cortège of cars drove up and I advanced to receive the Maharajah who, in the act of dismounting from his car, was seized with an attack of cramp, lumbago, slipped disc or whatever, and was quite unable to straighten up. At first I thought he must have inadvertently looped his top trouser button-hole over his collar stud, but I soon saw that the poor man was in acute pain. Although I had tried to foresee all contingencies, the one thing I failed to provide was a chair: there was nowhere I could offer him to be seated except on a potted plant, two pieces of ordnance made in Gamlen's day and now used to lend dignity to the Mint entrance, or the floor. Office chairs could have been brought within half a minute, but these were of a quality scarcely suitable for the support of the lowness of a Highness; so I sent post-haste for one of the best chairs from my own home. This took a minute or so to arrive, during which time I was acutely embarrassed by having to utter repeated words of sympathy while bent almost double myself in order to speak somewhere in the vicinity of the princely ear.

The age of aviation started to touch Hyderabad during my time there, and a small civil aerodrome was constructed at Begampet just outside the city. The inauguration ceremony was to be presided over by Her Highness the Princess Dureshevar of Berar, to whom an address of welcome was to be presented in accordance with local custom, printed on silk and contained in a silver casket. I sent one of the Mint officers to the silversmiths' quarter in the city, and by good fortune he triumphantly returned with a silver model aeroplane. True, it resembled the first flying machine of Blériot or of the Wright brothers rather than any modern craft, but I did not expect the Princess to be an aficionada of aircraft design. I felt the curious object to be entirely apt for the occasion, if somewhat bizarre. A silver tube was made in the Mint for containing the silk scroll, mounted on an ebony base with a silver inscription plate; and the whole contraption was topped with the silver aeroplane. I asked to be supplied with the wording for the inscription and was instructed from Bella Vista Palace, the residence of the Prince and Princess of Berar, to word it . . . 'Presented to HIH The Princess of Berar on the occasion of . . .'. As daughter of the last Caliph, the princess claimed to be an 'Imperial Highness'. But that would have implied seniority of rank not only over her husband, a plain Highness, but (perish the thought!) over her father-in-law, an *Exalted* Highness. However, I did as I was bid and had 'HIH' engraved on the inscription. No sooner had this been done than the order was countermanded from the Finance Office – to whom I was directly responsible. The 'I' was deleted. Another message came from Bella Vista insisting on the retention of the controversial 'I'. During the twenty-four hours before the opening ceremony I was subjected again and again to orders and counter-orders. I now quite forget who won the argument; but I was in a very difficult position. I either had to defy the royal family or my own administrative chiefs. Apart from that, every alteration meant filling in an engraved letter with silver solder, rebuffing the casket, and re-engraving the controversial title.

The chief bugbear of ceremonial was a formal document called 'the warrant of precedence'. This was a standard work of reference, revised at frequent intervals, for placing guests at table in order of 'importance'. It covered not only the personalities within the State but also those who were stationed in the British Administered Territories. For example, a brigadier in the State Forces was junior to a British brigadier but took precedence over a British colonel. Every civil officer

The author (fifth from left at the nearest table, facing the camera) at a typical Hyderabad banquet. This one was at the time of The Nizam's Silver Jubilee in 1937.

Falaknuma Palace, built by a Hyderabad nobleman, Nawab Sir Vikhar-ul-Umra Bahadur and later acquired by The Nizam. It was mainly used as a guest house for visiting royalties and viceroys. Edward Prince of Wales stayed here shortly after the First World War, and King Alfonso XIII of Spain stayed in the 1930s.

Chow Mahala Palace, one of several royal palaces, used for ceremonial occasions only. Before viceregal or royal banquets the cutlery would be re-gold-plated, done here by Mint servants under the watchful eye of palace officials. *(Photos: Raja Deen Dayal)*

and every nobleman in the State was given a nominal 'rank' in the military scale. This warrant was rigidly observed at all State banquets and at Residency dinners. It was also expected to apply at private dinners, but as the warrant was issued only to those who held some kind of official appointment, many an innocent hostess – for example, the wife of an officer in Secunderabad – might quite unwittingly trigger off some terrible social feud through sheer ignorance of the mysteries of the warrant, the very existence of which she might well not know. Through no fault of mine, the Mintmaster was ranked as a State brigadier and therefore I took precedence over a British staff colonel. But many a British colonel's lady took not at all kindly to being placed 'below' Guen, who might have been twenty years her junior in age. I well remember at one dinner a woman, old enough to have been my mother-in-law, was seated on the host's left while Guen sat on his right. Conversation turned to a play that had been on in London some years earlier. Guen said she had not seen it. The indignant lady opposite seized her chance. Smiling sweetly, she said to Guen 'Neither did I see it; but of course you and I would have been at school then'. Another point of precedence that often puzzled the newcomer to India was that although the senior lady sat on the host's right hand, the senior man sat on the hostess's *left* hand. This is the logical result if any party is made up of married couples only; but many a hostess made a gaffe by not realising this point. The safest thing for a hostess was to confine her dinner parties to six – three married couples. It was then impossible to avoid dividing the honours evenly.

One universal exception to the warrant of precedence was the supremacy of a *bride*. For six months after her marriage a bride would be placed in the most exalted place at table, however young she might be and however junior her husband.

Our two children were sometimes invited to go riding with the two little Berar princes – one of whom is now the 'Pretender' to the Nizam's ghadi. The princes' ponies were decked out in royal trappings while our children were given ordinary saddles and bridles. If one of the small princes felt like a change of mount, the trappings had to be changed from one pony to the other. At one stage the younger prince, then aged about five, pulled my daughter's hair. She, being a young woman of about the same age and of formidable temper, knocked her royal assailant flat on his back, to the secret amusement of some of the Berar household and to the alarm and consternation of Nanny, who doubtless expected swift retribution in the form of being trampled upon by elephants, or something equally imaginative.

XVIII

Indian Hotch-Potch

My memories of India, as I write, extend back through more than sixty years. Isolated incidents come crowding into my mind: they fit into no coherent story but form part of the backdrop. A few inconsequential loose ends are collected in this chapter, as they all help to build up a general picture of a world that has vanished for ever.

A favourite nesting place for bees in India is on the under side of a tree branch or of a wooden beam. It is a common sight to see great clusters of these insects, perhaps three or four feet deep, suspended like a bag from the lintels of a columned verandah. As our house had verandahs on three sides it was a popular swarming ground in the bee world. In his day, Gamlen had dealt with this problem in characteristic fashion. He had made, from old kerosene cans, a long rectangular box open at the top and fixed at the bottom to the end of a tall pole. The width of the box was equal to that of the verandah roof beams. Into this box would be poured a gallon of petrol and the whole device, borne by brave coolies, would be deftly thrust upwards against the cluster of bees in such a manner that nine-tenths of them were trapped inside the box. The remaining tenth flew about in wild excitement but, strange to relate, had never been known to sting their assailants. The trapped majority, which included the queen, being overcome by petrol fumes, fell into the box and were decanted onto the ground in a wet heap, to meet a fiery death with the help of a match. The system was effective; but the

187

surviving bees evidently passed on no warning of the dangers of swarming at the Mint House to their fellow creatures. Other bees kept coming back, being, like the human race, apparently incapable of learning the lessons of history. At one season of my first year in the Mint House I found I was consuming about five or six gallons of petrol in this way every week – an expensive form of defence. So I decided on a policy of live and let live. I just left the bees to hang in their clusters and took no notice of them. The policy seemed to work. The bees kept to their side of the bargain for a couple of years and then suddenly, without warning, violated the treaty by attacking Guen en masse. It must have been a terrifying experience for her, with hundreds of bees entangled in her hair and clothes. She was very badly stung. The khitmagar rushed over to my office, only a few yards from the house, in such a state of excitement that he confused subject with object, blurting out 'Memsahib istinging bees!' My first reaction was to think this was rather peculiar behaviour on the part of 'Memsahib', but sensing his alarm I ran over to the house, receiving a dozen or so stings myself en route. The house was filled with bees, and Guen was lying on a sofa in a state of panic. The only action I could think of in a hurry was to seize a bottle of whisky and pour it over her head. This was strangely effective: the bees became intoxicated within seconds; or perhaps the fumes of the liquor roused atavistic memories of the petrol box in which so many of their ancestors had perished. At any rate, they became inert almost at once. I then combed dozens of very drunk bees out of Guen's hair, and with a pair of eye-brow tweezers removed a host of stings that were sticking into her face, arms and neck like pins in a cushion. She was very ill afterwards and developed an alarmingly high fever; but it eventually passed, and she now has a theory that she will never suffer from rheumatism. Nevertheless, and most understandably, she remains strongly apiphobic to this day.

The shameless violation of the cease-fire agreement by the bees led me to devise a new 'secret weapon' which proved to be highly effective and also cheap. It consisted of a series of electrically live wires supported on insulated bobbins about an inch below the verandah beams. The bees would try to swarm, as before, but whenever a cluster bridged the gap between the wires they received a shock and dispersed. We had no more trouble from them.

A really tragic bee episode had occurred in Hyderabad many years earlier. A British Resident had died en poste and a state funeral was arranged. The troops were lined up outside the Residency and the gun-carriage stood at the foot of the main steps to receive the flag-draped coffin. As soon as the band struck up the Dead March the bees, who are no music lovers, attacked everyone in sight. The horses were stung and, terrified, bolted into the city trailing the gun-carriage behind them. The pall bearers were stung and they dropped the coffin. The crowd, the troops, everyone within reach was stung and chaos reigned. The feelings of the unhappy mourners may well be imagined.

Another potential danger was the scorpion.

Once, in Warangal, I was seated on a verandah in the house of the European mill manager there. Suddenly the mali started to wail and came running to the house to say he had been stung by one. My hostess took him to the back of the house and within a few minutes the victim reappeared grinning from ear to ear. The lady claimed to be able to 'charm' away scorpion stings and snake bites simply by making passes. HEH himself was reputed to have this gift, and it was said that he had given standing orders to be wakened at any time of the night if a victim should make a claim on his healing powers. It is not recorded whether anyone was brave enough to try; but this is suggestive of the 'King's Touch' for curing scrofula, last said to have been exercised in England by Queen Anne.

My fortieth birthday fell at a time when my family was away in the hills. At about 5.0 o'clock every afternoon it was my custom to walk over from my office to my garden to have tea there, often only as a break before a further bout of work. Being meticulous about such things, Guen had left instructions with the cook to make me a birthday cake; and on the day in question I was astonished to see a small procession approaching the tea table and bearing a large cake with forty candles on it. I congratulated the cook and sat back to relax and enjoy my tea and a slice of cake. Now at that time I was having serious labour troubles in the Mint. Suddenly the side gates of the garden burst open and a large crowd surged in to present me with a petition. At this time the War was almost entering its fifth year, and the days of docile labour relations were almost imperceptibly becoming affected by creeping communism – thanks largely to the public image of 'Good old Uncle Jo Stalin'. Trade unions, hitherto unknown in the State, were being organised and it was clear that one or two of the leaders were out for the good of themselves and not of the work people, who were very easily led. On this occasion the mood of the crowd was distinctly ugly. They were led by a man who was no employee of the Mint, but a known agent provocateur from outside the State and who had already caused trouble with the railway staff and at the cotton mills.

It would be hard to imagine a situation in which one could feel more foolish or at a greater disadvantage than when seated alone before a fiery cake and confronted by a hostile mob. However, the cake worked wonders. Thinking I was engaged in some mysterious rite or poojah, the crowd discreetly dissolved, leaving me with their petition to be examined in privacy instead of beneath the gaze of hundreds of pairs of eyes. I was spared the necessity of becoming involved in argument or of making an instant, and perhaps ill-judged decision.

When on a short holiday to Ootacamund, Guen and I had gone for a picnic on the Downs, where I had unfortunately sat in a cow-pat. On the way home we passed the Hyderabad Resident's house, and we thought it would be a good opportunity to slink in quietly and sign his 'book', as was expected of us by étiquette. Although the book was discreetly placed at a side door we were unfortunately spotted by the

Resident's lady who insisted on inviting us in. She must have been mystified by the fact that I firmly declined her offer of a chair, and wondered why I backed out of her presence as though before royalty, when we left. My peculiar behaviour was, of course, due to consideration for her brocaded chairs and the indignity of my rear view.

From time to time the Secunderabad Club committee would muster all available local talent and put on a cabaret. These were sometimes rather painful evenings but it would have been churlish to have stayed away. On one such occasion a young Belgian girl performed a swan dance in conventional ballerina skirt decorated with fluffy pom-poms. I was watching the uncertain gyrations of this young woman from the back of the hall in the company of an amusing Englishman who was quite incapable of whispering: his voice, even when lowered to minimum volume, had tremendous carrying power. His idea of a whisper was only a few decibels below a sergeant-major's parade ground voice. As the dance approached its climax, our ballerina balanced very precariously on one toe, wobbling rather violently. At that moment one of her pom-poms fell off. My stentorian friend uttered, in what he doubtless believed to be a stage whisper, 'My God! She's laid an egg!'

It was curious how the degree of friendship one could enjoy with some of the Indians was inversely related to the amount of official dealings one had with them. We had many Indian friends; but with a few exceptions our relationship with them was purely social. Inter-departmental jealousies seemed to sour friendships as soon as governmental transactions had to be conducted. The Public Works Department was a large organisation, and its chief engineers succeeded one another with remarkable rapidity, so that the number of ex-chief engineers drawing high pensions was considerable. One of them, who had long been a close friend of ours, was related to someone very highly placed in the State. As soon as he took office I started to fall foul of him. This was awkward, as I had many dealings with his department. I had powers to erect and maintain my own departmental buildings, such as electricity substations, stores, and so on, but for most public buildings, including the Mint House, the PWD was fully responsible. One of the first acts of this particular chief engineer was to attempt to take away from me the right to place even one brick upon another. This would have led to an impossible situation that would have seriously undermined the efficiency of my departments. I resisted, and won the argument. After that, I found my friend pernickety, obstructive and altogether difficult to deal with in the many matters where the interests of the PWD overlapped with mine; for example, in the laying of electric cables under public roads. Our former friendship degenerated into a state of cold warfare. I reported to him that in my view the roof of my house was unsafe, as the steel joists were rusted through in places. He inspected it and declared my fears to be groundless. I could do nothing about it because the Mint House was a PWD building. A few weeks later my roof fell in. Had it not been for our habit of sleeping on the verandah instead of in the bedroom we could have been seriously injured, or worse. I must confess to some satisfaction when I reported what had happened. The roof was rebuilt. The chief engineer retired shortly afterwards and, as we no longer had business dealings, we became quite friendly again.

One night at about two o'clock I was awakened by our cook in a great state of excitement. His wife was pregnant and she had 'bad pains in istomach'. As I had no wish to add accoucheur to my list of official titles, I hastily dressed and drove the woman, groaning all the way, to the large hospital in Secunderabad, where I had the greatest difficulty in finding anyone to admit her. A month later, the woman was discharged from hospital – still pregnant.

A terrible tragedy occurred when an Indian cinema went up

in flames in the heart of Hyderabad City and many people were burnt to death. The victims were all women and children, trapped in the purdah balcony. One brave woman, valuing life more than modesty, took off her sari and, using it as a rope, helped several people to escape before she made her own getaway.

The popular belief, echoed by the local press, was that the fire had been started by an electrical fault, and I came in for a good deal of criticism (although there was an official Electrical Inspector outside my jurisdiction, who was responsible for the safety of consumers' installations). HEH ordered a Commission of Enquiry to be set up under the excellent chairmanship of S T Hollins, the Director-General of the State Police. There were four other commission members, including myself. I had visited the scene of the disaster early in the morning after the fire. It was not a pretty sight or smell, with charred corpses lying all over the ground among the burned ruins of the building. The Commission sat for several days examining witnesses, some of whom had heart-breaking stories to tell. One member of the Commission was a fine looking large bearded nawab of very forceful personality: he was a political leader and possessed a dangerous rabble-rousing gift of oratory. He would fiercely examine witnesses with great skill. Suddenly, after hearing some sad story of a trapped child burned to death, he would leave the courtroom, go into an adjoining room and there sob his heart out. Then he would quickly regain control of his emotions, return to the courtroom and continue to bully witnesses.

From the conflicting evidence of the witnesses, some of whom talked of fireballs running round the electric wires and other such improbable nonsense, I soon became convinced that electricity was not the culprit. The management had sworn on oath that no films had been on the premises other than the reels in the projection room used for the actual performance. I was certain they were lying, so I asked the president to adjourn the enquiry to the scene of the fire, which had been under continuous police guard since the disaster, so that we might closely examine the débris. There we found box after box of charred films, reduced to ashes but clearly recognisable for what they were. Electricity was exonerated. The management were reprimanded, but otherwide escaped scot free.

We recommended the woman who had saved so many lives for the George Cross: I am glad to say she received it.

Towards the end of the War the English Electricity Company sent to India a trade delegation composed of some of their most senior engineers and executives. One member was a Dr Seewar, an international authority on hydro power. Although Swiss, he had spent most of his life in England and had cultivated a strong 'foreign' accent and way of speech as part of his build-up as a 'character'. It was most effective, and he was a very amusing companion. 'Gentlemen', he would say, 'let us take the bull by the corns!' A meeting was arranged between the State Executive Council and the Mission, and I was asked to attend. The Nawab of Chattari, then President of the Council, was a very dignified man but he clearly had no idea what the Mission was about. It had, of course, been sent in the hopes of securing trade for Britain in the reconstruction that was expected to follow the War, but the President seemed to think that the kind gentlemen had expressly come to offer their services, gratis, to the State. A good misunderstanding was had by all. On hearing the President addressed by his normal title of 'Your Excellency', Dr Seewar then called everyone in the room 'Your Excellency', including the gold-braided peons who handed round the cigarettes and lemonade.

One day I was visited by a certain Mr Roshan Lal who claimed, on what authority I know not, to be the Poet Laureate of India. He produced an impressive document to support his claim and asked that he might have the honour of composing an ode to me! He said this would take a week or two to complete, after which a presentation ceremony would be necessary. 'Recipient', said he 'will be seated in one chair at entrance to his house. On his right hand will be seated Recipient's wife. If Recipient's wife be absent, then one photograph of Recipient's wife shall be placed on chair beside Recipient. Poet Laureate will then read ode, after which Recipient will offer suitable honorarium to Poet Laureate. Honorarium must include the numeral 'one' to be auspicious; for example, Re 1, Rs 11, Rs 21, Rs 31, etc. Poet Laureate having received honorarium will render ispeech of thanks and will place written version of ode in hands of Recipient. Ceremony being concluded, Poet Laureate and Recipient will bid one another Godspeed and proceed about their lawful occasions.'

Since 'Recipient' could scarcely offer as little as one rupee, it was clear that the minimum 'honorarium' would be eleven rupees and that at least twenty-one or thirty-one rupees would be expected from a quadruple Nazim.

I thanked Mr Roshan Lal but explained that I was really not interested in receiving an ode as I did not think I was sufficiently important for such an honour. Roshan Lal was staggered Never in all his experience had anyone declined the honour of accepting one of his odes – an honour that was strictly rationed in its bestowal. I had insulted him. Tears flowed freely down his cheeks and after an emotional scene he departed. I have often wondered what masterpiece I may have missed. It might have been worth thirty-one or even forty-one rupees and even sitting through 'ceremony with photograph of wife placed on chair beside me', as Guen at that time was in England.

Mint affairs occasionally took me to Bombay, where I got to know the Master of His Majesty's Mint, Colonel (later Sir) Alastair Ransford. I profited on these occasions during the War to visit the dentist, as my regular dentist in Hyderabad had been locked up as an 'enemy alien'. Inevitably the time came when I had to be fitted with my first denture. After leaving the dentist I lunched with friends at the Royal Bombay Yacht Club, of which I was an up-country member. Having had no time in which to 'break in' my denture I found it quite impossible to enjoy my lunch with the beastly thing in situ, so I discreetly removed it from behind the cover of a table napkin. Unfortunately I dropped the offending contraption onto the floor; and before I could recover it a club servant had inadvertently kicked it across the room. It became necessary to embark upon an undignified game of 'hunt-the-denture' in the Yacht Club dining-room. The quarry was finally retrieved, and after a day or two of practice became duly tamed.

This unhappy episode brings to my mind the story of the bishop who was fitted with a new denture. While his dentist was cleaning and putting away his instruments the bishop was inspecting himself in the mirror to see how his mouth looked. Suddenly His Lordship ejaculated 'Jesus Christ!' The dentist turned round in horror and said 'I trust, my Lord, there is nothing wrong with the denture?' 'Ah! No, my dear fellow, No', was the reply. 'They fit perfectly. But this is the first time in twenty-five years I have been able to utter the name of our Divine Redeemer without whistling'.

An old Bombay friend of mine had married a few years before I did. His wife proved to be rather prolific; and by the time that No 4 arrived my friend had learned the hard way to know the financial worries of parenthood. When the new baby was born he took his eldest boy to see 'Mummy and the new little sister'. All the way to the hospital the small boy kept up a refrain of 'I want to see the stork, Daddy. I want to see the stork'. After a while 'Daddy' became exasperated. 'So do I', he said. 'I want to wring his bloody neck!'

Late in the War a munitions ship blew up in Bombay harbour. The damage was terrific and the dock area was more or less flattened. A friend of mine was in his chief's office at the moment of the explosion, and every window in the building was instantly shattered. His chief, with superb sang-froid, immediately picked up the telephone and asked for Pilkingtons. 'Reserve for me 2,000 square feet of window glass, will you

196

please', he said, and then resumed the conversation with my friend as though nothing had happened.

Hyderabad possessed quite a fine observatory, which collaborated with other observatories of the world in mapping out the heavens and cataloguing the stars. It came into being in typical Hyderabad fashion. Early in the century a wealthy nawab had brought a 9-inch telescope to amuse himself with. After losing interest in it he sold it to the State government who appointed a State Astronomer. In my day the holder of this office was Bhaskeran Shastri, a very pleasant mild-mannered Mysori. I spent many hours looking at the mountains of the moon and the rings of Saturn through his telescope and discussing astronomical theories with him. In my younger days I had been fanatically interested in astronomy and cosmogony, and in 1929 had evolved a theory based on the 'curvature of space'. I had been so convinced of the basic soundness of my theory that I had sent a short memorandum to Sir James Jeans, who had expressed polite interest but remained somewhat sceptical. Years later I saw my theory described in two books; one by Sir Arthur Eddington and one by Professor G. Gamow.

I have said elsewhere that the Hindu and Muslim communities lived more or less in harmony with one another in the State. Inter-communal rioting was very rare by comparison with what happened so often in British India. At a typical dinner party in our house we might in the same evening have Hindu, Muslim, Parsee and European guests in a perfectly happy atmosphere. Nevertheless there were undercurrents that were only per-ceptible to those who had the opportunity of penetrating beneath the surface. One particular nawab, a charming man who clearly modelled his conduct on the idealised 'English gentleman', keen on sports and of impeccable manners, told me one day that the British would always rule India and that he was happy that this should be so. I asked him if he never felt any wish for national independence. 'Independence?', he cried.

'How could we Muslims ever know independence with a huge Hindu majority in the Congress party?' I suggested that the best hope for India was to forget all about classifying people according to religion. 'Europe', I said, 'was torn by religious wars in the 16th and 17th centuries. Now we have friends without even knowing if they are Roman Catholics, Protestants or Agnostics. Religion with us is a purely personal matter: our politics are based on economic beliefs more than anything else'. This argument carried no weight with him. 'For centuries', he said, 'we Muslims ruled most of India by right of conquest, and we shall never allow ourselves to be governed by those Hindu bastards if you British should ever be foolish enough to quit this country'.

XIX

The Calm Before The Storm

Ever since our home leave of 1937 the tension in Europe had mounted with every new act of bombast on the part of the German Chancellor; and by September 1938 war seemed both inevitable and imminent. I took ten days' leave during that month in order to revisit the Nilgiri Hills where I had stayed for a few days in 1928, but which Guen had never seen. To take the car there from the Deccan it was necessary to put it on the train for part of the journey as there were no road bridges over the Kistna and Tungabhadra Rivers. After a night in a hotel in Bangalore we drove on to Mysore City, which we had last seen during the Dasserah festivities in 1935. The Public Works Department of Mysore State was at that time experimenting with the use of molasses, of which they had a surfeit from their sugar factories, as a road surfacing material. From the point of view of the motorist it was far from successful. By remaining sticky in the hot sun, the molasses could be splashed up onto one's exhaust pipe, where it was converted into goo-ey toffee that smelt to High Heaven.

In Mysore we lunched with Sir Martin and Lady Forster, a most interesting couple who had a big house just outside the city. Sir Martin had been a distinguished scientist, a Fellow of the Royal Society and the first Director of the Indian Institute of Science at Bangalore. He so greatly liked the State of Mysore that he decided to retire there. His Spanish wife was a very entertaining character who believed in speaking her mind. She had once visited Hyderabad where at a garden party she had found herself sitting next to an Indian wearing very shabby clothes. She asked him to point out the Nizam. 'I am the Nizam', said her companion. 'What! In those dreadful old clothes?' said Lady Forster. Instead of being offended HEH was highly amused; which speaks well of him. The Forsters' Mysore house was furnished in a curious blend of Indian and Spanish décor, which went rather well together. The curved Spanish style ironwork over the windows effectively kept out the burglars. The Forsters' daughter, Carmen, inherited her mother's personality, and we came to know her a few years later. She married Sir Donald Field, a high ICS officer of the best type who had served as Diwan to Jodhpur State. Our Nanny, after leaving our service, went to the Fields to look after their small boy.

The drive from Mysore to the Nilgiri Hills is very spectacular. After passing over miles of roads lined with fine banyan trees well populated with monkeys, the massif of the Nilgiris appears ahead like a great wall. The road then passes through many miles of some of the finest and densest jungle in all India, teaming with game – from elephant, tiger and panther to samba and other deer types. Vast bamboo clumps like great plumes mix with some fine timber, and a rocky river flows close to the roadside. Here the milestones are painted black, as it has been found that elephants like to uproot white ones and playfully toss them into the forest. Suddenly the Nilgiris come upon one, and the ascent of the Gudulur Chat road is a truly wonderful experience, with its innumerable hairpin bends and fine views over the jungle and plains. As one mounts higher and higher the climate and scenery change with incredible rapidity. After the hot and steamy jungle the air becomes cool, even cold, while the forest gives way consecutively to coffee plantations, tea, and finally to green downland covered in gorse, suggestive of Sussex or the Scottish Lowlands. Tropical vegetation disappears and the eucalyptus and ilex take its place.

The climate of the Nilgiris is superb. All through the year it is cold enough to enjoy an open fire, even in the daytime; but never cold enough to produce more than a rare touch of ground frost at night. There is a certain amount of rain and mist, but for much of the year the skies are bright and clear. The hills rise to nearly 9,000 feet and the four principal 'hill stations' are Octacamund (generally known as Ooty), Wellington, Koonoor and Kotagiri. Before the Second World War the hills were largely populated by retired British who, after a career spent in India, felt themselves to be too much out of touch with the home country to return there to live. It was also possible to live in the Nilgiris quite cheaply and in reasonable comfort. Many of these retired folk lived to great ages in these hills. The principal industry of the district was of course tea, with a small amount of coffee on the lower slopes. The scenery was a complex of downlands, eucalyptus forest and tea estates. The whole effect was entirely pleasant, and the air, strongly scented with eucalyptus and mimosa, was most invigorating.

Here then, in September 1938, Guen and I came for a short holiday. We stayed at an excellent private hotel at Koonoor, kept by an Australian couple. The food was good and the low buildings were covered with a riot of climbing geraniums. Our enjoyment during the first few days was marred by the near-certainty we felt that war would break out any day. It was the time of the Munich crisis. After Chamberlain's return to London we, like so many others, were deluded into believing that he had really brought home 'peace with honour'. Although disillusionment was to follow so soon, we were able at least to enjoy to the full the rest of our short stay in Koonoor.

The Nilgiri downs offer ideal picnic grounds where one seldom sees a living soul except near the occasional settlement of Todas, a primitive aboriginal tribe that lives in curious hive-like huts and regards the buffalo as sacred. Ooty was the summer capital of the Madras Government, and Government House was a delightful place set in an imposing park. Also at Ooty were the summer residences of many rajahs, nawabs, and officials from southern India. The Hyderabad Resident was one of those fortunates to have a fine house to retreat to, without expense to himself, during the hottest summer months.

Our holiday ended and we returned to Hyderabad. Not far from Mysore we stopped at Seringapatam to see the ancient palace of Tipu Sultan, implacable foe of the British and reputed secret ally of Napoleon the First. The dungeons of the Seringapatam Fort had been used to imprison British captives under appalling conditions. Another curiosity of Seringapatam was a slender, very 'flat' brick arch built by an eighteenth century engineer, not for any practical purpose but simply to demonstrate the principle of the arch in an extreme form. It oscillated like a spring beneath one's weight. Unfortunately, this arch was washed away in a heavy storm a few years after we had seen it.

It was not long after our trip south that it became quite clear that Hitler had only been buying time at Munich. Crisis followed crisis and the future began to look truly grim. We had a personal problem in that our second child was on its way. As with the first, we wanted the baby to be born in London, but there seemed to be a serious risk that we might become separated indefinitely if Guen travelled home to England and became stranded there. However, we took the risk: our daughter was born in London, and my family returned to Hyderabad a few weeks before the war broke out. So at least we were all together when the holocaust began.

Another problem was to know what I myself should do if war came. I was only thirty-six in September, 1939, and still thirty-five during the preceding crisis months. The possibility of military service had to be considered, and with it the problem of where to 'park' my family in that event, as they could not expect to have the use of the Mint House if I were no longer administering my departments. I mentioned the matter one day in conversation with Sir Akbar Hydari, who said that the State would in no circumstances agree to release me in the event of war. On checking with the Residency I was told that if the State government insisted on keeping me I would have to stay where I was, whether I wished it or not.

I then began to worry about how I should be able to fulfil my duties as a supplier of public services if India should be cut off from Europe by war. How would I get essential supplies that had to be imported? I therefore invested very large sums of departmental funds in building up stocks of stores. This brought from the government a load of criticism upon my head: the money spent could have been earning interest. As prices rocketed after the outbreak of war, and as supplies became increasingly difficult to obtain, this outlay of money paid the government handsome dividends; but I got no thanks for it. Had I not looked ahead in this way we should have been in a serious plight.

XX

The Phoney War and After

At first, the outbreak of the Second World War had but little effect on life in Hyderabad and Secunderabad. After the rather dramatic arrest of the German doctor at our dinner table nothing very much happened locally except that the bazaar shopkeepers raised their prices outrageously on all imported goods, and a few rather childish Europeans, mostly women, showed their inability to distinguish between genuine patriotism and narrow chauvinism. The Secunderabad Club had a good stock of Munich beer, for which the German exporters had already been paid; but in the eyes of a few club members anyone who drank the stuff after 3rd September, 1939, was a black traitor: the beer was only fit to be poured down the drain.

The very small local colony of 'enemy aliens' – a doctor, a couple of loose Austrian barons and a harmless trader or so – were interned, but their wives were still at large. Because we continued to be friendly with two of these wives, one of whom was British by birth, we were accused by a few fanatics of being pro-German. The husbands were held in the Military Detention Barracks at Trimulgherry, part of Secunderabad, and after a few weeks they were allowed to be visited by their wives. As I seemed to be the only person within range who had a smattering of German – Heaven knows it was little enough – I was asked to act as interpreter at these emotional meetings. It was a most unpleasant task. The commanding officer of the prison and I sat facing one another at a table, the interned husband was seated at

THE PHONEY WAR AND AFTER

one end and his visiting wife at the other. I first had to explain to each, in my very bad German, that they were not allowed to embrace or to have any contact with one another – presumably in case a file or weapon exchanged hands in the best traditions of the detective story. I then had to listen to their allowance of five minutes' conversation to ensure that no secret messages were exchanged. (Very possibly they were: I could only unravel about half of what was said!) For the most part the talk was just pathetic, with little more than affectionate platitudes and enquiries exchanged; but one elderly man who had seen the seamier side of Nazi Germany declared he was very happy 'because the prison officers are kind and no one has beaten me'. The Indian Police delved into the records of all the internees very thoroughly, and within a few months most of them, throughout India, had been released except for a few known Nazis, mainly from Bombay and Calcutta – representatives of the larger German manufacturing firms. None of these potentially dangerous characters was from the Deccan.

The local ladies formed committees for sending parcels and 'comforts' to the troops in France – all very reminiscent of the First World War – while I served on a State committee to decide how Hyderabad could best contribute to the war effort. Apart from raising of a general War Purposes Fund, to which all the local European civilians undertook to contribute a percentage of their salaries for the duration of the war, this committee achieved little during the first few months of its existence.

People still swam in the club pool, drank whisky on the club lawn, gave parties and went about their affairs much as usual, lulled by a false sense of security into a belief that Hitler had shot his bolt and had been stimied by the Maginot Line. The same garrison regiments stayed in Secunderabad, played polo and continued to live the life of the 1930s. After the short, swift holocaust in Poland Hitler seemed to be paralysed and the sabre-rattlings of Mussolini sounded rather less harshly. In this deceptive calm I sent my family to the hills for the hot season at the end of March, 1940. They went to a pleasant little place called Kodai Kanal in the Palni Hills near the southern tip of India. This hill station, much patronised by the Europeans of Madras, held a large quota of missionaries. It was said that there were two Kodais – Kodai Carnal and Kodai Spiritual.

The Fool's Paradise of the phoney war was rudely shattered in April, when Hitler invaded Norway and Denmark. Guen was approached in Kodai village by an American missionary who said 'Say! Your country has been invaded'. After a moment of stunned shock Guen said 'But what about our Navy?' The reply was even blunter than the first remark; 'I didn't know you had a Navy'. Just because Guen was blonde, the foolish missionary assumed her to be Norwegian.

The attack on the western front followed soon afterwards, and with the collapse of France no grounds remained for complacency. The world was treated to the sorry spectacle of a senile French marshal aping the salutes of his conquerors. The war in Africa began, and two or three regiments from Secunderabad were sent overseas. The local European civilians were mustered: the few who could be released for military service went away, while the rest of us paraded regularly on the maidan and rifle range as a sort of 'Dad's Army'. I found myself in the embarrassing situation of bayonetting sacks under the instructions of an Anglo-Indian sergeant who, in civil life, was one of my power station shift engineers. The Government of India, taking no chances after the evidence of fifth column activities in the German-occupied countries, interned *all* enemy aliens – including the women this time. Not until a year or two later, after very careful vetting of their records, were a few of the internees released. Internment, even under the most humane conditions, is no doubt unpleasant; but some of the German women deserved no sympathy. A group of them, while still enjoying their freedom, had held a champagne party at the Breach Kandy Swimming Club in Bombay (admissible to *all* Europeans of whatever nationality) to celebrate the sinking of the *Rawalpindi*. This, to put it mildly, was tactless.

My family returned from the hills after the monsoon had

broken; and from then on, for the rest of the war, Guen became a volunteer worker at the Osmania Hospital in Hyderabad City. On her very first day she had to assist in the operating theatre. She worked there in the mornings only and used to put me off my lunch with realistic and colourful descriptions of the unpleasant things she had witnessed and the duties she had performed.

The Government of India undertook to produce as much as possible in the way of war supplies, and the princely states were invited to cooperate. India was by no means an industrialised country, and much reorganisation was needed before she could make a useful contribution. A special Mission, under the chairmanship of Sir Alexander Roger, toured India and visited Hyderabad to see what could be done. With the agreement of the State government I offered to divert the Mint, as far as possible, from the production of coin to war work. The nature of the Mint machinery was such that it could serve a particularly useful purpose in feeding the arsenals with rolled metal strips and various pressings. The State Workshop, and even the Electricity Department workshop, also contributed what they could. Meanwhile I had rashly volunteered to start up a factory for making pocket-knives, some hundreds of thousands of which were needed by the army. We had to start by acquiring a building, manufacturing most of our own specialised machinery and recruiting as manager an elderly retired Anglo-Indian engineer who had served for most of his life in the Mint. The knives were to be of the 'boy scout' variety, each with two blades, screw-driver, tin-opener and 'a thing for removing stones from a horse's hoof'. A huge stock of buffalo horns was laid in to provide the side-plates, scrap railway tyre steel provided the metal for the blades and other parts, the necessary rolling mills and presses were installed and a host of fitters and blacksmiths was engaged. Somehow, things did not go well. The old manager was not equal to his duties and the availability of skilled workers was very limited. Thousands of parts were correctly made but the assemblers seemed to bungle their work; with the result that mountainous stocks of parts built up while the output of finished knives was pitifully small. I became almost demented with worry. Eventually, to my great relief, the whole of the Nizam's Knife Factory was bought up, lock, stock and barrel by a rich Indian industrialist who had access to skilled labour and management from outside the State. I have no doubt he did well out of it. As far as I was concerned I was well rid of it.

The GOC of the Deccan Command, General Maltby (who was subsequently transferred to Hong Kong and had to try to defend the colony against the Japanese invasion), was a good friend of ours. One day he asked me if I could make sun-compasses which were needed in huge quantities for desert warfare. Never having heard of a sun-compass I asked him what it consisted of. 'It looks like a soup plate with a knitting needle sticking out of it; and a box full of charts goes with it' was the reply. He supplied me with a sample and I volunteered not only to make sun-compasses but also to improve upon the design. My early naval training and my later surveying studies at London University had taught me enough about observational astronomy to convince me I could design a far more accurate and *chartless* instrument than the regulation pattern. I set to work and produced a prototype that proved to be remarkably accurate. Then followed a long bureaucratic war in which I could get no recognition of my new gadget, despite the fact that I asked for no reward or royalties: I offered the idea as a small contribution to the war effort. General Maltby had meanwhile left for Hong Kong and I had no champion. At one stage a friend of mine discovered my instrument in one of the military organisational offices in Calcutta, just put on one side with the case *unopened*. I then took my 'war' into high places; and at one time I had no less than three generals (including General Norton of Mount Everest fame) and a brigadier as allies. My hopes were raised when I was invited to give a demonstration of the compass to the Chief Sapper in

Secunderabad. I duly turned up at the appointed place where I found a whole bevy of brass-hats, before whom I put my instrument through its paces, feeling rather like 'the man with the vacuum-cleaner'. The demonstration was greeted in silence, broken by the voice of a much-bemedalled general, 'Too bloody highbrow for me to understand'. However, the sapper officer came to me afterwards and told me not to be discouraged as he could appreciate the advantages of my design. To cut a long story short, I finally received a polite letter from the Commander-in-chief in India, after the desert warfare in Africa had finished, to say that everyone was very impressed with my design, but commitments to the existing standard instrument precluded any change: it would have been better if I had put my ideas forward earlier! That was the end of a two or three years' bureaucratic 'war'.

Another device I concocted, at the request of a certain colonel, was a slide-rule for quick range-finding in gunnery. This time I had a prototype made within twenty-four hours and sent it by hand to the colonel. Apart from a signature in the messenger's delivery book, I never heard another word from him.

As the war progressed the difficulties of directing an electricity supply enterprise increased. Supplies became scarcer and dearer, and the stocks I had providently laid in before the war had become depleted. There was an exodus of skilled men to more profitable employment in the factories of Bombay and Calcutta. Shipments of plant were sometimes torpedoed, and we had to rely more and more upon improvisations. Mercifully at no time was there a total failure of electricity supply, not even for a minute, though at times it was touch and go. One of the results of the Roger Supply Mission had been the establishment of a Bren gun factory near Secunderabad. A colony of refugee Czech engineers and their wives (or Czech-mates, as I called them) moved in, a new village was hastily built for their accommodation and a large factory was erected for the purpose

209

of producing the guns. At a time when I could not buy for love or money a steel joist or a lathe, I saw crates and crates of new machine tools lying *unpacked* in the factory. This was particularly frustrating because the factory failed to turn out *a single Bren gun* throughout the war.

Another difficulty was coal supplies. My power house had always relied for these on the Singareni collieries in the State, but as industrial development grew apace in British India more and more coal had to be diverted elsewhere. My peacetime propaganda enjoining the public 'to use more electricity' had to be put into reverse: the slogan became 'Use *less* electricity'. The wits of course made the obvious sallies about 'useless' electricity. Minor local industries were booming with war orders, so it was the domestic consumer who had to tighten his electrical belt. A system of electricity rationing became necessary; and instead of gloating over curves of rising output, as in better days, I had perforce to find satisfaction from negative trends. By one measure and another some hundreds of thousands of tons of coal were saved; but my departmental revenues suffered acutely and I found it increasingly difficult to fund necessary investments.

In 1942 and '43 I had to contend with a few isolated cases of sabotage. Sand was found in the turbine oil and spanners were literally thrown into the works. The CID planted spies among the work people but the culprits were too slick to be detected.

Even Nature conspired to make things worse. A series of poor monsoons, aggravated by the pilfering of water by farmers from the stream that normally fed the Hussein Sagar Lake, caused the water to fall some twenty to thirty feet below the normal full level. The Hyderabad power house was built on the shore of this lake and was absolutely dependent upon its waters. By dint of blasting channels in the solid rock and installing pumps I was able to keep supplies going, though with increasing difficulty. One day in 1943, late in the monsoon season, I made a calculation that revealed that unless some new pumps which I had ordered from England arrived almost immediately, or unless I were saved by a miracle of late and heavy rains, electricity supply must surely and totally fail within three months. At that very moment I was handed a cablegram informing me that my new pumps had been lost at sea in a torpedoed ship. These pumps had themselves been replacements of others that had gone to the bottom of the sea a year previously. I felt like drowning myself in the lake while it still contained enough water for that purpose. That night it rained, and continued to rain for several days, most unseasonably, as it had never rained before. The lake rose fifteen feet and my troubles in that direction were miraculously over.

My worries were not lightened when my only European assistant, Captain 'Y', suddenly decided to leave me to join the army. Had his action been inspired by heroism he would have earned my respect; but in fact he had been offered some routine supply work in a depôt no more dangerously situated than Hyderabad, but with the prestige of an officer's uniform. I cannot conscientiously say that his use to me had ever been very profound, but at least it had been possible for me to offload onto him a mass of routine work so that I had more time to devote to the many new problems that were constantly claiming my attention. I felt sore that he had let me down at a time when at last he could have been of some use to me. However, his departure proved to be a blessing in disguise, for shortly afterwards it reached my ears that a Polish engineer, after escaping from Warsaw through the Balkans and the Middle East, having seen his home and city destroyed and his country ravished, and having endured great hardships, had been washed up by the tide of war into Bombay, penniless and seeking useful employment. I quickly pounced on him and *got* him.

Jerzy Roman had been a very eminent engineer in Poland before the War. He was also the brother of one of the ministers in Colonel Beck's cabinet that had been in power in the late 1930s. He had written a monumental textbook, all copies of which had been destroyed in the German attack on Warsaw in September, 1939. He was nearly twenty years my senior, a

brilliant linguist and a first class engineer. By rights I should
have been his assistant, and not vice versa. The Hyderabad
government treated him shabbily by paying him only a pittance,
but the poor man had suffered so much he was only too happy to
find an oasis and to do a useful job of work. His very charming
wife was a physicist, who had studied under Madame Curie.
The arrival of these two Poles in Hyderabad made a great
difference to our lives for four years; in fact they more or less
enabled me to preserve my sanity. They were both highly
cultivated, had lived in St Petersburg during the 1917
Revolution and later in Berlin, and shared a deep appreciation of
good music – especially Chopin, of course. Many an evening we
spent in their company talking the clock round on every
conceivable topic. I shall always be eternally grateful to Jerzy
Roman for his loyal support in those difficult years and for the
valuable work he did in helping me.

Only a few days after Roman joined me Hitler attacked
Russia. As the German armies penetrated more deeply
eastwards, and as my face grew longer and longer, Roman
remained quite unruffled. Like all Poles he was an intense
patriot, and he regarded both Germany and Russia as inveterate
enemies. Of the two he seemed to regard Germany the lesser of
the two evils, but perhaps I am wrong there. He clearly hoped
that the two giants would exhaust themselves to a standstill. His
view of the psychology of his two national enemies was summed
up quite simply. 'I can spend an evening drinking with a
German', he said, 'knowing all the time that however jovial he
may be he will inwardly be regarding me as his inferior – as a
'Polak'. I can spend an evening drinking with a Russian, who
will treat me as his equal and swear eternal friendship with tears
rolling down his cheeks: tomorrow he will happily cut my
throat'.

Roman's political views reached the ears of the Hyderabad
Police, by whom I was advised to pass a discreet warning to my
new assistant that it would be unwise to speak disrespectfully in
public of our gallant Russian allies.

After the end of the Phoney War, and as the grim Hot War progressed, the social life of Hyderabad and Secunderabad became of course much simpler. A few official state dinners and garden parties still took place, but private entertaining among Europeans became more or less restricted to informal gatherings of four to six friends in one another's houses. This was really far more enjoyable than the flamboyance of former times, though less romantic in retrospect. The staple liquid diet of the European in India, Scotch and soda, soon became both very dear and very scarce: thereafter one was faced with a choice between abstention or the sampling of some very strange country-distilled liquors. After buying an experimental bottle of Indian 'whisky' and finding it rather horrible, I received a visit from a Bombay friend of mine when my family was in Ooty. On the evening of his arrival I had to attend a meeting and could not welcome him in person. I told a servant to offer my guest a bath and a drink until I could join him. Returning to the house and seeing my friend seated with a glass in his hand I suddenly remembered the parlous state of my liquor supplies. 'What have they given you to drink?', I asked. 'Some excellent rum', was the unexpected reply. Having no rum in the house I realised he was in fact drinking the country 'whisky', but as my friend came from Jamaica and knew what rum was, I thought his reaction somewhat odd. So I helped myself from the same bottle, tuned my mind into 'rum' instead of 'whisky' and found it quite palatable. Thereafter I offered my guests *rum* and everyone seemed quite happy.

Mails continued to get through from Britain to India fairly regularly, though the sending of duplicates a week later was a wise precaution against the losses that occasionally occurred. Censorship caused a good deal of delay. A woman friend of ours worked in the Bombay Censor's office, and she told us that the most violent source of anti-British propaganda was the American missionaries, who talked of imperialism, exploitation and political suppression. These do-gooders did not seem to understand that their own government in the Philippines was no

213

more successful than the British Indian government in raising the lot of the teeming millions of the tropics. That is a problem that has not yet been solved, and probably never will be solved by *any* government. The post-war Indian government has certainly done no better in this respect than the British did.

At a distance of some thousands of miles it had been difficult to view the war in proper perspective, or to visualise life in wartime Britain. News films got through and were shown in the Secunderabad cinemas. The sight of London burning in the blitz was heart-rending, and gave the impression that very little of that city could still be standing; but letters from home sounded quite cheerful in spite of everything.

In the last months of 1941 there was a welcome breathing space for us. First, we were able to get away for a few days' rest at Mahableshwar, a very beautiful hill station to the south-west of Poona, formerly the summer capital of the Bombay Government. I had not seen the place since my bachelor days in the 1920s. Here the climate was good, the scenery fine, and we made some good friends. Above all, the war news seemed to be improving. Shortly after our return to Hyderabad the State government extended an invitation to the officers and ship's company of HMS *Coventry*, then in Bombay harbour for repairs after a long spell of gruelling service in the Mediterranean campaign. At the Mint House we acted as hosts to one of the officers while the rest of the guests were spread around other homes in Hyderabad and Secunderabad. If there was one thing the State knew how to do really well it was *entertaining*. Without doubt all the naval guests enjoyed themselves enormously. A brief return to pre-war gaiety seemed not only justifiable but obligatory. We gave parties for the officers and the men, and they in turn heartened us all with a boost to our morale. In the following year we were devastated to learn that HMS *Coventry* had been lost at sea in action. We never knew how many of our friends went down with her: no more letters came from any of them.

XXI

The Hectic Years

Hardly had our naval guests departed when the news of Pearl Harbour burst upon us, and in the months that followed we learned of the depressing advance of the Japanese forces over south-east Asia. The Secunderabad garrison was further depleted by the despatch of more regiments to the East until little more than a skeleton force remained behind. The Government of India was faced with the problem of how to train new armies without weapons, so a new task fell upon me. I produced large quantities of *dummy* weapons, such as service rifles and 3-inch mortars. Some local wit, parodying President Roosevelt's famous expression, dubbed my workshops as 'The Dummy Arsenal of Democracy'. These dummy weapons had to be made in the State workshops and in the Electricity workshops, so as not to interfere with the work of arsenal-feeding from the Mint.

Suddenly, in 1942, all war work in the Mint had to be suspended to meet a new and more urgent crisis. We had to embark upon the greatest coinage production programme that had ever been attempted in the history of the Mint.

A basic principle of minting is that the intrinsic value of the metal content of a coin must not be so low as to undermine confidence or to encourage forgeries; but, even more important, it must never approach too closely the face value of the coin. Obviously, if the instrinsic value should exceed the face value, it

215

would pay to melt coins for the sake of their metal content, or at least to hoard them as bullion. In expectation of a rise in the price of silver, the Government of India had debased their coinage early in the War, from 91.6% to 50% silver content: and HM Mints in Bombay, Calcutta and Lahore had done this smoothly over quite a long period. Because Hyderabad State bought its silver bullion from China – then in the throes of the Sino-Japanese War – I tried to persuade the State government to follow suit. My pleas fell on deaf ears. After Pearl Harbour, as the Japanese hordes advanced rapidly westwards, my warnings mounted in crescendo. 'At least', I begged, 'amend the Currency Act to *legalise* debasement so that practical action can be taken at the drop of a hat'. But the government continued to follow a policy of masterly inactivity until it was almost too late. When it became apparent that even Burmah would be overrun they at last took panic. The Currency Act was hastily amended and I was authorised to debase the currency. This was easier said than done. The price of silver continued to rise, and at one time the intrinsic value of a rupee actually exceeded its face value. Almost overnight silver coins vanished underground, where they were either melted or hoarded. Even the low denomination cupro-nickel and bronze coins were in danger of a similar fate. The shortage of coin in the markets was causing great hardship. At one time only eight silver rupees could be exchanged for a ten-rupee note, and the greatest difficulty was experienced in paying out wages to large bodies of labour – as, for example, in the Mint itself.

The situation called for very urgent action, and the Mint took upon itself the unprecedented burden of remonetising the entire currency of the State, to meet the needs of some eighteen million people. Matters were aggravated by the lack of reserves of bullion and base metals, and by the fact that the coin famine coincided with a greatly increased demand for coin due to the stimulation of local industries and public works resulting from wartime activities. Rapid debasement was the only solution, but this was difficult to effect. The problem was partly to find

The family, including Paddy the golden retriever, with our Terraplane car, which was considered very modern at the time, and which took us on many a picnic. The rocky background is typical of the Deccan landscape.

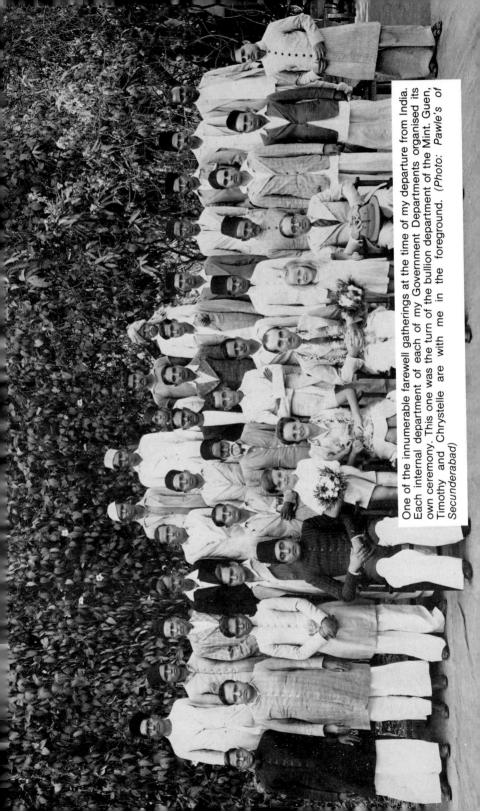

One of the innumerable farewell gatherings at the time of my departure from India. Each internal department of each of my Government Departments organised its own ceremony. This one was the turn of the bullion department of the Mint. Guen, Timothy and Chrystelle are with me in the foreground. (Photo: Pawle's of Secunderabad)

enough old coins to melt, and partly to find enough copper, nickel and zinc with which to alloy them. Fairly large stocks of silver-rich coin could be withdrawn from the treasuries and banks, but nickel was of a more serious nature.

It had happened that a year or two before the War a consignment of nickel bound for the Hyderabad Mint had been accidentally dropped into Bombay harbour when being unloaded from the ship. The loss had been covered by insurance; but now it had become worthwhile to salvage it and to refund the indemnity to the underwriters although, literally and metaphorically, it was a 'drop in the ocean'.

This problem of nickel shortage worried me desperately until I suddenly realised that the solution was staring me in the face. Why was nickel unobtainable? Because it was going to the arsenals for the manufacture of .303 rifle ammunition. And so to the famous Kirkee Arsenal, near Poona, went I; where I found that thousands of tons of scrap cupro-nickel were obtainable. I bought wagon-loads of the stuff from the British Ordnance Department. By calling in every old rupee that came into the banks and treasuries from circulation, and replacing it with the new coin, the process of remonetisation gathered momentum. The staff of the Mint was not very large when the trouble started, and it had to be supplemented by some hundreds of completely untrained men at a time when skilled labour was desperately scarce. The machinery was old and had never been expected to produce more than a fraction of the output now required. As it was virtually impossible, even if the time were available, to import new machinery, I had to make what machinery we needed in the State Workshops. The new silver alloy, known as quaternary silver, was a difficult metal to work; and my burden was not eased by an eruption of labour troubles and of sabotage.

The main problem was to strike coins quickly enough: they were needed in scores of millions. But the Devil was driving and the obstacles were gradually overcome. The Mint, groaning beneath its burden, working twenty-four hours a day and seven days a week, and trying to make skilled artisans from raw coolies, began to turn out an ever-increasing quantity of coin until, by June, 1944, the output reached the prodigious figure of nearly three-quarters of a million rupee pieces in a single day. Often, something like ten tons of silver were being melted daily. These are figures that would not have shamed some of the largest mints in the world, equipped with every modern device and well staffed with experienced engineers and artisans.

The re-coining of the silver was not our only task. The cupro-nickel anna had to be replaced with a bronze coin of the same size, and a new small bronze coin (one-sixth of an anna) was produced in huge quantities. Gradually the crisis was mastered, and by the end of the War the output had fallen considerably.

Early in the currency crisis it was thought advisable to alleviate matters by printing one-rupee treasury notes. This was easier to propose than to effect, since the Government of India Security Press at Nasik was too busy with its own burdens to be able to help the State. So we had to print them ourselves. The government's Central Press produced them on locally made paper and the notes were of excellent quality. A daily output of 300,000 one-rupee notes was maintained for many months, and these undoubtedly helped to stave off disaster during these difficult times. Although these notes were printed outside the Mint, they all had to pass through the Mint treasury for checking and counting, adding greatly to our other tasks.

The thought that so maddened me during those anxious times was that the whole crisis had been entirely unnecessary. If the State government had listened to me in good time, the entire remonetisation could have been completed quite smoothly and without panic before the price of silver had rocketed. The British Indian Mints were spared the agonies that were so unnecessarily thrust upon me, because sound foresight had been exercised. How often did I say to myself 'This is the job I rashly volunteered to do without salary in exchange for a rent-free house only?'

To help me in the minting crisis I was lent the services of one of the Czech engineers from the Bren gun factory. This young man somehow failed to endear himself to the Mint staff, and I was constantly diverted from more useful work by the necessity of trying to keep departmental peace. Eventually, when his enemies had put sugar into his petrol tank, the Czech left me in a rage and I never saw him again. It made very little difference.

Before supplies of nickel had become available from the arsenal, enabling the remonetisation programme to get into its stride, I had been forced to consider ideas on the lunatic fringe of practicability, such as striking rupees in leather, hardboard or other cheap impressionable materials – a sort of compromise between metal and paper currency that would have enabled me to use existing dies; but fortunately we were never reduced to such extremities.

By normal standards, dealing with the coinage crisis was more than a full time job for one man; but I still had my other departments to run, and I was beset with troubles in the Electricity Department too. Quite apart from torpedoed supplies, I was presented with a more or less insoluble equation in that my coal supplies were being curtailed and at the same time there was a greatly increased demand for electricity for local industries that had been stimulated by the war. The rationing of *domestic* electricity was only a partial, and very troublesome, answer. It was still possible to buy oil fuel fairly easily, so I was forced into buying some old secondhand diesel engines from two Bombay cotton mills, reconditioning them, and building – without the help of the PWD this time – an auxiliary power house, complete with oil storage depot and crane. The Swiss representative of Sulzer Bros., Emil Weber, was most helpful in providing me with the services of a diesel engineer for a few weeks and in taking a personal interest in the reconstruction of these old engines. Emil Weber has remained my good friend ever since, and we met from time to time either in Switzerland or in England until his death in 1983.

Meanwhile the Japanese had over-run Burmah and were poised to strike an apparently defenceless India. Some of the Indian politicians, in the best tradition of the Vicar of Bray, loudly declared they had no quarrel with Japan and prepared to jump over to the other side of the fence if this should become expedient. Subhas Chandra Bose actually *did* jump, and went to Japan. A subtle change of attitude towards the Europeans could even be detected among some of the Hyderabadis. Indian labour, hitherto docile, showed signs of militancy, and I had no option but to suspend a handful of known agitators from the labour force of the Mint and Electricity Departments when a few isolated acts of sabotage occurred. The gentle Mahatma Gandhi cannot escape all responsibility for a wave of violence that swept over India during the darkest hours of the War.

ARP committees and black-out rehearsals made further demands upon my time. Petrol rationing was introduced into the State and food rationing followed. These measures added to the burdens even of the Stamps Department, for I had to print the ration books. It was not surprising that in a feudalistic state the size of the food ration was linked to the salary of the individual! At any rate, the food rationing in Hyderabad was never very austere, even to the humblest: their diet was more limited by their purse than by their ration book.

It was a curious feature of the War that the really bad news always seemed to come through during the hot weather, when one's vitality was at its lowest ebb and one was least able to cope with it. The collapse of France, the loss of Greece, the reversals in Africa and the fall of Burmah all occurred when the thermometer registered about 115°F in the shade in Hyderabad. There was one particularly grim time when the Far East had fallen and the Japanese had made air raids on Calcutta, Colombo and on one or two places along the east coast of India. The raids, as such, were not heavy, but were sufficient to cause something like panic among the Indian population. Even as far inland as Hyderabad a large part of the labour force fled from

220

the capital for a few days. The British Government chose this time to send Sir Stafford Cripps on a mission to India in an attempt to reach a political settlement with the Congress Party. At such a time London could not bargain from a position of strength, and it is not surprising that the Mission failed. The 'saintly' Ghandi showed signs of militancy. There seemed to be nothing to stop the Japanese from over-running India. Apart from the paucity of defences, the air raids had already demonstrated the degree of chaos that could be triggered off by a few squibs.

One night during that black period, when my family was in Ooty, I dined quietly with the Director-General of the Hyderabad State Police and the British Commanding officer of the Deccan District. During the meal, news arrived that a Japanese fleet had been sighted sailing westwards in the Bay of Bengal. This looked like the beginning of the end. We speculated about the enemy plans. The police were very much awake and had learned much from interned Japanese who had been masquerading as Chinese restaurant keepers all over India. It was expected that the enemy would land on the east coast somewhere to the north of Madras and strike across towards Bombay, cutting India in two and relying on panic to dislocate the transport system. With my family to the south and myself to the north of this assault line I wondered if and when we would ever be reunited. I had received absolutely no instructions from high places whether, if such a contingency had arisen, I should stay at my post to keep public services going or whether I should adopt a 'scorched earth' policy and destroy, or put out of action, vital machinery. No doubt such instructions would have come through if the occasion had arisen; but it was worrying not to know what would have been expected of me. I have little doubt that I would have been told to keep electricity supplies intact, for three-quarters of a million people would have been deprived of water supply and sewerage if the electricity had completely failed.

Whether the reported sighting of a Japanese fleet was false, or whether the ships turned back for some good reason, I never learned. Perhaps they decided that their lines of communication had been overstretched. At any rate, while the enemy paused, and while the forces under Sir William Slim held them at bay, troops and weapons started to pour into India. Secunderabad again became a major military base. Whereas before the War we had been at least on nodding acquaintance with nearly every British officer in the garrison, the cantonments now became swollen with swarms of uniformed strangers: and a very welcome sight they were too!

The blackest days had passed: the tide of war began to turn and better news started to come in. Meanwhile, however, my own duties had been becoming more and more arduous. This is not a hard luck story: I am fully conscious that I can count myself fortunate by comparison with the millions of real sufferers from the war. Nevertheless, the strain of extra burdens and worries greatly tired me and I suffered acutely from insomnia. In the lone watches of the night I would fret about this and that while I waited for the next hour to be struck by the guard on Gamlen's bell. Water shortage, one of my most acute anxieties until September, 1943, made my ears sensitive to the sound of a dripping tap a quarter of a mile away. (To this day I cannot abide the sound of water running to waste.) Many a time I would get out of bed at two or three o'clock in the morning, dress, and walk round the Mint or power house – partly to keep everyone on their toes and partly to break the unendurable monotony of a wakeful night. At times I would almost give way to despair. Would I ever see England again? Were my children to grow up among the Anglo-Indians in an alien land? Then, when at last I might be growing drowsy, I would be rudely jerked wide awake by the raucous shouting of the muezzin only just on the other side of my garden wall, calling the Faithful to prayer and the Faithless to wakefulness.

When I received a cablegram informing me that all my antique furniture and other possessions in store in England had been destroyed in an air raid I was able to shrug it off philosophically. What was this by comparison with what others had lost and were losing? To be honest, I must confess that this attitude was not attributable to any noble sacrificial streak in my character: it was simply due to a state of apathetic exhaustion induced by overwork. It is well that the loss occurred when it did. In better times I would have been devastated.

However, these fits of depression were only one facet of life, which in other ways continued to be interesting and, at times, even enjoyable. In 1941 I had rented a cottage in Ooty for the duration of the war. There I sent my family for about five months every year to escape the rigours of the hot weather in the plains; and there too I occasionally escaped for a week or ten days of 'casual leave' to preserve my sanity. The joys of sitting by the fireside in a cosy room with the smell of burning eucalyptus wood in one's nostrils, and of sleeping under a blanket at night, were indescribable after the harsh heat and interminable cares of the plains.

On one of these short leaves I was accompanied by another Englishman in the train to Mysore, from where we travelled by bus through the dense jungles and up to the highlands of the Nilgiri Hills. At dusk the bus stopped for a few minutes at a small mountain village and an officious little Indian approached us, saying 'From where do you come and what is your business in Ootacamund?' As he wore no uniform I was on the point of telling him to mind his own business when he added 'I should like to know your names please'. My travelling companion rose to the occasion by saying in a strong Indian accent 'We have come all the way from Europe in a bus, and my name is Adolf Hitler'. Not to be outdone, I added 'And my name is Hermann Goering. We are escaping from the Russian armies'. That night, just after I had gone to bed, there was a ring at the door and I admitted a British police officer. 'I understand you arrived from Mysore this evening and gave unsatisfactory answers to enquiries made by one of my inspectors', said he. I explained that if police inspectors expected cooperation they should either wear uniform, or show some kind of credentials. The officer, at first annoyed at having to turn out late at night, was soon laughing. I asked him how he had traced me, and he produced a label off my suitcase, bearing my name and address. The inspector had not been so dumb: he had told the bus driver to tear off the labels from our baggage when we were not looking. But the poor little man must have been bitterly disappointed that he had failed to make the most sensational catch of the war since Rudolf Hess.

The establishment of an RAF base at Begumet, close to Hyderabad, was like a new breath of air. Group-Captain Wallis and several of his officers became good friends of ours and I was once invited to take part in a paper chase, for which the Group-Captain very kindly lent me a mount. It was the nearest approximation to the hunting field I had known since 1931. The horse pulled like a steam engine and I was remarkably sore afterwards, but it was a great occasion. We also became very friendly with two aircraftsmen, both of whose names were Jim. The Jims came regularly to the Mint House, and they both enjoyed listening to good music played on my gramophone.

The lack of music, even in peace time, was one of the great drawbacks to life in India for those who, like myself, derive great pleasure from it. So, during the war, with the help of a Secunderabad padré named Groves, we founded a Gramophone Society which met one evening every week. Members agreed to lend such records as they possessed and to meet in each others' houses in turn. Many dozens of pleasant evenings were spent cheaply in this way and we had a membership of about fifty or sixty.

A young officer whom we came to know during the war bore a famous Scots name but was of uncertain nationality, having been born in Egypt and having many of his cosmopolitan relations scattered all over the world. He told us of 'Aunt Arabella' who lived in Trieste. In the 1914/18 war Aunt

Arabella had been an Austrian and therefore an 'enemy': her name was not mentioned in the family in those days. In 1940 poor Aunt Arabella had, willy-nilly, become an Italian and was again an 'enemy'. I never discovered whether she was reinstated in the family graces after Italy became a 'co-belligerent'.

Before the War I had found it possible to live like a lord and at the same time to put by some modest savings, but as the war progressed, prices rose so sharply that the process had to be reversed: from time to time I had to send to England for funds, dipping into my savings so as to be able to make both ends meet. For some time I was reluctant to ask for more salary while the War was still on; but when the Mintmastership, which had previously been almost a sinecure, became a full-time and nerve-racking occupation I felt justified in asking for some financial recognition in view of the fact that I had originally accepted that office without remuneration (other than rent exemption) when the duties had been light. This reasonable request was countered by a slick retort. For reasons of accountancy, the government had allocated one-quarter of the salary, which I had agreed to accept for the directorship of the Electricity Department, to the Mint budget. Although this made not a penny of difference to me, the government argued that I was, in fact, being paid for my Mint duties. With a war on, and with an acute coinage crisis also on, I could hardly drive my argument to the extreme threat of resignation; particularly as I was a virtual 'prisoner' in that I knew my resignation would not be accepted. However, a new situation arose that *did* drive me to the threat of resignation, if only to test the waters.

All executive departmental heads were answerable to a minister through the intermediary of a Secretary to government in the ministry concerned. Because of Gamlen's personal evolution from the Mintmastership into other activities, I had always been responsible to the Finance Minister through the Finance Secretary. I had served under two Secretaries who, being laymen, had confined their influence to matters of

225

finance and policy. Now suddenly the government appointed a new Finance Secretary – an *engineer* from the Public Works Department. This engineer, who had held a comparatively junior position when I had been directing four departments, would, I felt sure, intervene in technical matters. It was a situation I would have found humiliating: it would have amounted to an obligation on my part to accept technical orders from a man who had been junior to me and who was not versed in the technologies of my departments. I refused to accept the position and said I would resign if the government persisted. There was a stormy scene with the minister, who accused me of trying to dictate to the government. I replied that I recognised the government's absolute right to appoint whomever they wished as Secretary; but that *they* should recognise *my* right to resign if I found my working conditions unacceptable. I was far from sure of my position in view of the fact that just before the War it had been made clear to me that I would have to 'stay put' as a 'key man'. However, much had happened since then, so I approached the local British military commander. His reply confirmed that the position was still the same: I would *not* be free to accept a military commission unless the State agreed to release me. This they would not do, so I was truly 'stuck' with an unpleasant situation.

In the middle of all this shemozzle a new Finance Minister appeared. This was Ghulam Muhammed, who later became Governor-General of Pakistan. I had been warned that Ghulam Muhammed was very anti-British; but at my first interview with him I found him most charming and sympathetic to my cause. He at once re-shuffled the secretaryships so that I would not have to serve under an engineer. I had won my point by the skin of my teeth.

Throughout the coinage crisis the new minister was friendly and helpful. He grasped at once the seriousness of the currency situation and he cooperated with me to the full. It was not until later that I saw another side to his character.

While my troubles were at their height, yet another blow was threatened. Captain 'Y' relinquished his commission in the Army. I know nothing of the circumstances, but he wrote me to ask me to give him back his old job. I wrote to say that I regretted that the post had been filled and that I could not possibly spare his successor, whose services were quite indispensable. Captain 'Y' then wrote to the Residency to ask that pressure be brought to bear upon the State government to reinstate him. Ghulam Muhammad sent for me, and I implored him at all costs not to let Roman go as I just could not carry on without him. Fortunately the Minister knew and liked Roman. He had also made enquiries about the military appointment that Captain 'Y' had 'relinquished'. To my intense relief Ghulam Muhammed said that Captain 'Y' would be reinstated over his dead body and that Roman would remain at all costs. Yet another crisis had been successfully solved.

XXII

Farewell to Nabobery

As the currency crisis slowly subsided, so did the war news improve. It soon became clear that the coming of peace could not be far off and our spirits started to rise. But as the Russian armies swept westwards my Polish friend, Jerzy Roman, showed no signs of jubilation. It was from him, through the small colony of his compatriots in Bombay, that we first heard of the Katyn Woods massacre long before the news of it had shocked the world. At the time I dismissed, as mere propaganda, the suggestion that anyone but the Nazis could have perpetrated such an outrageous act, but Roman just sadly shook his head. His old father was in Lithuania and his brother, the ex-minister, was under house arrest in Bucharest, both under German surveillance. As the Russians advanced he began to fear greatly for their safety, particularly as his family was of the minor nobility. His fears were later justified: none of his close relations survived the Russian occupation.

Although much of the element of crisis had gone out of my work, the cold hand of bureaucracy continually made life more difficult. Government interference in petty affairs was sometimes excused by the imposition of 'war controls' but was more often inspired by sheer officiousness. One particular instance of this nearly caused me to have a riot on my hands. Since time immemorial there had been a decree, more honoured in the breach than in the observance, that Urdu was to be the sole language of governmental departments. In practice this could not be enforced, particularly in an organisation like the Electricity Department that had many dealings with the outside world of importers, manufacturers, collieries, oil companies and so forth. Moreover, to three-quarters of the population of the State Urdu was a language almost as foreign as English: Telegu was the prevailing tongue of the capital. Business therefore had to be conducted multi-lingually. Printed forms and bills appeared both in Urdu and English, while correspondence was conducted in the language best suited to the addressee. It had always been the custom of my department to prepare the monthly wage sheets in roman numerals. At six-monthly intervals circulars would regularly be issued to all departments – mine were not the only offenders by any means – reminding them that Urdu was the official language of government and instructing them to mend their ways. All such circulars had always been ignored for thirty-seven years, both by Gamlen and myself and by several other departments. The interesting feature of these circulars that particularly tickled me was that they were always worded in *English*. This was about as inconsequential as the famous case in which an unauthorised subordinate in a London Ministry was accidentally sent a 'classified' file. After perusing it, the subordinate initialled it in accordance with normal government procedure. His superior, on discovering that a mistake had been made, sent back the file to his subordinate with a note saying 'This file was sent to you in error. Please erase your initials and initial the erasure'.

One day my garden was invaded by an angry mob, many hundreds strong and in an ugly mood. They had been told there was no pay for them because the auditor had refused to pass the paysheets which had, as usual, been prepared in roman numerals. I 'phoned the auditor to tell him I was directing the mob to *his* house; so he hastily rescinded his veto and I had no more trouble on that score.

My relationship with the new Finance Minister, Ghulam Muhammad, had at first been excellent. I again broached the suggestion that my vastly increased responsibilities in the Mint merited at least *some* salary. He invariably agreed in principle, but postponed action by means of a subtle hope-raising hint. 'My dear fellow', he would say, 'I could grant you a Mint salary at any moment simply by an istroke of the pen; but I have in mind *something much better* for you'. The 'something much better' remained elusive.

I had long decided to leave India as soon as the end of the war would release me from 'captivity'. I had had my fill, and was still young enough to seek fresh fields elsewhere. Moreover, the problem of educating our children was looming up. Both of them had been taught by Guen, who was not only excellently qualified to do so but who also had a natural flair for teaching. But the boy was approaching an age when home education, however good, would not be enough.

Then, like a bolt from the blue, I received an offer of employment from a famous British firm of consulting engineers: it was to be implemented as soon as I could get my release from the State. As the firm also had an office in Calcutta they offered to use my services there until I could obtain a passage to England. (It was, of course, a foregone conclusion that the homeward rush that would follow the end of the War would result in long waiting lists for passages and a system of 'priorities'.) I accepted the offer *sine die* but did not at first disclose it to the State government because I did not for one moment think they would release me until the war was over and might meanwhile make life even more difficult for me.

Next, Ghulam Muhammed's 'something much better' came along. Instead of being the Director of the Electricity Department with jurisdiction only over the capital city and suburbs, I was to become Chief Electrical Engineer to the State. This meant taking charge of several small electrical under-takings in the provinces (hitherto run by the Public Works Department), direct involvement in certain ambitious plans for hydro-electrical development in the State, and also taking over yet another complete organisation – the Telephone Department. This impressive offer was accompanied by a sting, or rather *two* stings, in the tail. As these additional duties would be onerous I would have to relinquish the Mint and Stamps Department (fair enough), and as the new arrangement amounted to a *change*, and not an *extension* of duties, I would continue to draw precisely the same salary as in the past. But the most unkindest cut out of all was that as soon as a new Mintmaster had been appointed I was to relinquish the Mint House. No alternative government quarters were to be allotted to me, so I would have to rent a house at my own cost. The upshot of this 'generous' offer was that I was to be thrown out of a house that had been our home for ten years, and would be financially far worse off, as rents had risen sharply during the War.

To put it mildly, I was furious, and immediately applied for my release from the State. The Resident assured me that although the War was still on, the situation had now changed and he would raise no objection from his side. I then went to see Ghulam Muhammed, from who I expected opposition. To my surprise he was most affable, even after I had told him what I thought of his 'offer'. He expressed gratitude for the work I had done in saving the State currency from collapse and promised me a substantial cash bonus in recognition of this. He also told me it had already been settled with the Residency that, like my predecessor, I was to be awarded the OBE. He quite understood that I wished to return to my native land and he even agreed to let me remain in occupation of the Mint House until I was able to leave Hyderabad. Meanwhile I was still Mintmaster, etc. *and* Chief Electrical Engineer. These promises somewhat mollified me. I informed my future employers that I would join their Calcutta office as soon as I could do so.

Needless to say, I received neither the cash bonus nor the OBE. But the meanest thing of all was that after twelve years' service with the State I even had to pay my own passage home as well as those of my family. The 'one further return sea passage' included in my 1937 agreement was interpreted by a niggardly government as being a return to *India* only. Even the *Indian* civil officers of the Nizam's State Railways were entitled to a sea passage to and from Europe for themselves and their families once every three years; while I, an Englishman engaged in England, was to be dumped in India and left to find my own way home. Although Gamlen had been pensionable, I was not. I had contributed to a Provident Fund which provided me with a capital sum of just over £1,000, half of which was simply the repayment of my own money: the government's contribution, over twelve years, amounted to just about £50 a year including interest. Unlike the 'lent' State officers from the ICS, Army and Indian Police, I was a lone wolf, without the support of the Government of India behind me to ensure fair play. It seemed clear to me that Ghulam Muhammed's anti-British reputation was well founded. I have little doubt that my 'promotion' to the Chief Electrical Engineer's post had been engineered by him in terms that he knew I would never accept, so that one fewer British civil officer would remain in the State. While there had been a crisis, and he had needed my help, he had been willing to play along with me; but now, with the crisis past and the end of the War in sight, he discarded me like a used duster. His policy of reducing British influence in India was fair enough from his point of view, but he might have spared me the cheese-paring pettiness of which I was made the victim.

The last formal function I attended while still in State service was the laying of foundation stones for the Tungabadhra hydro power and irrigation project. The Tungabadrha River flowed along the boundary of the Nizam's Dominions and the Madras Presidency. The construction of a huge dam across the river called for an initiation ceremony on each bank. I was present at both in my capacity as Chief-Electrical-Engineer-under-notice. An RAF Dakota plane was lent for the purpose of transporting the Resident, the Prime Minister and three or four others including myself to a landing field near the Hyderabad end of the projected dam. Meanwhile a special train carried the Prince of Berar and a host of State officials who preferred wheels to wings. In true Hyderabad tradition a splendid lunch was dispensed in a vast marquee on the Hyderabad bank. Speeches were made all about the close accord between the two governments and a foundation stone was laid by the prince. After lunch the whole assembly had to be transported in a special train over some eighty miles of track by way of the nearest bridge in order to reassemble at the Madras end of the dam site, about two miles as the crow flies from where we had lunched. This time the Governor of Madras acted as host, and we were regaled with tea and more speeches saying what we had more or less already heard. After that, a second foundation stone was laid by the Governor on *his* bank. The return train journey was made by night to bring us back to the point on the opposite bank and we flew back to Hyderabad the following morning.

Packing up our home was a long, and in some ways a sad business. I felt I had been shabbily treated, but in spite of the troubles and worries of the past years I had no regrets. I was only forty-one – quite young enough to start on a new career – and the Mint House had certainly been a splendid setting in which to start family life. I was desperately tired and felt the full weight of the preceding twelve years, but at that age it is possible to recoup one's energies very quickly when the pressures have been eased. (In point of fact I was trekking on foot across the hump of the Himalayas into Ladakh within two or three weeks of leaving Hyderabad.)

We auctioned our furniture and 'junk' very well, and were invited to spend our last few days at the State guesthouse, as the Mint House was then empty. I thought this very generous of the Prime Minister, the Nawab of Chattari, who had sanctioned it. While there, Guen's watch was stolen – probably by one of the guesthouse servants. Thinking it would be churlish to make a fuss of the incident while we were State guests, we let the matter drop. After we had left Hyderabad I received a bill for board and lodging during our stay at the guesthouse!

As the day of our departure approached I was reminded of similar days in 1935 when Gamlen had retired. Ceremony after ceremony had to be endured. Bad ispeech followed bad ispeech. Layers of garlands were placed round our necks – even the children's. On our last evening we were invited to dine with the Bijliwallah's Association, when an 'ode' was read out to me. The text, printed on silk, was presented to me and I have it to this day. It listed in verse all the State appointments I had held, and included the dubious heptameter . . . 'Chief Electric Engineer to Hyderabad Istate'.

Crowds of tearful Indians saw us off at the station, and the emotional stress might have been acute had I not remembered the weeping that had accompanied Gamlen's departure and the smiles that had greeted me on the following day. The crocodile is always ready with his tears, and I had become rather cynical about Indian emotions.

And so I departed, the last of the Nizam's Mintmasters. For a while I was succeeded by an Indian Acting Mintmaster, but no one was ever confirmed in that office again. My Polish friend, Jerzy Roman, took over the appointment of Chief Electrical Engineer, again with a further salary cut. He was treated so shabbily by the State government that he too left after a year or two. He and his delightful wife, Jadwiga, became US citizens and he obtained a professorship at a technical college in Michigan. Jadwiga died in the 1960s and Jerzy, a grief-stricken old man, put fresh flowers on her grave every day for the rest of his life. In his retirement he took to painting watercolours which, as with everything else he undertook, he did very well. He died in 1979.

My work during the twelve years I had spent in Hyderabad had offered many disappointments, a few triumphs and some unusual and unforgettable experiences. Life had never been dull, and always busy.

Three years later the whole structure of the State collapsed like a house of cards. The power and dominions of the Nizam were swept away, and with them went the halli sicca currency. In this modern age it can be argued that there is no place for such feudal anachronisms as was Hyderabad, a vast Hindu country ruled by a Muslim majority. But where tradition is concerned, reason and sentiment often conflict with one another. I, for one, feel some regrets at the passing of a régime which, with all its faults, was at least picturesque; and I am glad to have known it intimately.

Tamám shud

Glossary

Note on spelling. When words are transcribed from an Asian into the Roman script, a certain amount of tolerance in spelling must be allowed. Some people have strong views on the relative merits of 'Bakhshish' and 'Bucksheesh' – I refer, of course, to the spelling and not to the substance – but I regard it as rather unimportant as long as the meaning is clear: I have simply used the spellings that are commonly used. A word of warning about the letter 'Q' is advisable for the benefit of those who have no knowledge of the Arabic, Persian or Urdu script. This letter does not, as in English, have to be coupled with the letters 'U' (to give a 'kw' sound): it is simply a very gutteral version of the English 'K', to be uttered somewhere in the region of the uvula and if correctly pronounced it sounds like a rather rude noise.

Ag	fire
Ali Hazrat	His Exalted Highness
Amerah	hospitality, entertainment
Ashram	a philosophical or religious colony of eccentrics, a sort of monastery or convent
Babu	an Indian clerk
Baghloos	ceremonial belt of cloth of gold
Bahadur	brave: used as a title by those of noble rank, regardless of whether it is merited or not

236

Bakr Id	a Muslim festival
Bakhshish	gratuity, largesse
Baradari	literally 'twelve doors'; an open-sided pavilion formed by arches – usually 3 × 4
Bijli	electricity
Bijliwallah	electrician
Burra, or Barra	big
Burra Sahib	boss
Barqi	lightning, electricity
Bat	1) matter, subject 2) vernacular
Batti	lamp
Battiwallah	electrician, electrical engineer, lamp-lighter
Bazaar	market, shopping street
Begam, Begum	lady of rank, wife of a nawab
Bund	dam or barrage
Chahiye	it is necessary
Chapatti	cake of unleavened bread
Chaprassi	a liveried office messenger (*see* peon)
Charpoy, charpai	simple bed; literally 'four-feet'
Chatti	earthenware water pot
Chota	small
Chota hazri	early morning tea
Chota peg	a small measure of whisky
Dak	post, mail
Dak bungalow	post-house, rest-house
Daman	a large, but harmless snake
Dar-ul-Zarb	Mint
Dasserah	an important Hindu festival
Dastar	a head-gear peculiar to Hyderabad
Dastar-i-mubarak	the 'auspicious headgear' or royal crown of Hyderabad
Deccan	south; the southern central plateau of India

Devdi	a nobleman's palace or mansion
Dhobi	washerman
Dhobi-ghat	laundry
Dhoti	garment used by Hindus to wrap around the legs
Diwan	chief minister, prime minister
Durbar	ceremonial court assembly
Fakhr	pride
Fakir	a Muslim holy man
Fasli	Muslim solar calendar
Fateh	victory
Fez	red 'flower-pot' headgear worn by Muslims
Firman	decree
Firman-i-mubarak	'auspicious decree' or royal edict
Ghadi	throne
Gharry	a horse-drawn cab, 'Victoria'
Ghat	hill, mountain pass, steps
Godown	corruption of the Indian word 'gudam' – a store or warehouse
Guru	Hindu spiritual teacher
Gurudwar	Sikh place of worship
Hai	is, is present
Halli sicca	literally 'current coin'; the name given to the coinage of Hyderabad State
Hazri	breakfast
Hijri	Muslim lunar calendar
Himru	brocade
Hindi	the principal Sanskrit-based language of India
Hissar	citadel; fortress
Holi	an important Hindu festival
Hukka, Huqa	a hubble-bubble pipe in which the smoke is drawn through water and thence by tube to the smoker's mouth
Id	religious festival

Id mubarak	'happy festival'; a greeting like 'happy Christmas'
Id-ul-Fitr	Muslim festival to mark the end of Ramzan, the month of fasting
Jagir	a vast feudal estate
Jagirdar	a feudal lord; owner of a jagir
Jama	Friday, the Muslim Sabbath
Jama Masjid	the principal city mosque
Jemadar	1) sergeant (military)
	2) senior chaprassi or peon; commissionaire
	3) in Hyderabad, the feudal commander of levied troops
Jung	war
Ke waste	for
Kharita	official communiqué, through diplomatic channels, from the Viceroy to a ruling Indian prince
Kharma	Buddhistic destiny
Khas-khas	a fragrant grass
Khitmagar	male Indian servant, high in the domestic pecking order, butler
Kothi	mansion
Ki	of
Kotwal	senior commissioner of police
Kummerband	belt
Lekin	but
Lota	brass vessel used by Hindus for ablutions
Machan	tree platform used by big game hunters
Mahakma	department
Maharajah	a major Hindu prince
Maidan	plain; field; parade ground; park
Malan	female gardener
Mali	male gardener
Masjid	mosque

Memsahib	European married lady; corruption of 'Madam Sahiba'
Mizaj-i-sherif	ceremonial exchange of visits
Moharram	a month of mourning in the Muslim calendar
Mubarak	auspicious
Muezzin	Muslim crier, calling the Faithful to prayer at the prescribed times of day
Mullah	Muslim priest
Munshi	teacher of oriental languages
Naib	deputy, or assistant
Nauch	dance
Nawab	a Muslim gentleman of rank, sometimes a Muslim ruling prince
Nazar	ceremonial presentation of money to a prince
Nazim	director
Nirvana	Buddhist concept of blessed absorption into the Eternal Spirit
Nizam	dynastic title of the rulers of Hyderabad State (pronounced to rhyme with 'his arm')
Pagri	turban
Paigah	of very high rank, ducal
Pan	a parcel of nuts and spices wrapped in a 'pan' leaf and secured by a clove; to be chewed
Papadam	very thin, brittle form of biscuit, eaten with curries
Peon	a liveried office messenger (*see* chaprassi)
Pradesh	province
Puchna	to ask
Pujah, Pooja	Hindu prayers
Pukka	ripe, mature, thorough

Pukka Sahib	a dyed-in-the-wool British bore who has spent most of his life in India and cannot stop talking about it
Punkah	fan
Purdah	literally 'curtain'; system of keeping women in seclusion
Rajah	a minor Hindu prince or nobleman
Rajkumar	Heir Apparent of a Hindu princely house
Rajpramukh	provincial governor (post-Independence)
Ramzan, or Ramadan	a month of fasting for the Muslims
Rani	wife of a rajah, or a noble Hindu lady of rank in her own right
Rat	night
Rat-ki-Rani	climbing plant with strong sweet smell at night; literally 'Queen of the night'
Razzakar	a corps of dedicated Muslim fighters pledged to defend Hyderabad State against Hindu aggression
Sadhu	a Hindu holy man
Sagar	lake
Sahib	gentleman
Sahiba	lady
Sahibzada	prince
Sahibzadi	princess
Salaam	literally 'peace'; a greeting
Sarf-i-khas	Crown property
Sari	national garment worn by Indian women
Satiyagraha	doctrine of civil disobedience
Se	from
Sherwani	a long tunic worn by men, especially Muslims, in India
Shikar	hunting, big game shooting
Swaraj	doctrine of Indian Home Rule
Syce, sais	groom
Taluqdar	collector, or chief civil officer of a district

GLOSSARY

Taman shud	This is the end; 'finis' (Persian)
Thik	correct, all right
Tiffin	lunch
Toghra	monogram
Topi	hat; pith helmet formerly worn by 'pukka sahibs' and other Europeans
Turrah	a spray of gold thread used to embellish the royal dastar-i-mubarak, or crown of Hyderabad
Urdu	the principal language of Indian Muslims, based on an Arabic/Persian vocabulary grafted onto a Hindi grammar and using the Arabic/Persian style of script
Verandah	covered terrace, often forming a feature of Indian houses
Yar	friend
Yuvarajah	a senior member of a Hindu princely house
Zenana	women's quarters; 'seraglio'

Index

INDEX

North Warwickshire Hunt, 85

O

Observatory, The Hyderabad —, 197
Omar Khan Sirdar, of Afghanistan, 96
Ootacamund ('Ooty'), 9, 65, 190, 201, 223
Ordnance Department, 217
Orphanage, Victoria Memorial, 36, 99
Osmania Central Technical College, 37, 71-72
Osmania Hospital, Hyderabad, 207
Osmania sicca coins/currency, 126
Osmania University, 72, 134
Osmansagar reservoir, 140, 172

P

Paddy, the golden retriever, 98-99
Padmaja Naidu, 98
Paigah(s)/Paigah nobles, 6, 88, 132
Pali Hill, 25
Paper currency, 128, 218
Paramount Power, The, 3, 9
Parsee, 10
Patiala State, 125
Peons, 113
Philatelists, 132
Pickthall, Muhammed Marmaduke, 98
Playing cards, Moghul, 176
Pocharam, 172
Police, The Mint —, 156, 157
Police and Revenue Member of HEH The Nizam's Executive Council, 9, 50
Political Minister/Secretary, Hyderabad, 177, 179
Poona, 83
'Prickly heat', 25
President of HEH The Nizam's Executive Council, 8, 89, 96, 136, 142, 194, 233
Prime Minister (see President)
Princely India, 1
Power House, Hyderabad City —, 35, 43, 210
Purdah system, 7, 103-106

Q

Qadr Yar Jung Bahadur, Nawab, 94
Quaternary silver coins, 217
Qutb Shahi kings and queens of the Deccan, 2, 52, 173

R

Rahman, Sir C.V. FRS, Director of the

Indian Institute of Science/Lady Rahman, 111
Railway, The Nizam's State —, 10, 48, 179
Rajkumar of Mysore, The, 110
Rajpramukh of Andhra Pradesh, 12
Ramzan, 44, 107, 109
Ransford, Colonel A., Master of HM Mint, Bombay (later knighted), 195
Rationing of electricity/food, 210, 220
Rawalpindi, RMS, 15, 16, 206
Raymond, Monsieur, 8, 10
Razakars, 12
Reed, Sir Stanley MP, 14
Regular State Forces, Hyderabad, 7
Remonetisation of the Hyderabad State currency, 216-219
Residency, Hyderabad, 9, 45, 49, 141, 177
Resident, The —, Hyderabad, 9, 90, 141
Rewentlow, Count and Countess, 147
Roger Supply Mission, 207, 209
Roman, Jerzy and Jadwiga, 211, 212, 227, 228, 234
Roshan Jal, 'Poet Laureate of India', 194-195
Ross, Sir Ronald, 47
Rotten Row, 84-85
Round Table Conference, London 1933, 33
Royal Bombay Yacht Club, 17, 25, 76, 195
Royal Mint, 135
Royal Naval Colleges, Osborne and Dartmouth, 14

S

Sabbath, The Muslim — (Friday), 123
Sabotage, 210, 220
Saif Nawaz Jung Bahadur, Nawab, 7
St Francis Xavier, 30
St John's Wood barracks, 85
Saklaji Street, Bombay, 20-21
Salar Jung Bahadur, Nawab I, 7, 90, 126
Salar Jung Bahadur, Nawab III, 7, 90-92, 109, 146-148, 152
Salsette Island, 22
Salvage, 129, 217
Santa Cruz, 25, 76, 82
Sarf-i-Khas, 4
Satyagraha, 98
Scorpion(s), 189
Secunderabad, 9, 35, 177, 204

247